Regimes of Violence

Also by John Protevi
Published by the University of Minnesota Press

Political Affect: Connecting the Social and the Somatic
Life, War, Earth: Deleuze and the Sciences
Edges of the State

Regimes of Violence

Toward a Political Anthropology

John Protevi

 University of Minnesota Press
Minneapolis
London

The University of Minnesota Press gratefully acknowledges the generous assistance provided for the publication of this book by the research fund support of Phyllis M Taylor to the Department of French Studies at Louisiana State University.

The Publication History at the end of the book gives original and previous publication history for the writings compiled in this book.

Published by the University of Minnesota Press
111 Third Avenue South, Suite 290
Minneapolis, MN 55401–2520
http://www.upress.umn.edu

ISBN 978-1-5179-1874-3 (hc)
ISBN 978-1-5179-1875-0 (pb)

Library of Congress record available at https://lccn.loc.gov/2024062209

Contents

Preface

I wrote the essays that form the base of this book from 2016 to 2023 in response to invitations; they weren't all composed from a unified standpoint. To form them into a book I make arguments that, even if they don't form a straight line, do at least follow a set of related themes. The main readers I envision are those in the "Theory" fields of the humanities and social sciences, though of course I would be delighted if the book found readers further afield. Among the sources I use are philosophical works by Deleuze and Guattari, mixed with works on evolutionary and cultural anthropology; on psychology, philosophy of mind, and enaction; on history; and on sports.

Although I am an expert only in the first area, I hope to have traced a path through the literature that is informative for nonexperts while defensible in the eyes of experts. Because of the wide range of topics I deal with, I cannot enter into a detailed evaluation of most points, though my wish is to be fair to positions other than my own. In other words, this is a synthetic book, linking wide-ranging fields by perforce somewhat shallow threads, rather than an analytic one, making incremental progress by small steps in work on a carefully defined problem. Furthermore, while I establish what I think are plausible lines of thought, I don't claim neutrality, so, in addition to all the unconscious ways in which writers reveal their orientations in fine distinctions, points of emphasis, and shades of nuance, when push comes to shove, I consciously choose left-wing positions.

I hope that those who follow the paths laid out here can reinforce these lines of contact between disciplines. It should be interesting for philosophers to see these concrete applications of philosophical works, and, while I don't think practitioners in other fields need philosophical concepts to do their everyday work, should they find the concepts I lay out here to be thought-provoking when they consider the ontological and ethical implications of their practice, so much the better.

The book develops and expands lines of thought worked out in preceding works published by the University of Minnesota Press, especially *Edges of the State* in chapters 1, 2, 5, and 6. I've tried to avoid outright repetition except in a few places where I thought it best to maintain consistency in my formulations. Some passages strongly resonate with others across chapters and previous books. To keep this book to a reasonable length, at times I refer readers to longer analyses I've done elsewhere.

In what I have discovered is a relatively common experience, I had a hard time writing during the Covid years. I had written the ideology and berserker rage essays in 2016 and in 2018 respectively, and I was able to write the Capitol essay in the summer of 2021, but that was it from spring 2020 until spring 2022. When we could drop our masks in spring 2022, I felt a surge of creative energy and wrote the Covid paper, the sports paper, and the statification and marronage essays between then and spring 2023; the Introduction was written in the summer of 2023. I devoted the fall of 2023 to revising.

Acknowledgments

For help with this project, I would like to acknowledge Quentin Badaire, Jeff Bell, Robert Bernasconi, Emanuela Bianchi, Camille Chamois, Tony Chemero, Jon Cogburn, Amy Cohen, Claire Colebrook, Bastien Craipain, Andrew Culp, Anya Daly, Miguel de Beistegui, Natalie Depraz, John Drabinski, Jeanne Etelain, Shaun Gallagher, Deborah Goldgaber, Jairus Victor Grove, Lama Hantash, Andrew Johnson, Leigh Johnson, Ed Kazarian, Julian Kiverstein, Gokhan Kodalak, Stavros Kousoulas, Len Lawlor, Michelle Maiese, David Morris, Rodrigo Nunes, Lucy Osler, Davide Panagia, Charles Pence, Andrej Radman, Jason Read, Anne Sauvargnargues, Eric Schliesser, Guillaume Sibertin-Blanc, Jan Slaby, Daniel J. Smith, Daniel W. Smith, Henry Somers-Hall, Greg Stone, John Sutton, Adriel M. Trott, Daniela Voss, Charles Wolfe, Dan Zahavi, and an anonymous reviewer of the manuscript for the University of Minnesota Press.

For institutional support, I would like to acknowledge Louisiana State University for sabbatical leave in fall 2015 and fall 2022, which provided time free from teaching and administration.

Mostly, and as always, my loving relation with Kate Jensen enabled me in so many ways that my writing is just one aspect of my life with her.

Finally, I dedicate this book to the memory of my mother, whose words to the priest performing the last rites were to ask him to lead the congregation in a prayer for world peace.

Introduction

Bioculture and Bodies Politic

> Violence is found everywhere, but under different regimes and economies.
> —Deleuze and Guattari, *A Thousand Plateaus*

We live politically; we are all bodies politic. We compose societies, and they shape our corporeal being deeply. Although our living politically is biological—it is literally a form of life—there is no such thing as a raw, natural, aggressive urge that underlies human violence. While we inherit defense mechanisms, they work only when triggered culturally.[1] The many forms of violence in human ways of life, individual and group, local and global, are regulated in "regimes," so we should investigate how they set their limits of legitimacy and illegitimacy, so that we might change ours, operating in the leeway granted us by the fact that there is no natural urge to war.

In this Introduction I first treat one of the basic theses of the book: Humans are biocultural all the way down and all the way back. Then, I'll look at regimes of violence, the way in which many violent acts are regulated by cultural practices that, by taking advantage of our neural and behavioral plasticity, implant patterns and triggers of action. I will then argue that, despite its heartbreaking frequency nowadays, war, as organized group-level violence, is not a necessary consequence of human nature, a fate to which we are doomed (a notion I will develop at length in chapter 1). I will conclude with a forecast of the chapters to come.

Bioculturality

This book takes a biocultural stance, with a moderate social constructivism, a modified sociological functionalism, and an anti-progressivism concerning social formations. To take up the last point: States are not the telos of social formations, which is a good thing, as many of them entrench domination and exploitation, even if we seem to be stuck with them and might as well try to use them as we can. Regarding the moderation of my social constructivism, while I believe many human capacities are deeply embodied via socialization, I am far from precluding consideration of our biological nature, as deep embodiment is possible only as a result of a developmental plasticity that is an evolved inheritance. Because interdependent social living was necessary for our deep ancestors, such plasticity is nonetheless compatible with an inherited predisposition to prosociality, or tendency to act, because of cognitive and emotional investment in social patterns, in ways that enact those very patterns.[2] To avoid reifying such patterns, we must see that prosocial actions constitute social patterns in "upward causality," yet we are constituted as subjects capable of action by being subjected to practices—continuing through life but especially intense in childhood—that accord with those patterns in "downward causality." As I will have occasion to repeat often, prosociality does not always mean that people help one another, for indeed it is a prosocial act to punish those who violate norms, just as it is to reward norm-followers, and to experience joy when norms work out in ways that accord with our expectations. Thanks to this prosocial investment, many of our thoughts and desires are shaped in ways that produce acts which reproduce the social patterns in which we were raised, hence the problem of investment in patterns that hurt us and many of our fellows. To differentiate between acts that produce joy for the actor by lowering the self-affirming interactive capacities of the recipient and those that increase such capacities for actor and recipient, I will use a modified version of the Spinozist distinction between passive and active joy. Hence, those acts which hurt the interactive capacity of both actor and recipient (their ability to engage in acts of mutual empowerment) will be named de-socializing acts, and when that de-socializing produces joy in the actor, I will call that fascist joy. This accords with my definition of fascism as the desire to live in a world of asymmetrical power relations, a vertical world of command and obedience, hence a world in which self-originating mutual empowerment is stamped out. Acts that increase the potential for futher "horizontalizing" or "rhizomatic" acts of mutual empowerment will be called active joyous acts. Finally, mine is a modest functionalism, as social reproduction will leave room for struggle and innovation in response to—and formative of—social patterns. Human social formations admit of centripetal and centrifugal movements: Social formations are traversed by processes that reinforce how things have always been done as well as experiment with how things might happen differently. The ratio of the strength of those forces to each other determines the relative stability or turmoil of a society.

To think the human characteristic of bioculturality, we must overcome the separation of biological and cultural anthropology; biology and culture are aspects of concrete human life, living politically, rather than separately existing levels or realms. This overcoming is called "integrative anthropology" by Agustín Fuentes (2009, 2015), which means that if you separate biology from culture for analysis, you must synthesize them for understanding. Problems arise, though, when your method becomes your metaphysics. You can analyze life from the morphological, physiological, and neurodynamical perspectives on an organism, but "biology" is not a separate realm to which you add "culture" to end up with a human being. "Biology" and "culture" are abstractions, useful for precise thinking about mechanisms but dangerous when reified as "levels" to be addressed temporally, as if first you assure survival and then you add a dollop of culture on top. Instead, culture and biology always coexist in living politically; in a slogan, you can study digestion all you want, but no one has ever eaten "food" as opposed to this or that meat, grain, seed, or insect, produced by certain practices and consumed in a particularly meaningful way.

I will use the term "bioenculturated human being" to express the concrete whole of living politically.[3] From this perspective, the patterns, triggers, and thresholds of the affective cognition that is the stuff of experience, the way in which human lives are lived, are produced via transgenerational subjectification practices modifying a plastic being in its development. That plasticity is a biological inheritance. The somatic and the social are not separate levels but processes linked in a spiraling interweaving at three temporal scales: the long-term phylogenetic (we inherit a plastic capacity for living in interdependent niches), the mid-term ontogenetic (we develop our embodied capacities as we are embedded in practices), and the short-term behavioral (as developed bodies politic we act and react to our material and semiotic encounters). Our bodies politic are in process; we live politically by somaticizing our socialization—that is, by digesting and incorporating material and semiotic inputs we produce our bodies politic. The interweaving of soma and society means we cannot think of biocultural human lives as mere input/output machines passively patterned by their environment (that way lies a discredited social constructivism) or passively programmed by their genes (an equally discredited genetic determinism).

Developmental Systems Theory

To make sense of bioculturality, I now turn to an important school of thought in contemporary critical biology: "Developmental Systems Theory" (DST), which developed from the writings of Richard Lewontin (2002), Susan Oyama (2000), Paul Griffiths and Russell Gray (Griffiths and Gray 1997, 2001, 2004, 2005), and others (Oyama, Griffiths, and Gray 2001).[4] A recent article by Griffiths and Stotz (2018) provides a précis of DST:

> DST analyses development, heredity, and evolution in a way that avoids dichotomies such as nature versus nurture, genes versus environment, and biology versus culture. In this framework, *development* (ontogeny) is the reconstruction of a life cycle using resources passed on by previous life cycles. DST takes *heredity* to encompass both the stability and the plasticity of biological form, which are complementary aspects of the recurrence and modification, in each generation, of a system of genetic, epigenetic, and exogenetic developmental resources [citation omitted]. The prime focus of a DST account of *evolution* is the life cycle— the series of events that occurs in each generation of a lineage. The process of evolution is the differential reproduction of variant life cycles. (225)

I want to expand a bit on three concepts associated with DST: plasticity, niche-construction, and life cycle. The bioenculturated human being is developmentally plastic—that is, it is neither a simple blank slate nor a determined mechanism. Instead, our biological inheritance is to be open to the subjectification practices we undergo in our cultural embedding, practices that work with the broad contours provided by the genetic contribution to development to install culturally variant triggers and thresholds to the patterns that are our common heritage. Griffiths (2007) uses the example of fear to make this point, but the same holds for the emotion of rage we will discuss in chapter 3: "The empirical evidence suggests that in humans the actual fear response—the output side of fear—is an outcome of very coarse-grained selection, since it responds to danger of all kinds. The emotional appraisal mechanism for fear—the input side—seems to have been shaped by a combination of very fine-grained selection, since it is primed to respond to crude snake-like gestalts, and selection for developmental plasticity, since very few stimuli elicit fear without relevant experience" (Griffiths 2007, 204).

A second key notion for our notion of bioculturality is "niche-construction." Developmental plasticity on the ontogenetic level is never a mere mechanical stamping process, even if disciplinary practices attempt to instill as much behavioral conformity as they can. But we cannot see evolution as the adaptation of organisms to independently changing environments (the organism thus being reactive). Rather, DST follows Richard Lewontin (2002) and others in focusing on the way in which bioenculturated organisms, in their practices, consciously and unconsciously shape the environment they live in and in which their offspring will live (Fuentes 2017). Bioenculturated human beings thus play a role in selecting which environmental factors are most important for them and their offspring. Thus, evolution should be seen not simply as the change in gene frequency (a mere "bookkeeping" perspective) but as the change in organism–environment systems—that is, the organism in its constructed niche (Griffiths and Gray 2005).

Allied with niche-construction, a third key notion is that the "life cycle" should be considered the unit of development and evolution. For DST adherents, the developmental system considered in an evolutionary perspective is the widest possible extension of developmental resources that are reliably present (or better, re-created) across generations. The "life cycle" considered from an evolutionary perspective is the series of events caused by this developmental matrix that recurs in each generation (Griffiths and Gray 1997, 2001, 2004). The evolutionary perspective on the notions of developmental system and life cycle is thus different from the individual perspective, where events need not recur: A singular event might play a crucial role in the development of any one individual, but unless it reliably recurs, it will not have a role in evolution; DST thus avoids the specter of Lamarckism. In their evolutionary work, DST thinkers thus extend the notion of epigenetic inheritance from the intra-nuclear factors of chromatin markings to the cytoplasmic environment of the egg (an extension many mainstream biologists have come to accept) and beyond to intraorganismic and even (most controversially) to extra-somatic factors—that is, to the relevant, constructed features of the physical and social environments (for example, species-typical brain development in humans needs language exposure in critical sensitive windows) (Griffiths and Gray 1997, 2001, 2004; Jablonka and Lamb 2005).

One of the consequences of adopting a DST perspective is that we can replace the term "innate" with "reliably produced given certain environmental factors." For DST, traits are not simply pre-programmed, as the traditional sense of "innate" might lead one to think, but are the product of a dynamic developmental process influenced by genetic, epigenetic, and environmental factors. This perspective allows us to analyze how different societies cultivate distinct patterns from similar biological endowments. For example, rather than genetically inheriting a predisposition to violent behavior, we inherit the potential to develop certain behavioral patterns, including those involving violence, which may be triggered by specific culturally meaningful signs. It is precisely the meshing of cultural practices and the various types of subjects called forth by them, producing a distribution of cognitive and affective patterns, thresholds, and triggers in a given population, that are to be analyzed in the study of regimes of violence.

Regimes of Violence

A regime of violence consists of the implicit norms or explicit codes that make sense of and that initiate, continue, or end, the sort of violent acts that are characteristic of a particular social system. Such norms need not be formally encoded in linguistically transmitted rules; there just has to be a developed habitus in the group, a felt sense that is evoked by violent acts that is prevalent enough and accurate enough to maintain a pattern of behavior characteristic of that society.[5] The notion of regime of violence means that violence is not a natural impulse but is always enacted in socially normative ways, indicative of the history of a community.[6] Now, of course that doesn't mean that a norm can't be violated, but violation itself is a normative concept. You can't condemn murder if you have a purely population–biology perspective and are just talking about mortality rates. Then it's all just killing; there's no murder. There are then two limit cases in considering regimes of violence: a Hobbesian state of nature, which is a maximally loose regime of violence, wherein there is no murder, just killing when it is perceived to be necessary; and, on the other hand, an absolute pacifism, such a highly restricted normative structure that all violence is a violation of the code, and so all killing is murder.

   That violence occurs in regimes doesn't mean that violent acts don't sometimes seem to erupt without warning; it just means that, upon reflection, most acts of violence can be made sense of by the codes of a society, even if some are so strange that we must resort to categories of bewitchment, possession, or perversion.[7] There can, of course, be clashes of social formations such that violent acts understandable by one side are so foreign to the codes of another that, as we will explore in chapter 5, they appear senseless to the victims, "too different even to be hated" (Deleuze and Guattari 1977, 151–52, citing *Genealogy of Morals* [Nietzsche 1977, 2.6]).[8]

Mode of Being of Regimes of Violence

Regimes of violence exist in dispersed concrete acts of individuals and groups; to understand them, we need to study the formation and implementation of "affective ideologies" (chapter 2) at the intersection of the regime and the act—that is, we need to study the ways in which individual subjects, sometimes embedded in institutions, though sometimes atomized "lone wolves," are molded to enable or inhibit a range of violent acts. A regime of violence is normative; in any one system, there are right and wrong ways to be violent, even though those norms can be contested in large and small ways, all the way from civilization-shaping events, as in the rise of the "Big Gods" of Axial Age religions (Norenzayan 2013), to smaller contestation via changing mores (I experienced corporal punishment in Catholic elementary schools during the Baby Boom in ways that would not be tolerated today in many segments of American society).

Furthermore, a regime of violence is an aspect of a wider social system, intertwined with political (decision making), cultural (sense making), and productive/distributive (economic) patterns. To use Deleuzoguattarian terms, a regime of violence is the "form of content" mediated by the "regime of signs" or "form of expression" of a social formation.[9] Content for Deleuze and Guattari is composed of formed matter; the "substance of content" or finished product of a production process is a "body." In concrete human socialization, "matter" is the habits and potentials of people, often very young but in principle of any age, who are subjected to, and hence subjectified by, training practices that form them in such a way as to be prepared to be useful for the social formation in which they are inserted. Child-rearing and other training practices produce people with capacities, inclinations, and triggers of potential action; the rationalizing of such processes takes the form of disciplinary practices that produce "docile bodies" ready to be put to work in a variety of other practices (Foucault 1979). A regime of signs, or "form of expression" of a social formation, governs the putting to work of those trained bodies; they are composed of "order-words" that change the social status of bodies. Via order-words, bodies are put to work or set into an "expression" or functional structure. That is to say, human beings are socially conditioned into roles of which a regime of violence is an aspect of what is expected of them, both as subject and object of violent acts, for to be the target of violent acts is also a role in a regime of violence.

In this sense, violent acts are formations of matter: They are ways in which bodies (human bodies and material objects such as rocks and swords) are mixed together with resulting damage to the human bodies; these acts are produced by bioencultured human beings whose acts are conditioned, incited, damped down, unleashed, or otherwise modified by "order-words" such as stereotypes, commands, encouragements, and invectives. These order-words produce an "incorporeal transformation" or change in social status that makes possible a certain treatment of bodies. For instance, let's think of a body before a firing squad. The command "fire" transforms the status of that body from that of the condemned, to be led to the post, to that of the legitimate target of the shots; that change allows the firing squad to shoot at the body at the post. Accompanying that incorporeal transformation from condemned to target is the mixing of the bodies of the bullets and the victim; after the act, with the order-word of the examiner pronouncing death, there is another status change, wherein the body is now treated as a corpse, to be accorded whatever treatment is customary, such as burial, exhibition, cremation, or what-have-you.

Variation in Regimes of Violence

For Deleuze and Guattari, regimes of signs and regimes of violence vary with social forms, which themselves are defined by "machinic processes." I will provide detailed descriptions in subsequent chapters, but for now, here is a brief preview. The main social forms I will be concerned with in this book are "primitive society," State, and nomadic society.[10] (This trio is something of a motley, as in *Anti-Oedipus* the three forms in "universal history" are primitives, State, and capitalism; and nomadic societies appear only in *A Thousand Plateaus*.) Primitive societies operate via a territorialized network of immanent horizontal obligations that saturate a social field, coding material and libidinal production via "mobile blocs of debt." States are a project of centralization, hierarchy, control, and exploitation; they are described in terms of "overcoding" in *Anti-Oedipus* and "capture" in *A Thousand Plateaus*. Nomadic societies are a social form dedicated to mobility as well as to the formation and occupation of open spaces; by extension from their point of highest intensity in the Steppe nomads, we can find "nomads" in any form that flees, undermines, or resists command structures.

Although each of these formations interacts with others *in concreto*, they are distinguishable in concept. Deleuze and Guattari draw their description of primitive societies from a variety of anthropological sources, but a major focus is the Amazonian societies studied by Clastres (1989, 1994; see Viveiros de Castro 2019 and Badaire 2023). To break up the notion of "primitive society" that Deleuze and Guattari use, I note that these societies would be classed as sedentary horticulturalists with village and chief structure, as opposed to the nomadic foragers on which I will concentrate in chapter 1. In all these "societies against the state" we find positive anti-State mechanisms, such as refusal of overproduction as well as the refusal of central political power. Deleuze and Guattari's notion of State is involved with the Marxist notion of "Asiatic mode of production" (Sibertin-Blanc 2016; Badaire 2023). For Deleuze and Guattari, the term "nomads" refers primarily to the Steppe nomads, rather than to nomadic foragers, as is the case for most anthropology.

The "machinic processes" (characteristic means of arranging material and semiotic flows) of these social formations are capture, prevention-anticipation, and "war machines" (Deleuze and Guattari 1987, 435). States operate by "overcoding" and "capture." The former turns the qualitative into the quantitative, changing ritual territory, activity, and exchange into measurable and hence comparable units of land, work, and money. The latter is extraction of a surplus: rent from land, surplus labor from work, and taxes from currency (443–44). Primitive societies prevent or ward off the formation of State-central hierarchies, and war machines are, at their point of highest intensity, shown in the way in which Steppe nomad social life is organized. The corresponding regimes of violence are, for the State, primitive accumulation or the structural violence that simultaneously constitutes capture and the right to capture; this is in effect the monopolistic appropriation of violence, which is legitimated for state agents at the same time as it is coded as "crime" for nonstate agents. For primitive societies, the regime of violence, according to Deleuze and Guattari, is "struggle," or the performance of serial violence in so-called status-driven "ritual war." (We will untangle the "primitive" regime of violence in chapter 1, distinguishing revenge, feud, status raids, and war as anonymous intergroup violence.) For Deleuze and Guattari's "nomadic" societies, typified by the Steppe nomads, the regime of violence is "war," which, while it can take the form of violent action directed against established States, can also mean revolutionary change directed against any sort of predictable fixed order (1987, 422–23). What we contemporaries mean by war as inter-State conflict is for Deleuze and Guattari the result of the State capture of war machines and their transformation into "armed forces" put to political ends.[11]

In chapter 5, I will discuss the relation of state and nonstate regimes of violence, adding to Deleuze and Guattari's list the social form and regime of violence of maroons, those who flee states (and may possibly found states in certain circumstances). I will narrow that focus when, in chapter 6, I discuss the regimes of violence of mastery and marronage in the Atlantic slavery system. The regimes of violence of foragers and maroons are often related to the state but have their own, often anti-State, specificity. I won't deal too extensively with Deleuze and Guattari's most-well-known regime of violence, the Steppe nomad "war machine."[12] Nor, by dint of a lack of training and by an overwhelming literature on the subject, will I discuss terrorism, one of the most important dimensions of many contemporary regimes of violence.[13]

Social Formation	Machinic Process	Regime of Violence
State	Overcoding / capture	Primitive accumulation / structural violence / crime versus policing / war as political aim
Primitive (territorialized)	Prevention–anticipation	"Struggle"
Nomadic (forager)	Prevention–anticipation	"Reverse dominance hierarchy" / revenge
Nomadic (Steppe)	War machine / mutation	War as armed struggle when confronting state
Nomadic (generalized)	Mutation	Revolutions confronting command institutions
Maroons	Autonomy-seeking flight / refuge	Liberating violence / defense / raid

Comparison of State, primitive, nomadic, and maroon social formations, machinic processes, and regimes of violence.

Physical and Social Violence

I will use a quite flat notion of violence, in line with, to use one example among many, what Johanna Oksala in *Foucault, Politics, and Violence* (2012) says is a "very narrow" way of treating violence as "intentional bodily harm that reflects the sense in which violence is generally held to be categorically objectionable" (8–9). However, I will also slightly widen this sense, but not so far as what Leonard Lawlor (2016) calls "transcendental violence" (that which inhabits the "fundamental structure of experience" [xi]).[14] Nor will I discuss what we could call "ontological violence"—a Nietzschean ontology of force leading to thinking of concrete objects as the result of processes of violent integration, appropriation, and exploitation. Similarly, I won't pursue what we could call "interpretive violence"—that which chops up the world, taking this as that, the very form of discursive thought (what Žižek 2008 calls "symbolic" violence; in this vein, see also Murphy 2012, a wonderful tour of the "ubiquity" of images of violence in contemporary Continental philosophy). Hence, I don't want to say that philosophical thought is violent in breaking with habit or with a dogmatic image of thought, that we must destroy Oedipus, or that we must think that identity or subject formation is inescapably bound up with the violence of excluding others. Going beyond sheer physical violence, but not so far as ontological or interpretive violence, I will extend the notion of violence to "social violence." In what I call a "dynamic interactionist" view (Protevi 2013), and as I discussed in the section on bioculturality, human beings are webs of social and somatic interaction. On this basis, I want to consider social group norm enforcement via shunning, ostracism, and exile as forms of social violence, as they cut us off from the relations that constitute ourselves.[15] Cutting off your relations is cutting into your being and can show up in depression and perhaps "weathering" (stress-related rapid aging), as we will discuss in chapter 8. To be clear, even this social violence is regulated by a regime. In any one society, there are justified acts of social violence when applied to bullies and shirkers, and there are unjustly applied insults, as well as denigrating or dehumanizing categorizations. An insult is different from rebuking someone for breaking social expectations. An insult is an unjust harm to dignity; it says someone is not worthy of the esteem owed them by their social standing. Systematic insult is both socially violent and can worryingly lower the threshold for the targeting of people with physical violence by others or by oneself (self-identifying with demeaning categories can lead to physical self-harm).

A major reason I want to include the category of "social violence" is that these regulatory practices are a key to the anti-state and anti-war effects of the economy of violence of pre-state and nonstate societies (what Boehm 2012a and 2012b call a "reverse dominance hierarchy"): They keep societies to a personal and egalitarian regime of violence, avoiding the installation and maintenance of state violence via armies and police, and avoid the anonymous group violence of war. This focus on nonstate societies will be a departure from almost the entirety of contemporary political philosophy and political theory, which—after a few pro forma nods to the anarchist tradition—almost always looks at the economies of violence of concern to states as that which holds the monopoly on the legitimate use of violence: crimes, wars, and terrorism, matched by police, armed forces, and security forces.[16] "What justifies this or that level of state violence?" is the question for these fields. That's not to say that "security studies," as a branch of the political science subfield of "International Relations," doesn't tackle the complexity of what is variously called "fourth-generation warfare" or "post-Westphalian conflicts," but even those for the most part look at how states deal with that which escapes their control and threatens their economy of violence.

Physical violence produces pain by hurting bodies and damaging tissues, and social violence hurts us by cutting our relations. To use some Spinozist notions, both forms of violence forcibly impose a sadness that marks the diminishing of your power to affect and to be affected, to engage a wide and mutually empowering range of encounters. In being the victim of violence, your world shrinks, as memorably described by Elaine Scarry (1987), though it can be rebuilt, as movingly shown by Susan Brison (2003). Violence is transitive and uninvited, for the most part, although ambiguity holds in some other cases. In some initiation rites, flesh is marked, and pain is produced, but we could say this violence is transitive but invited as the initiates welcome the rites in principle (Clastres 1989; see also Deleuze and Guattari 1977, chapter 3). A recognized pattern of ongoing violence, or recognition of its possible actualization, often serves to constrain action by activating motivation to avoid the source of pain. Hence violence can shape the field of action. That's not to say all power ("action on the action of others" per Foucault 2007) is violent in act, but the possibility of power involving violence, especially when considering "sovereign power," is always there.

For most of this book, I'll be talking about direct physical and social violence, but I'll expand it in the last chapter to talk about distributed harms

of American racism, where social violence is, some claim, physically registered in the phenomenon of weathering. That harm has connections to historical patterns of direct physical and social violence but also is constituted
by economic limits and residential segregation and their impact on, among
other factors, poor food quality, lowered healthcare accessibility, limited
recreational facilities, and psychological stress from microaggressions.[17]

Human Nature Is Not Essentially Violent

I will discuss human nature in more detail in chapter 1. Here I would like
to offer just a brief defense of the idea that group violence is not an essential attribute of our living politically, even if it occurs with distressing regu-
larity in all-too-many circumstances; in fact, I don't think we should think
in terms of essences (fixed and stable sets of necessary and sufficient conditions) at all as a rule, and especially not when discussing human nature.[18]
While all social systems regulate violence, I don't think that means we as
a species are somehow predisposed to violence either at the group or individual level. Peace is not what prevents the default setting of war from
breaking through, and we are rather pacific in the vast majority of daily
interactions.[19] By the same token, war is not the failure of our achieving
our peaceful essential nature.

Instead of thinking in terms of essences, we should think of human
nature in terms of what Deleuze and Guattari call multiplicities: the patterns, triggers, and thresholds of a set of interacting intensive biocultural
processes. A multiplicity is an irreducibly diverse sheaf with resonances,
feedback loops, and rhythms among its processes; ontologically speaking,
it is virtual—that is, it is a set of potentials embedded in those intersecting processes; it exists only dispersed in the concrete instances that ensue
when certain thresholds in the relation of those processes are met.[20] Thus,
while violence, individual and collective, is certainly part of our potentials,
it is not our essence, as violent acts are produced only when certain social
and somatic processes intersect at the right intensity. Violence is not a natural drive we barely keep in check, even if, in certain extreme cases, we find
ourselves caught up by a berserker rage. As we will see in chapter 3, a berserker rage depends on the meshing together of evolutionarily developed
mechanisms along with culturally imposed triggers, but we are no more
essentially defined by rages than we are defined by sculpting or painting.
Nor are we "predisposed" to such rages any more than we are predisposed

to anxiety attacks, depressions, or diabetic comas. Rather, violent acts, while they are made possible by evolutionary inheritances such as eyesight, arm strength, and neurological defensive postures, are performed by bioenculturated beings whose actions are triggered by situations and order-words regulated by a regime of violence. Hence, I want to insist that sharing and peaceful cooperation are equally potentials whose actualization is within our grasp, as they are well attested to in our evolutionary past. The question I will pursue in chapter 1's study of the selection pressures productive of human nature will not turn on the *possibilities* of individual and group violence or cooperation, but on their *frequencies* during the long evolution of our species.

On the individual psychology level, I don't think all human tendencies are straightforward adaptations from a putative "environment of evolutionary adaptedness" (EEA) seen as a restricted set of problems posed by the environment of our nomadic forager ancestors. Rather, as I will sketch in chapter 1, plasticity, niche-construction, and ecopolitical experimentation prevent that sort of passive adaptation or "lock and key" picture. On the cultural level, while I do think ways of life (reward and punishment systems, both material and symbolic, for both child-rearing and adult life) can enter into competition, especially when war becomes a rational option, I will present anthropological claims that allow us to doubt that war was frequent or intense enough to be considered the default setting for pre-state intergroup relations.[21] In fact, a quite radical strain in current anthropological research suggests that flexible social networks among contemporary foragers might let us question the basic social ontology of "groups," let alone inter-group conflict, as features of our evolutionary past (Bird et al. 2019). But even if we stay with the notion of groups, we shouldn't always assume inter-group conflict; we can't gainsay translation, multilingualism, and cultural diffusion as possible, and indeed frequent, inter-group relations.

Forecast of the Book

Part I: Political Living. In this part, I first lay out an argument for a notion of human nature as biocultural (we live politically; our bodies and minds are linked together by social practices that become deeply embodied). I will emphasize our significant capacities of joyful sharing; I do so with the help of an analysis of regimes of violence that render suspect the notion of early inter-group violence that was frequent and intense enough to serve as a selection pressure for the prosociality that marks our species. I then investigate affective ideology as the psychological mechanism by which regimes of violence regulate social reproduction.

Chapter 1: Human Nature. By delving into recent anthropological literature on human evolution, I hint at what we might become if we build upon the potentially joyous cooperative aspects of human nature. This is not an instance of the naturalist fallacy. I'm not saying we *should* joyfully share *because* that's our nature. I am saying joyful sharing is not impossibly swimming against the tide of an essentially egoistic and competitive human nature. All I want to do is clear a space for a world that is a more peaceful and cooperative world than we have today; I will show it's not an impossible dream from which we are precluded because of a bellicose deep history that has embedded a xenophobic strain in human nature.

Chapter 2: Affective Ideology. In this chapter I emphasize social psychology rather than anthropology. As I have argued that prosociality, *qua* intellectual and emotional investment in social patterns, is typical of bio-enculturated human beings, in this chapter I examine how prosociality is concretized. How does a regime of violence regulate and motivate acts directed at the reproduction of social patterns? I will claim that ideology, when seen as a flawed belief system, is inadequate to explain the use of violence in coerced social reproduction, but that a notion of "affective ideology" would do the trick.

Part II: Political Psychology. Given that we live politically, such that our social practices guide our sentiments and actions even in the case of violence, here I present two limited cases of regimes of violence. First, I examine berserker rages, which are phenomena that, at the limit of a regime of violence, show a violence so extreme that it leads to a loss of autobiographically maintained narrative identity. Second, I present a case study of *esprit de corps* in team sports that does not see sports as mere sublimated violence but, building on chapter 1's analyses, as an expression of joy in cooperative striving based partially on resonant bodily effort.

Chapter 3: Berserkers. In this chapter, I follow the leading idea of an "inhuman gaze" to explore the perceptual-motor effects and possible episodic memory inhibition in extreme cases of the "berserker rage." I first locate berserker rages in a taxonomy of aggressive behavior as out-of-control reactive aggression triggered by blocked flight in a high-danger situation. I then sketch its military implications and follow that by presenting a plausible neurological substrate. I then zero in on the most extreme manifestations, the so-called blackout rages—or, in technical terms, "Transient Global Amnesia" (TGA)—in which episodic memory is inhibited or attenuated, even though there is retention of affective-charged sensory fragments.

Chapter 4: *Esprit de Corps.* If human nature is not an essence molded by an evolutionary history in which group conflict was a major factor, then sports is not sublimated violence, as sublimation implies an essential deep drive that needs to be diverted. Joy from shared resonant motion is just as indicative of the multiplicity of human nature as is violence triggered by threats to self and others. The discursive fields of relational autonomy and collective intentionality seek to disrupt the notion of human individuals as self-enclosed subjects relating to the world via representation and calculation; instead, they look at human flourishing through mutually affirming social relations. I present a case study in which we can see several themes in the scholarly literature exemplified in a real-life event. The event in question is the Megan Rapinoe–Abby Wambach goal in the quarterfinals of the Women's World Cup of 2011, one of the greatest in all soccer history.

Part III: Political Anthropology. In this section I turn to political anthropology and the relations of state and nonstate peoples. I interrogate Deleuze and Guattari's use of Pierre Clastres by bringing to bear the work of James C. Scott on the regimes of violence embedded in processes of imposing a state form on nonstate people and on the regimes of violence involved in flight from states, especially by those who would be condemned to lives of servitude, exploitation, and arbitrary "masterly" violence were they to be forced to remain in states.

Chapter 5: Statification. I improve upon Deleuze and Guattari's somewhat cavalier dismissal of historical processes of state formation by examining *Anti-Oedipus* and *A Thousand Plateaus* in the context of new anthropological research on early states. I distinguish pure abstract machines from mixed-concrete assemblages. As an abstract machine, "the State" is the limit of the processes of overcoding and capture. Similarly, there are tendencies in all concrete societies to primitive territoriality, nomadic mutability, and other limit conditions. In other words, "the State" has never existed, no more than pure "primitivity" or "nomadicity," as all concrete social assemblages are mixtures of tendencies. In some cases, however, the tendency toward centralization, hierarchization, and "legibility" (ability of flows to be measured) is so strong that we call them, empirically, "states."

I look at the contingent encounter of both endogenous and exogenous factors as plausible mechanisms for some instances of state-formation.

Chapter 6: Marronage. I examine the figure of the maroon, that is, the runaway enslaved person. Here again the concept of a regime of violence is foregrounded. I will concentrate on the plantation slavery system of the New World, though I believe that what I say, insofar as I incorporate work by James C. Scott on southeast Asia, will illuminate marronage in other circumstances. I will show in a materialist but not reductionist manner that the analysis of the maroon regime of violence lets us see the social structure and geographical features of maroon communities through the lens of "marginality"—that is, the search for a form of life that best enables, though of course it doesn't guarantee, the independence of maroons faced with the massive violence capacities of the plantocracy. I don't want to say that my analysis is a total reduction, as I won't try to derive their art and music and religion from their regime of violence, so I don't want to say that the cultural life of maroons was nothing but preparation for war, but I certainly think war is a central factor in their form of life.

Part IV: Political Events. Here I bring together philosophical, anthropological, and enactive cognitive science analyses of regimes of violence in two case studies that examine the political violence of the January 6, 2021, invasion of the U.S. Capitol, and the structural violence of U.S. racism found in the fate of an "essential worker" in the management of the Covid-19 pandemic, respectively.

Chapter 7: The Capitol Invasion. I present a case study of the January 6, 2021, invasion of the U.S. Capitol. Something happened at the Capitol: an event, a drama, a haecceity, a case. Many others have interpreted the meaning of the actions, so rather than simply repeat their efforts, I want to contextualize the meanings of the event by looking at the "political affordances" of the Capitol as they elicited political actions and bodily affects in a politically charged built environment. I look at how features of the building solicited actions that are ordinarily mundane but were spectacularly out of place when performed by those people that day at the Capitol. In particular, I'll look at how the dais in the Senate chamber prompted prayers by Jacob Chansley, the "Q-Anon Shaman," in the simultaneously grandiose and paranoid "Trumpian ecumenical" style.

Chapter 8: Covid-19 in the United States. I present a case study that is both heartbreakingly concrete and illustrative of wider trends: the story of the life and death of Shenetta White-Ballard, a nurse at a senior care facility and hence an "essential worker," who died after exposure to Covid-19 at work. I provide a Foucauldian analysis of the long development of "bio-power" regimes for public health and disease management, culminating in the development in the last forty years of a regime of neoliberalism, financialization of daily life, and risk management as we are subjectified as "self-entrepreneurs" responsible for health decisions for self and family. Moving still closer to the present, I look at race and Covid-19 in the United States, specifically the notion of "preexisting conditions" or "comorbidities" and their relation to "weathering," the thesis that chronic stress in populations suffering anti-Black racism will accelerate aging as measured by telomere length. Hence, when faced with the Covid-19 pandemic, those who are negatively racialized and precariously employed, deprived of a robust social safety net so that they are left as life-management agents responsible for both self and family, face an intense entanglement of financial and viral risk management. Turning briefly to enactive accounts, we see that searching for epistemic solutions itself imposes a physiological cost that contributes to weathering.

Conclusion. I bring together the philosophical, anthropological, and political themes of the book to consider a politics of joy that, while it takes seriously the awful spectacle of the passive fascist joy of fusion into a crowd transfixed by a transcendent leader, nonetheless tries to show what an antifascist life would look like when it seeks to maximize mutually empowering active joyous encounters.

Part I

Political Living

1

Human Nature

We live politically; our bodies and minds are shaped by our upbringing. While cultures vary, we are all bioenculturated. Such bioculturality means I should clarify my notion of human nature. Although we all know that we're on dangerous ground when we talk about "human nature," I think it's worth the risk.[1] It's risky, as thick or content-laden versions of that concept have long been used to justify exclusions, hierarchies, and command structures based on, among other things, the need to arrange society so as to put the dependent to work to provide the thoughtful with the leisure necessary to contemplate reality,[2] or prod the lazy into achieving what is the rational productivist nature of their betters,[3] or the need to rein in, via culturally induced rational control, a fearsomely violent and hyper-individualist human nature that only external control keeps in line.[4] Not to mention the claims that the construction of "the human" in Western modernity was forged in the flames of colonial power as both anti-indigenous and anti-Black.[5] "Political living" means not simply that we live together in organized societies but that a restricted sense of "politics" as particular forms of striving within and across societies influence how we think our "nature," how our bodies shape our minds. Those accounts of a lazy, violent, or "primitive," overly emotional human nature (expressed by all but the few) held in check by culturally induced top-down cognitive control (successfully internalized by the few, externally imposed on the others via coercive institutions) leave us with a pessimism that forecloses many political reforms based on positive and bottom-up care and cooperation capacities, which are labeled as idealistic fantasies.

But we needn't settle for those stories; we should intervene in that discursive field. And that intervention shouldn't abandon the rhetorical power of appeals to human nature or the concepts of evolutionary anthropology; as there's plenty of human nature talk in our political lives, we should tackle it head on. Even in acknowledging the importance of considering evolved human nature, however, we need not concede science to "biofatalists" (analyzed by Barker 2015) or to "evoconservatives" (analyzed by Buchanan and Powell 2018) who stress the limits that their version of human nature puts on efforts to institutionalize joyous cooperative inclusivity. We should, rather, insist that it's better science to explore the complexities of human nature as biocultural flexibility with a prosocial default setting. This keeps the door open for social formations whose highly restricted regimes of violence minimize organized war, exploitation, and domination. All societies have regimes of violence, but there are better and worse regimes, and we shouldn't let certain bellicose views of human nature keep us from attempting to institute better ones than those we have now. In wading into evolutionary human nature discourse, there is always a danger of nonspecialists like me combating one just-so story with another, even if, rather than daring a "how actually" assertion, I hedge my bets with a "how possibly" narrative (Kitcher 2011), or even a "how probably" narrative (Kumar and Campbell 2022). I trace a path through the literature which shows that joy in sharing is not only a possible factor in the evolution of human prosociality but that it is instead arguably a more important one than anger in war. I will not be able, unfortunately, because of limitations of space and my own training, to produce definitive surveys of the literature or knock down arguments against those emphasizing frequent and intense war. But I can, I think, point to interesting new research that might not be known to some of my readers.

I should justify treading on such controversial ground; why shouldn't we just wait out the resolution of the conflicts among the experts? Here I can appeal to the interventionist aspect of this chapter. The inter-group conflict story is out there already (e.g., one example among many, Bowles and Gintis 2013; for criticism of that work, see Sterelny 2014 and 2021) and showing that it's not the only story on hand—in other words, showing the variability in early regimes of violence, such that nonwar violence regimes were possible and indeed quite plausibly frequently occurring— has political benefits in expanding the range of what is possible for us given our human nature; hence this chapter is an anti-"biofatalist" maneuver in the sense of Barker (2015). In other words, there are contemporary political benefits to establishing that xenophilic joy in cooperation and sharing is not swimming against the tide of an essentially individualist and egoist human nature alleviated only by conflict-sharpened group bonds. As should be clear, this is also not a story of activist politics against strict science, as the group conflict story itself has its own political entanglements (as shown strikingly in Segovia-Cuéllar and Del Savio 2021).

In this chapter I begin with a sketch of Evolutionary Psychology as a foil to my notion of human nature. Next, expanding upon the Introduction, I present a sketch of my definition of human nature as bioculturality with a prosocial predisposition, using as a guiding thread through the human evolution literature the relative lack of attention to joy as a consequence of and motivation for sharing. I then present a discussion of the regimes of violence found in our past.[6] Having put forth a plausible account that early nomadic foragers did not encounter frequent and intense war as a part of their regime of violence, I conclude with a discussion of research showing interdependent cooperation with daily and occasional contacts from near and far, from family, friends, and strangers, as the selection pressure for prosociality.

Evolutionary Psychology

Among the contemporary perspectives on human nature, that of Evolutionary Psychology will be my foil. Given the huge and often highly technical literature it has provoked, this can be an only all too brief primer, useful solely for situating my position.[7] By most accounts, Evolutionary Psychology was formed as a successor to the sociobiology made famous by E. O. Wilson (1975; see Ruse 1985 and Kitcher 1987 for the early controversy). Like its immediate ancestor, Evolutionary Psychology is highly controversial, with passionate critics and defenders. While sociobiology just looked at evolutionary determinants of behavior, Evolutionary Psychology includes the study of proximate psychological mechanisms (motivating psychological states), which it distinguishes from ultimate explanations. Such ultimate explanations are grounded in evolution by natural or sexual selection in the Environment of Evolutionary Adaptedness (EEA), which can date back as far as several million years ago in the evolution of our hominin ancestors, before the establishment of the genus *Homo,* and as far forward as the late Pleistocene, around 20,000 years ago. Both natural and sexual selection requires variation in fitness-affecting heritable traits that are selected for (or, alternatively, less-competitive traits are selected against) by natural and social environmental pressure, with differential reproduction of traits in succeeding generations.

Evolutionary Psychology sees its proximate mechanisms as psychological "modules" (closed software programs that compute solutions to problems); such modules are adaptations—that is, holdovers which direct actions that, when performed by our ancestors, led to successful solutions to common problems of EEA that helped differential reproduction. Sometimes we find mismatches between what we have inherited—an adaptation formed in the EEA—and the way we live in modern mass society, as in the oft-repeated slogan "Stone Age minds in modern skulls." For the biofatalists, such mismatches set limits to further changes in society that risk provoking even more psychological mayhem than we now suffer when our mental modules fire as they are presented with cues that might have been rare for our ancestors but are all too common today.[8] Finally, among the commonly accepted Evolutionary Psychology notions of living politically in the EEA most relevant to this chapter is the view that, in addition to intra-group violence, inter-group violence was frequent and intense enough to serve as a selection pressure for prosociality, in the form of intra-group norm development and enforcement allowing a coherent and motivated force leading to success in battle. Sometimes this is tied to a narrative linking contemporary war to chimpanzee inter-group violence.[9]

The approach to human nature I present below is identifiable as both psychological and evolutionary, though it departs from standard Evolutionary Psychology in the following ways: (1) a Developmental Systems Theory approach to evolution focusing on life cycles rather than genes (see above in the Introduction); (2) a moderate neural and behavioral plasticity (allowing for a moderate social constructivism) as our major adaptation, rather than massive modularity; (3) an emphasis on joy as a proximate mechanism;[10] (4) a less bellicose version of the EEA; and, linked with that, (5) a networked social structure rather than an aggregation of closed bands into larger tribes.

Because of its importance to my approach, the social structure argument should be treated here. According to an important recent article (Bird et al. 2019), early nonstate foragers may not have had hard in-group versus out-group organization but instead an extended network system such that residential, kinship, productive, and ritual activities do not line up with each other as they do in "small-scale" societies with a concentric circle pattern. In such "small-scale societies," you add together relatively small and closed families who live, work, and pray together in close geographical proximity to get bands and then add together bands to get tribes, with each step progressively widening the geographical area without, however, severely disrupting the core family structure. I say "relatively" closed because any ethnographically informed small-scale society theory accepts some measure of a "fission–fusion" pattern with some movement within and between bands. We could say that at the limit of a fission–fusion pattern we pass over into a network model, which is the tendency of the analysis by Fry (2006, 168–69). By contrast with group-bonded social formations, in Bird et al.'s picture of a network society ("large societies" in their terms), those you live with aren't necessarily the ones with whom you forage, nor are they necessarily your kin, nor do they necessarily perform the same ritual roles at the same sites. If we can accept the hypothesis that "large societies . . . are inherent features of the Pleistocene spread of modern humans" (Bird et al. 2019, 106), then we face radical revisions to our picture of early human social life. Briefly put, the assumption that "inter-group conflict" was endemic to the EEA becomes questionable, as these hypothesized network living practices mean you can't assume that "inter-group conflict" was the default setting if relatively closed "groups" were not a good description of early social formations. In this picture, group-bound "small-scale societies" are not the kernel that expands via aggregative fusion to later form cities and states but are rather the limit case of fission, the breakdown into restricted clumps, of early network society.

The consequence of this revision most important for this book is that a defensible position in contemporary anthropology claims that we have wrongly retrojected the xenophobic regime of violence generated by later "small-scale society" necessary to protect group-bound material wealth accumulation onto the xenophilic and anti-command regime of violence generated by early "large society" networks operating by "relational wealth" (Bird et al. 2019, 105–6). (Note that the networked society hypothesis, even if it leads to questioning frequent and intense inter-group conflict as a prominent part of our ancestral regimes of violence, does not deny personal or individual violent acts as part of those regimes.)[11]

Human Nature: Biocultural Plasticity Predisposed to Prosociality

My definition of human nature is "a multiplicity or virtual differential field of biocultural processes insisting in different existing actual assemblages of politically inflected affective cognition."[12] A multiplicity is composed of the virtual patterns, triggers, and thresholds of a set of interacting intensive processes; multiplicities are not essences—that is, fixed and stable sets of necessary and sufficient conditions. Rather, they are the matrix for processes of actualization producing at times novel entities whose interactions feed back into the virtual multiplicity to change it.[13] "Virtual" is a term of ontological modality—a pattern of walking does not exist in the same way any one actual series of steps exists, but it is nonetheless part of the real world (Webster 2023). Rather, we should say that the virtual pattern "insists" on those actual series. "Actual" here means distinctly formed and identifiable: A step, as the meeting of foot and ground, is distinct from the steps that precede and follow it. An assemblage is a set of actual interacting processes in which thresholds in the patterns of those processes—in the relations among the processes—trigger qualitative changes in the behavior of the system. For instance, a walk can change from strolling to jogging to running. The walking assemblage is informed by the "ambulatory motion" multiplicity it actualizes or, if you like, "incarnates."

Assemblages are biocultural: Movement patterns vary across cultures and cycle back to shape the bodies and minds that are taught to walk or dance or run in a particular way for particular reasons from childhood on. The basic viewpoint here, then, as explained in the Introduction, is that humans are biocultural: We have evolved to be open to our cultural imprinting or, in other words, we might say that our nature is to have our nurture become second nature. While this is close to social constructivism, I do think most humans have an inherited predisposition to prosociality (which doesn't mean it always appears). The preliminary definition of "prosociality" we'll use is "cognitive and emotional investment in intra- and inter-generational social patterns that constitute us as subjects, including altruistic acts." The term "altruism" here refers to acts that aid another at some cost to the agent.

Let me clarify the relation of prosociality to altruism. "Prosociality" is a wider term; a prosocial act is one that, because of cognitive and emotional investment in social patterns, reinforces those patterns. You get invested in patterns by imitation, by desire to make loved ones proud (affirming their investment), by myth, by formalized religion, by pain of initiation, and so on, in sum by what I will call in chapter 2 "affective ideology." So, if altruism is behavior that helps others at cost to oneself, then you can be led to behave altruistically by prosocial motivations. (You might even be led to behave egoistically by prosocial motivations if your social patterns praise such actions via some sort of "greed is good" training.) There is a vast literature on altruism in philosophy and anthropology; an important distinction is put forth by Kitcher (2011) between biological and psychological altruism. Both assume a cost to the agent, but the former concerns acts that help the reproductive success of the recipient (and hence can be performed by quite simple organisms) while the latter concerns acts intended by the agent to help the recipient. In the latter case, such help might indeed show up in improved reproductive success, but it need not. To clear space for psychological altruism, Kitcher helpfully critiques the hypothesis of pure psychological egoism. Pure altruism would be self-sacrifice. The psychological egoism explanation is that you may want to leave a great name behind or avoid what you expect might be crushing levels of survivor's guilt. But while such explanations might make sense from a third-party perspective, as explanations of motivation they require such complex mental gymnastics that they are implausible compared with the hypothesis of altruistic help of another in quick and direct action under the severe time constraints that are sometimes encountered.

From a third-party or economic perspective, altruistic acts can indeed be recompensated in reciprocity, either directly by the recipient or indirectly by someone motivated by the agent's reputation. (There must be a time lag between act and recompense; if they occur at the same time, the act is an instance of "mutualism.") Hence, there's no pure gift, there's always an expectation of some return; we know and feel that gifts impose obligations. But the recognition of an expectation of return doesn't seal the deal for pure egoism either; self-interest is deeply rooted but not all-encompassing, as there's always a risk in putting yourself "out there"; it's not a gift if it can't be refused or inadequately paid back, and the purely egoistic act would be to not take the risk at all. There's always an impure economy of gift and return, a rationality of risk and reward, as we learned from Mauss. A pure gift, like pure egoism, is impossible or mad. But while there are no pure gifts, there are gifts and there is sharing.[14]

As I mention in the Introduction, in my sense of the term, "prosociality" does not mean that people are always good and kind to one another but rather that we are rarely neutral to the cultural practices we are raised in that shape our minds and bodies. We are instead very often so cognitively and emotionally invested in them—some norms matter so much to us—that punishment of norm violators ensues. Obviously, cultures vary widely in content, but it seems that early-childhood prosocial development is cross-culturally robust (Callaghan and Corbit 2018).

Prosociality has second- and third-person aspects, as well as cognitive and affective aspects. Regarding cognition, neurotypical humans have second-person intersubjective understanding capacities, or "theory of mind."[15] Acts characteristic of third-person cognitive prosociality are those concerned with our relation to social patterns, which can range from traditional accounts emphasizing practical syllogism application of cases to explicitly formulated norms (that can be accessed in everyday life when we ponder moral quandaries or in legal institutions) to phenomenologically inspired approaches emphasizing our immersion in background fields and an embodied habitus that gives us a "feel for the game." I'm especially interested in the affective aspects of prosociality. Yes, you have to understand other people and their social roles in order to interact with them effectively, but you also have to care to make sure that interaction will be helpful to them. The second-person affective aspect includes helping and sharing, which appear early in human infants (Tomasello and Warnecken 2008). The third-person aspect in affective prosociality is emotional investment in social patterns: Humans buy into norms; justice matters to us. Of course, just because a population is invested in a social pattern doesn't mean that everyone benefits from it. Here, in what Deleuze and Guattari (1977) call the direct libidinal investment of the social field, you run into the "Spinoza problem": How can people in some circumstances desire to be dominated, exploited, and subjugated? Not all social patterns benefit all members of the society equally, but sometimes even the dominated want more domination: No one should be free; we should all be commanded by a strong leader! Accompanying the acts derived from this desire for a world in which command is the only social relation we find what I called "fascist joy" in the Introduction, the perverse joy in shrinking someone's world, in destroying any of their social relations other than obedience. In chapter 2 I will take up this notion once again, using the concept of "affective ideology."

Joy and Human Nature

My guiding thread into the labyrinthine evolutionary anthropological work on human nature will be something that has been often overlooked in discussions that focus on the supposedly xenophobic regimes of violence of our ancestors: the evolution of our capacity for joy in sharing and cooperation.[16]

The economics of food sharing, involving concepts of reciprocity, mutualism, kin selection, free-riding, and the like are well studied (e.g. Kaplan and Gurven 2005; Jaeggi and Gurven 2013), but I haven't seen much on joy in food sharing. The current work is a bit of a dismal science; we can't forget that barbecues can be fun, even if they are not pure gifts but involve expectations of payback. The only proximate mechanism I've seen mentioned is satisfaction from punishing free-riders (West, Griffin, and Gardner 2006). Gratitude, or at least keeping track of obligations, is often mentioned (McCullough, Kimeldorf, and Cohen 2008 see gratitude as an adaptation for prosociality). Schino and Aureli (2009) mention "emotional bookkeeping," which for them "may be at the basis of the primates' ability to reciprocate over extended time periods" (46). At the limit of pure giving, we find the notion that keeping track of obligations too closely is unseemly for close relations. Here, Gurven and Jaeggi (2015, 6) see this as akin to the notion of "generalized reciprocity" that they credit to Sahlins (1972, 193–94).

Here is a short phenomenological description of joy.[17] I assume a modest unity of human psychology (this is a chapter on human nature, after all), so I think we can extend this description across many cultures and far back in history. Although I will argue for a second-person relational notion of joy in chapter 4, here, for purposes of pursuing an immanent critique of adaptationist discourse, I will restrict myself to a first-person analysis. I think of joy in sharing as an uplifting feeling of contentment and satisfaction, a feeling that things are going well and are as they should be. When it's part of a series with a reasonable expectation of continuation, it shades into happiness as a long-term feeling (Walker and Kavedžija 2015). I'll speculate that such joy is an exaptation (the repurposing of a mechanism that was selected for other reasons) of the emotional tonality of successful parental care for offspring, spreading to encompass the experience of good relations with other kin (however that is defined by the society in question), as well as for friends, neighbors, and visitors. For the purposes of this chapter, then, I think it's fine to see joy in sharing as a proximate mechanism with an ultimate explanation, though as I discussed in the Introduction, the Developmental Systems Theory view is that the unit of selection, the locus of that explanation, is the developmental system (everything that is reliably transmitted to offspring, including social practices), not just genes per se. I also don't have a problem with talking about the evolution of joy in relation to kin selection (obviously, given the notion that it's exapted from parental care) or in relation to direct and indirect reciprocity—the expectation, however muted or prominent in the moment, of a return when in need is part of this complex feeling.

Although ritual objects are shared (and indeed food sharing will be highly ritualized in many circumstances), I will concentrate on food sharing. Even with potentially monopolizable goods (that you could keep only for family consumption), you can still share them as public goods ("everyone is welcome at the feast!"). Such sharing doesn't preclude expected reciprocity with hosting a feast, even if the payback is prestige, as in the limit case of sumptuary giving. What's important is that it is shared and that an expectation of return is generated either directly by the recipient or in a circuit influenced by reputation. It's certainly the case that gift economies can have competitive aspects or political angling, and it's certainly not the case that all sharing is always and everywhere done without grudging or grumbling, nor that it is received with angelic gratitude. But that sharing can be joyous, and that the experience of joy can be highly motivating, is something we need to foreground, despite the reluctance to do so by those who concentrate on the political economy of food sharing to the exclusion of the experiential element.[18]

As I mentioned, I find a lack of attention to joy in the evolutionary literature. I'm going to treat this as a symptom of the predominant view of the Environment of Evolutionary Adaptedness (EEA) as riven by intergroup conflict sparked by competition over scarce resources, rather than one with both competition and cooperation as possibilities—and, indeed, with networked (rather than "inter-group") cooperation as plausibly more frequent than competition and conflict. Hence, I'm going to look at how our joy in sharing could be considered as an adaptation; this means that the putative joy in sharing and the cooperation of our ancestors were adaptive when that joy was experienced by others as an honest signal of willingness to continue in a reciprocal food-sharing relation. The ultimate explanation of such sharing would be "resource variance insurance," because, by reinforcing what we will explain below as "risk-buffering" social mechanisms, it could plausibly have helped people in their struggle—not primarily or perhaps even often against rival humans but together with them against the variable nonhuman elements of their environment.[19] As I will explain below, this is an adoption of Kropotkin's "mutual aid" thesis, which is found, albeit in a minor key, in Darwin himself.[20]

Anthropological Debates over the Regimes of Violence in Human Evolution

Joy in sharing always occurs in the context of a regime of violence; the limited cases wherein joy vanishes in a humiliating pure gift or pure theft are never free of the possibility of exchanging violence for the original offer. To provide a reasonable reconstruction of the regime of violence in early human evolution, three important anthropological debates are, first, challenges to the long-dominant "Chimpanzee Referential Doctrine" (CRD) for the Last Common Ancestor (LCA) for the *Pan* (chimpanzees and bonobos) and *Homo* lineages; second, scarcity and competition in the EEA; and third, whether, in the *Homo* lineages, inter-group "coalitionary violence" was widespread and intense enough to form the primary selection pressure for human prosociality.

The Chimpanzee Referential Doctrine

The CRD posits extant chimpanzees as the best model for the LCA of the *Pan* and *Homo* lineages (Vaesen 2014; Gonzalez-Cabrera 2017). If you reject the CRD, you can remain agnostic as to the LCA and begin your analysis of modern humans within the hominin line, maintaining that chimpanzee, bonobo, and human traits had independent evolutionary origins; or you can adopt a "mosaic" conception of the LCA, such that it should be modeled with both bonobo-like and chimp-like traits. If you accept the CRD, you're pushed in the direction of a deep-roots theory of violence and war. This brings us to some high-stakes issues in moral psychology. If you accept the CRD, conscience is a top-down cognitive control of emotions that drives one to dominate others. Conscience is rooted in fear of group punishment—that is, conscience is an adaptation to "social selection," which is the violent marginalization or elimination of would-be dominators by an egalitarian group, up to and including capital punishment (Kitcher 2011; Boehm 2012a and 2012b; this is named "political selection" in Del Savio and Mameli 2020; see also Mameli 2013). Such "herd" production of conscience is, *pace* Nietzsche, not a late, post-state, cultural psychological struggle but a straightforward and early pre-state one. But in this picture, joy in collaboration vanishes and, in its place, would be mere relief at behavior that doesn't attract punishment, or at best satisfaction at having followed ethical precepts.

If you accept conscience as derived from fear of punishment directed at dominators, that doesn't mean you have to throw up your hands, but your main path to social improvement is to reinforce and / or supplement the teaching of explicit moral principles by child-rearing practices and social institutions of detection and punishment of dominance bids resulting from failures of conscience (Kitcher 2011). If you reject the CRD, conscience is still top-down but has two origins: physical punishment for dominance bids but also social punishment (rebukes) for failed care and cooperation such as quitting or nonsharing (called "partner control" in Tomasello 2016). Here, emotion doesn't have to be *only* a primitive source of trouble to be controlled so that later evolved and rationally based care and cooperation can have room to operate; it can *also* include a positive impulse to care and cooperation that can be nurtured. So, if you reject the CRD, it's easier for you to root the normative standard of active joyous encounters of care and cooperation in human nature.[21]

Scarcity and Competition in the EEA

The standard view of the EEA is one based on scarcity and competition. This is what Widerquist and McCall (2017) call the "Hobbesian Hypothesis." Note that it is always difficult to reach directly a picture of the EEA from contemporary foragers; a prime axiom of contemporary anthropology is that they are not in any way "living fossils" but fully integrated into a contemporary niche that has long been in contact with state societies. Nonetheless, we can say that because foragers in contemporary life are often pushed onto marginally productive land, if they have lives that do not always and everywhere consist of desperately scrounging for survival, it's arguable that foragers in the EEA, with their pick of prime locations, would themselves have had reasonably secure lives, at least in part and sometimes, if not often.

In the 1960s, in a celebrated piece, Marshall Sahlins proposed that contemporary foragers were affluent because they kept consumption in check by adhering to an immediate return economy (Sahlins 1972; Widerquist and McCall 2017 summarize recent research that nuances Sahlins's often overly enthusiastic account). Despite the pushback, Sahlins's insight that affluence is the relation of desires and resources merits further thought. So, what really is a "subsistence economy"? For Pierre Clastres (1994, 105–18), a strong influence on Deleuze and Guattari (see below, chapters 5 and 6; Sibertin-Blanc 2016; Viveiros de Castro 2019; Badaire 2023), it is a European prejudice to say that subsistence is a constant scramble at the edge of starvation, dissolution of the community, or resource-focused war. According to these "subsistence economy" prejudices, such a society does all it can just to let its members attain a minimal survival. Yet, Clastres notes, we also see in first-contact narratives complaints about the "laziness" of natives: They do what they need and then lounge about. So, it is an odd kind of edge-of-starvation "subsistence" if natives are healthy and have plenty of leisure. For Clastres, "primitives" thus have all the time they would need to develop surplus if they so desired. They do not work for a surplus because they are not forced externally. Their living politically is based on a refusal to produce a storable excess; instead, they produce for their immediate needs.

Moving from the restricted case of Clastres's studies of Amazonian sedentary horticulturalists to another form of nonstate immediate return societies, nomadic foragers, when they do in fact produce a surplus by killing a large prey animal, that abundance is consumed in festivals to which neighbors are invited. So, while nomadic foragers refuse "work" *qua* labor aiming at surplus, they have some degree of leisure and affluence (although Widerquist and McCall 2017 describe Sahlins's position as outdated, they do show that most contemporary anthropologists at least acknowledge that life with periods of abundance for those of our ancestors in the EEA is not *a priori* ruled out).

War and Prosocial Human Nature

Since Darwin's suggestion in *The Descent of Man,* it's been widely thought that war as inter-group violence was an important selection pressure for altruism and prosociality in human evolution (e.g., Bowles and Gintis 2013). According to this narrative, we are the descendants of victors in warfare.

> When two tribes of primeval man, living in the same country, came into competition, if (other things being equal) the one tribe included a great number of courageous, sympathetic and faithful members, who were always ready to warn each other of danger, to aid and defend each other, this tribe would succeed better and conquer the other. (Darwin 2004 [1871], 113)

The thesis that widespread pre-state warfare provided the selection pressure for prosociality is bitterly disputed. The basic question is whether war was frequent and intense enough to serve as a selection pressure, not whether war was possible. I will treat the position skeptical of frequent early war at length in the next section; to prepare for that, here are some preliminary considerations. First, there is evidence back to 300,000 years ago or so of widespread exchange networks, implying cooperation (indeed cooperation among pre-sapiens and among other primates [Pisor and Surbeck 2019; MacDonald et al. 2021]). So, the question really is not the possibility of competition or cooperation but the frequency of each, and indeed the superior rationality of cooperation. If early humans were smart enough to figure out how to wage war (something that requires high levels of communication and cooperation, as Kissel and Kim 2018 and Glowacki 2024 show), then they were smart enough to see the advantages of minimizing war.

As I mentioned above, my position can be said to build on Kropotkin's position, which we could call "inclusive Darwinism," in which both competition and cooperation can be forms of "struggle for existence" and hence selection pressures. Following Kropotkin, I can make two main points, one concerning the form that competition takes and the other concerning the relation of competition and cooperation. I claim that keeping both points together is a better way of being true to Darwin than a sole focus on competition. The first point concerns the form of competition, as intra-species competition—which can itself take two forms, intra-group and inter-group (*if* the species can be said to have a group-based social structure)—is only one form of competition, as there can be inter-species competition. Second, Darwin also allows struggle (and hence selection) to be conducted between a species (or indeed between a species and the other species that it cultivates or reliably engages with in order to compose its niche) and its environment. Given this last possibility, in which cooperation is the winning move, we have to investigate the ecological conditions for any one species over its evolutionary history, as difficult as that might be, and not simply assume that competition is the only form of struggle for existence; in some situations, intra-species cooperation, and that taking the form of both intra-group and inter-group cooperation, might be the best move given certain circumstances, with those circumstances being susceptible to modification in niche construction (which could indeed take the form of modifying inter-group relations). And all that, mind you, assumes that "group" is a good descriptor of the social dynamics of the species during a stretch of its evolutionary history, a point upon which I will elaborate further.

With these in mind, I would say that if we were essentially or even simply strongly predisposed to xenophobic violence because of a warfare selection pressure—whether or not that is continuous with or similar to chimpanzee lethal raiding (Wrangham 1999)—military and police training efforts would be toward control, when in fact the effort has to go to enabling (Grossman 1996; Roscoe 2007; Protevi 2008 and 2009). Now such enabling has, to be sure, made great strides with training using live-fire, realistic targets aiming at reflex and quick-decision or "shoot / no-shoot" engagements. We can, of course, extend this analysis of training to the living conditions, initiation rites, and other training procedures of gangs, guerrilla groups, and so on. Not only do we "have to be taught, carefully taught" to hate, as *South Pacific* tells us, we have to be trained to kill. So instead of saying only, as many would, that we are primarily descendants of victors in inter-group fighting—those best able to harness fear and anger in battle— we can also say we are descendants of those best able to foster sharing. Now, even if their inter-group violence wasn't prevalent, persistent, and intense enough to serve as a selection pressure (Kissel and Kim 2018), everyone agrees that early foragers fought at times, within and between groups. That is to say, they had a regime of violence, even if "war" wasn't one of its elements.[22] As we will see, within-group fighting includes equality-protecting "reverse dominance hierarchy" or, more simply, killing would-be alphas.

The Regime of Violence of Nomadic Foragers

On the Non-Ubiquity of Foraging

To begin our discussion, we should take seriously the thesis of Graeber and Wengrow (2021) that many of our pre-state ancestors were neither nomadic nor all that egalitarian. Graeber and Wengrow's fascinating book is a self-conscious political intervention into popular discourse; it is staunchly *contra* Rousseauian (or at least it argues against how Rousseau is seen in mainstream discourse). Among their targets is a tendency in the popular imagination to neglect the political experimentation of non-state peoples.[23] So, I take seriously their point that, in the time period they discuss (from roughly 40kya to the present), the state form is not a telos of social development but something in which we've gotten "stuck" and could possibly get away from. On a longer timescale, however, encompassing the entire *Homo* lineage, we can still talk about the centralized, hierarchical, and "legible" agricultural State's becoming the hegemonic social form supplanting, though never completely eliminating, forager egalitarianism.[24] The timescale for the deep history of forager egalitarianism is measured in hundreds of thousands of years. Although theirs is a noteworthy work, Graeber and Wengrow's decision to concentrate solely on recent archeology (dating back some 40,000 years) preempts any discussion of that deep history (Scheidel 2022 and Lindesfarne and Neale 2021 criticize them on this neglect). By getting rid of an alleged environmental determinism (it is possible that such a determinism is present in the popular imagination), Graeber and Wengrow rush toward an idealistic voluntarism in their desire to open some space in the political thought of our days. It is an admirable effort, especially when seen as a book for the general public. But, in discarding the evolutionism of nineteenth-century anthropology (a straight line from clans to tribes, chieftainships, empires), they discard the biological/evolutionary anthropology of the twenty-first century; thus, they discard the key concept of niche construction. Niche construction is a materialistic concept, but not deterministic; many species, by their own efforts, provide themselves with the means to modify their own environmental conditions, and by doing so they modify the selective pressures for future generations. Niches under-determine social formations; they provide broad viability constraints but don't optimize (Fuentes 2017, 2018). There's room for drift and for "schismogenesis," the process of self-distinction from a neighboring culture.

Nevertheless, despite these nuances, it is worth taking Graeber and Wengrow 2021 seriously. The networked egalitarian mobile foraging lifestyle ("large societies" in the terms of Bird et al. 2019) is only one form of human social organization; it might indeed be in some cases, as Graeber and Wengrow say, only a seasonal variation, with "small-scale" sedentary groupings at other times (see also Singh and Glowacki 2022). If we no longer want to say that there's a specific point in history in which sedentarism replaces nomadism, what we can say is that there does seem to be a time in which the ratio of sedentarism (even if only seasonal) to nomadism seemed to shift in favor of the former. At that point sedentarism and nomadism are more like options chosen as circumstances change than stages passed through in some march. This optionality picture would support only a mild rachet effect of sedentarism and groupishness, as you still have networked life and widespread contacts as possibilities, even if small-scale groupishness becomes more prominent with sedentarism. Certainly, we always have to remember Scott (2017; see chapter 5) that states are not the telos of social development and that people ran for the hills to escape them. Further, you can't just say that those who flee state life are irrational

(Widerquist and McCall 2017 remind us that even if states could claim to improve the median person's living conditions, they evidently don't confer enough benefits on the most disadvantaged to cause them to eschew flight). In other words, even if you want to say (counterfactually) that nonstate life was a state of nature in a Hobbesian sense (that is, a regime of violence constantly poised at the edge of descent into conflict), even that was preferable for those who fled states to life as a slave or as a member of a coerced labor class.

So, even if not ubiquitous, egalitarian mobile foraging is a social possibility, and it deserves to be counted as an expression of a plastic and niche-constructing "human nature." Hence, we should study foraging not for the essence of a peaceful human nature but for its egalitarian and anti-war mechanisms (even if Boehm's analyses are mostly of males treating other males, as Kumar and Campbell 2022 point out), which include its regime of violence. If, as we will argue, nonstate foragers did not live in a condition of near-constant war, then war could not serve as a selection pressure for intra-group cooperation, prosociality, and altruism, as is quite often argued, starting with Darwin himself. Despite current research showing more variability than previously acknowledged among currently living foragers (Kelly 2013), we can cautiously speculate that early nomadic forager societies were most likely egalitarian; that they had, if not the full networked society hypothesized by Bird et al. (2019), at the least frequent visiting, rendering group identity fluid; that they probably had a gendered division of labor with little specialization within genders (though see Lacy and Ocobock 2023 for a speculative discussion of Paleolithic women hunters); and that while there was most likely a prestige gradient relative to prowess, discussion was the decision-making process; hence, while there was rhetoric and persuasion, maybe even veiled threats, there was no explicit top-down command (Kelly 2000; Boehm 2012b; Sterelny 2014).

Arguments against Frequent and Intense Warfare in the EEA

First, a discussion of the definitional issues. There are looser and more strict definitions of war on offer in the anthropological literature. On the one hand, we have loose definitions tying it to "coalitionary violence," allowing for a continuity with chimpanzee inter-group violence (e.g., Wrangham 1999), and on the other, strict definitions of war as anonymous inter-group violence (Kelly 2000), distinguishing it not only from chimpanzee violence but also from other human regimes of violence. We will adopt the strict definition, as our object in this book is to differentiate regimes of violence, and Kelly's strict definition allows us to distinguish murder, revenge killing, group execution, and feud. Wrangham's capacious notion of "coalitionary violence" brings together execution, feud, status-motivated raiding, and war as population and territory capture. Hames (2019, 159–61) pushes back against Kelly-style strict definitions in favor of Wrangham's notion of coalitionary violence in order precisely to allow discussion of the continuity of human and chimpanzee violence; this then allows him to accuse his "Rousseauian" targets of "redefining" warfare, which seems to me to be a case of begging the question in favor of Wrangham's loose definition.

Here are some arguments against the assumption that competitive conflict (glossed as "war" by loose definitions) is the default setting for intergroup relations in human evolution. I don't present them as if they have settled the question and quieted the universal war proponents. I simply present them as an intervention into the discourse that focuses on early war. Recall also that the question here is the relative frequency and intensity of conflict, not simply its possibility. We can call these "anti–universal war" arguments (for an in-depth account covering many of these arguments, see Fry 2006, 162–83). I will treat eight arguments in four linked pairs. The first two arguments concern faulty evidence: (1) lack of archeological evidence and (2) faulty inferences from current nonstate life. The next two concern political economy motives for war: (3) lack of profitable targets and (4) the benefits of sharing. The next two concern the tactics of war: (5) defensive technology and (6) psychological implausibility. The final two arguments concern social structure: (7) social complexity and (8) networked lifestyle.

The first two arguments concern faulty evidence. The archeological argument, laid out by Ferguson (2013a and 2013b), is that there are just not enough mass graves in the archeological record of pre-state life to provide evidence of frequent and intense war before roughly 10,000 years ago. Second, the critics of frequent war also look askance at using current violence rates among contemporary nonstate peoples as transparent access to our evolutionary past (thus treating them as "living fossils"), by reminding us of the need to look at them in the context of state contact and subsequent territorial constriction and rivalry over trading rights (Ferguson 2008; Widerquist and McCall 2017). Fry (2013, 17) recounts how some deaths attributed to contemporary "hunter-gatherer" societies in universal war accounts were actually victims of killers from state societies, thus vitiating the use of high mortality rates in such societies as indirect evidence of the high mortality rates of early war.

The next two arguments concern political economy motives for war. The "lack of profitable targets" argument operates from a materialist perspective (thus abstaining from considering status-seeking ritual war)[25] and claims that early foragers were unlikely to wage frequent and intense war as there was nothing material to gain. Sterelny (2014) notes that foragers have no territorial motivation to attack, as they do not invest much labor in the land and have no interest in permanent occupation (though this point is nuanced in Scott 2017, which notes that permanent settlement is compatible with foraging when people can establish a settlement in a site, such as resource-rich wetlands, where they can remain in place and allow the resources to come to them, rather than their being compelled to chase the resources). In fact, per Kelly 2005, peace between foraging groups allows more efficient resource exploitation: The two sides are not afraid to go to the border of their territories, as they would be if border raids were frequent. The closely related "benefits of sharing" argument centers on the notion of "risk buffering." The idea is that the sharing of food can create webs of social obligation that can be called upon in times of need (Kaplan and Gurven 2005; Mameli 2013; Pisor and Gurven 2016; Pisor and Surbeck 2018). A history of conflict will impede such sharing, while a history of cooperation will improve your chances of receiving help when you need it. As meat in particular is difficult to store, you might as well share it when you have a lot of it, and if you share it with other groups as well as within your group you are widening and deepening your "relational wealth" and providing a sort of insurance against possible future shortfalls. Plus, should inter-group food sharing be done in a festive rather than grudging way, the joy involved would further entrench the relationships so formed.

Next, we find two arguments concerning the waging of war. The defensive-technology argument is laid out by Kelly (2005), who sketches a geo-eco-techno-social multiplicity that results in a period of "intrinsic defensive advantage." The geographical aspect is that defenders know their territory and can hold ambush positions. The ecological aspect is that low population density means that defenders can flee if needed. The technological aspect is that lethal throwing weapons allow inflicting dam-age from afar on invaders with low risk to defenders. The social aspect is that invading parties would be nonspecialists while defenders would have throwing skills developed in hunting. Kelly concludes that, faced with such a defensive advantage, contemporary foragers increased fitness by "eschewing efforts to achieve intercommunity dominance in favor of egal-itarian relations of friendship, mutuality, and sharing" (Kelly 2005, 15297). These same contemporary mechanisms could then, Kelly claims, be plau-sibly imputed to nonstate peoples in the upper Paleolithic, around 20,000 years ago. The psychological implausibility argument is laid out by Sterelny (2014): It's implausible that war provided a selection pressure for our evolved traits of intra-group cooperation, given that a major method for reinforcing such cooperation would be social selection against bullies in the group (via Christopher Boehm's idea of insult, shunning, exile, or kill-ing as strategies of "reverse dominance hierarchy" [Boehm 2012a and 2012b]). For Boehm, the contemporary nomadic forager's economy of vio-lence has an anti-state effect by preventing centralized power of the would-be alpha or dominating "head." Here we find individual acts of fighting and murder, and group responses of ostracism, exile, or killing—that is, "capi-tal punishment." Intra-group anonymous violence is a void category for nomadic foragers as everyone knows everyone else in the group. To the extent that these regimes resonate with those of the evolutionary past, we find another aspect of the anti–universal war arguments, as frequent and intense war does not seem compatible with early forager social selection, as that would entail also selecting for violence-prone people who can solely direct their aggression outside the group.[26]

The last two arguments concern "social structure." The first, Kelly (2000), concerns social complexity. Kelly distinguishes personally directed revenge, which for him is the dominant form of violence in unsegmented socie-ties (those without internal structure), from feud, which is possible in the regime of violence of segmented societies (those in which marriages and other social ties are regulated across subgroup formations such as lin-eages). For Kelly, only segmented societies allow feud, in which we find group duty on the side of the victimized avengers coupled with group lia-bility on the side of the offenders. Hence feud—as opposed to personalized vengeance—would, via the logic of "social substitutability," allow target-ing any member of the other group. A society without feud, then, would be, *a fortiori*, without war *qua* fully anonymous inter-group violence. The last, most radical argument is put forth by Bird et al. (2019). Because of its importance, we have discussed it more fully at the very start of this chapter. To recap briefly, the notion of networked society means that war as anonymous "inter-group" conflict is put into question as these hypothesized network living practices mean residential, kin, economic, and ritual roles of foragers are so varied and fluid that strict group boundaries are difficult to establish. Hence, "group size and mobility vary with the distribution of resources in anthropogenic landscapes: landscape-scale legacies of resource use modify foraging trade-offs and feedback on mobility" (97). In other words, it's hard to have inter-group conflict as a default setting if "groups" *qua* relatively closed "bands" aren't the basic social structure.

To protect against any accusations of "Rousseauism," I would like to emphasize, at the risk of repetition, that the above anti–universal war arguments should not be taken to mean that there is no evidence of early forager personal violence or vengeance. Furthermore, Sahlins notes the way that the principle of mobility which governs nomadic forager society means that its regime of violence includes infanticide and senilicide (both studied in Hrdy 2009). Our study of the forager regime of violence focused on its anti-state and anti-war effects. Anti-war practices do not imply the absence of individual, personalized acts of fighting or murder. In fact, they presuppose such acts as problems whose solution is found in a group response of permitting individualized vengeance targeting only the murderer. Boehm cites cases among contemporary foragers in which a serial murderer is killed by his own kin and then the corpse is presented to the victim's family; this is quite clearly an anti-war gesture aimed at forestalling feud (Boehm 2012b, 259; see also Glowacki 2024). According to Boehm, then, vengeance is an anti-war process; it prevents escalation to feud and, further on, anonymous inter-group violence. So, for Boehm, contemporary nomadic forager regimes of violence are (intra-group) against the formation of states, and (inter-group) against the outbreak of war. A cautious analogy with early human social life would thus hypothesize the presence of such anti-war practices in the EEA.

A Nonbellicose Hypothesis for Evolved Prosociality

I have presented arguments that violent inter-group conflict was not frequent or intense enough to be a selection pressure for prosociality—that is, affectively loaded and normatively laden communicative cooperation.

On this point, Kissel and Kim (2018) agree that rather than being a selection pressure, war is made possible by previous adaptations for communicative cooperation. So, if we are not only (or even mainly) the descendants of victors in war, then we are (at least also) the descendants of cooperators whose joyous sharing in times of plenty, and even grudging sharing in times of crisis, avoided war. Now, if war is not so widespread in human history to have served as a selection pressure for prosociality, what were those selection pressures? The alternative story on offer stresses "interdependent" cooperation, in the form of collaborative breeding (Hrdy 2009) and obligate collaborative foraging (Tomasello 2016); for the combination of these two, see Tomasello and Gonzalez-Cabrera (2017) and Tomasello (2019).[27] For the interdependence theorists, these, and not warfare, were the selection pressures for anger control or "self-domestication" and for cognitive and affective capacities for joint attention allowing for the development of prosocial capacities of care and cooperation beyond kin, even to the point of psychological altruism, in which the ends and needs of others motivate our action.

Human Self-Domestication

An important recent alternate movement to the early interdependence theories of Hrdy and Tomasello is the "Human Self-Domestication" (HSD) hypothesis, which tracks neurological, endocrinological, and anatomical divergences from the last common ancestor of the *Homo* and *Pan* (chimpanzee and bonobo) lineages (Hare 2017). The HSD hypothesis emphasizes late human evolution and assumes an inter-group conflict setting. I accept that contemporary humans show diminished reactivity and increased self-control, per the HSD proponents, but I reject the narrative that prosociality is an adaptation to an environment saturated by frequent inter-group conflict. The HSD hypothesis assumes that emotional control is a late development led by internal forager group punishment of bullies and shirkers, under the pressure of inter-group conflict (it hence runs counter to Sterelny's psychological implausibility objection I treated above). But the HSD hypothesis, in making reference to bonobos, shows deep-rooted environmentally conditioned plasticity: If we want to invoke an evolutionary parsimony principle, then, since when resources are plentiful and female defensive coalitions and reproductive autonomy are possible for bonobos, then our LCA should have behavioral plasticity conditioned by its natural-social environment.[28] Hence, we are back to criticisms of the CRD, which ask us to break the assumption that chimpanzees are our best model for LCA.

Recent publications critical of the HSD hypothesis push the development of emotional control further back in time and link it to tolerance of strangers. For instance, Shilton et al. 2020 criticize the HSD hypothesis by emphasizing the human similarity to other social mammals (whose relative pacificity derives from their natural social living) rather than to domesticated animals (whose produced pacificity replaces a previous wild aggressivity). They do agree with the HSD hypothesis when they "suggest that what underlies human social evolution is selection for socially mediated emotional control and plasticity." However, they push the roots of this development much further back than the HSD hypothesis to "two overlapping stages . . . one preceding the emergence of language and the second following it . . . [early hominin] practices both profited from and promoted an increase in emotional control and prosociality" (16). A second critical article (Sánchez-Villagra and van Schaik 2019) accepts HSD but allows us to distance ourselves from the xenophobic group defense model implied by HSD proponents. Sánchez-Villagra and van Schaik first emphasize that contact with strangers is an important component of the HSD hypothesis. Two components of the HSD hypothesis in animal studies are "selection against fear-induced aggression toward strangers, and . . . increased tolerance toward strangers" (140). If contemporary humans display such emotional effects of HSD, then, the authors argue, these effects would be the result of frequent early xenophilic encounters. The benefits of such contacts are resource variance insurance and an increased possibility of trade. They further claim that language is a key component of early exchange, allowing for tracking of relations and honest signaling of friendly intent.

Prosociality and Tolerance in the EEA

Let us now consider treatments of an EEA with important tolerance and even xenophilic components. Recent works in the literature on early tolerance look to different explanations of fire control, choosing cultural diffusion (spread by learning across groups) over demic (population movement) explanations (MacDonald et al. 2021). For this strain of thought such diffusion of fire control requires inter-group (and even inter-species) tolerance

(Pisor and Surbeck 2019) and involves possibly large social networks (Bird et al. 2019) with fluid groups, a long juvenile period for skill learning, and a long lifespan for skill refinement. These trends intensify with Levallois stone-tool technology about 300,000 years ago. The literature on early tolerance suggests that for too long we've been stuck with the xenophobic male defender of the group as an image of evolution, but there had to have been traders and cross-group relators. Instead of seeing only Ares among our ancestors, we should also see Hermes. This line of thought allows for evolved egalitarian sentiments to contribute positively to mutualistic cooperation. The selection pressure here would be, in addition to contributing to the provision of material sustenance, collective self-defense against nonhuman animal predators and so-called power scavenging in which hominins cooperatively chased predators from their kills.

The nomadic forager regime of violence did indeed enable our ancestors to develop ways to detect and punish bullies and shirkers and so to suppress our dominance-enabling hair-trigger temper and violent reactive aggression, as in the HSD hypothesis. But I would argue that our ancestors also genuinely and positively developed a xenophilic emotional structure that can motivate us, their descendants, to search for the joy we directly find in cooperation, sharing, and helping. This means that foragers don't settle for cooperation simply out of the fear that not cooperating would unleash the bullies and shirkers that lurk within all of us (Gaus 2015). For most people today most of the time, I hazard to say, it's a little bit of both. It's not impossible to find pure examples of bullies and cooperators, pure devils and pure saints, but either pure state seems relatively rare. What we have to watch out for is having our social structures tilt toward rewarding bullies and shirkers, which might end up, by taking advantage of plasticity and niches constructed around artificial scarcity, producing a prosociality of egoism, a cognitive–emotional investment in looking out for number one (Satz and Ferejohn 2005 give an externalist reading of Rational Choice Theory that looks like this). But such plasticity also means we can work with human nature, and not against it, to work toward institutions that would support a hortatory ideal of acting so as to spread active joy. It's a matter of nurturing a deep capacity for care and cooperation, and expanding it so it is without qualification, not a matter of desperately fighting a single deep drive to dominance.

I obviously don't want to say that all is sunshine and light in human history; this book is titled *Regimes of Violence,* after all. But I do want to say, given the importance I accord to plasticity and niche-construction—we are shaped by environments partially shaped by our ancestors even as we shape our descendants—that constructing minimalist regimes of violence is a possible, albeit difficult, goal for a world dominated by the regime of violence of states dedicated to the expansion of racialized and gendered capitalism.

2

Affective Ideology

This is the second chapter of Part I, in which I look at the interaction of social patterns and individual subjective motivation in composing a regime of violence. This chapter is a bit more contemporary and socio-logical than the historical and anthropological themes of chapter 1, but the resonances should be evident. For instance, as we have seen that prosocial-ity can require punishment of norm violators, in this chapter I examine the affective buy-in required of people's acting violently in support of social patterns.[1]

The discursive field proposing ideology as a key psychological compo-nent in social reproduction is well trodden. Deleuze and Guattari, who loved to needle received views, produced one of their best provocations in the claim that "ideology is an execrable concept" (1977, 344; 1987, 68). Why are they so harsh? They think standard treatments of ideology are too cognitive, too concerned with the falsity of beliefs that hide an unen-cumbered view of social reality from our minds. Instead, they want to look at the orientation of desires rather than the falsity of beliefs. In my terms, they want to look at the affective side of bioenculturation: what turns people on, what are their fears and hopes, what surges and urges push them to act, when their regime of violence calls for it? According to the tradition, ideol-ogy is supposed to preempt or at least minimize the overt use of force in social reproduction. Why bother bringing out the arms to put down trouble when you can work on people's minds to prevent trouble in the first place? But is producing an ideology powerful enough to do that itself worth the trouble? Some scholars in fact hold that contemporary societies have ren-dered ideology otiose via sophisticated forms of coercive reproduction and their attendant collective action problems that bring the affective into play (Rosen 1996). As long as the police and courts are efficient enough to stop would-be revolutionaries from acting for fear of being isolated, identi-fied, and punished, you don't need to bother to work on minds. Although I appreciate Rosen's insight, I don't share his position; I think ideological

buy-in on the part of a critical portion of the enforcers of coercive reproduction is necessary, but only with a notion of ideology expanded to include
the affective. If we restrict ideology critique to identifying cognitive errors
(category mistakes and false empirical generalizations as generating bad
beliefs, and confirmation bias and resistance to rational revision of beliefs
as keeping them in place), then we risk missing an essential component
of unjust social systems: the production of emotional commitments that
accompany those beliefs and that allow for the punishment on which part
of the effectiveness of coercive reproduction rests.

To tie this chapter to the overarching themes of the book, I want to say
that affective ideology is how prosociality is transmitted and reinforced:
You have to learn how to act in the ways expected of you (culture does
have cognitively accessible content), but you also have to be motivated to
act in ways that reproduce social patterns, including, crucially, those charged
with the violent enforcement of those patterns. In concrete terms, then,
affective ideology is the psychological component of a society's regime of
violence. In this chapter I'll look at the theories of ideology of Deleuze and
Guattari and that of Jason Stanley to articulate the notion of "affective ideology" and how it intersects with regimes of violence.

To show how we can arrive at the study of affective ideology, I propose
that it is one of the concrete applications of a political philosophy of mind,
a term I will now explain.

Political Philosophy of Mind

To study human ways of life, we need a political philosophy of mind that
goes above, below, and alongside the subject. Subjects don't just appear; they
are constituted by social and somatic practices that precede and surround
them. These practices are those that, in their myths, stories, and background
assumptions, shape our minds in their rational and affective patterns and,
in their training, exercise, and initiations, shape our bodies in their neural
and endocrinological patterns. In such a political philosophy of mind, we
go above the subject to a pre-personal field of politically analyzable subjectification processes, below the subject to physiological and neural mechanisms and alongside the subject to technological adjuncts. The trick here
is to avoid a structural determinism in which subjective actions are simple extrusions of subject positions, while of course also avoiding a liberal
atomization of subjects in which social processes are mere aggregations of

individual action. A successful political philosophy of mind must therefore avoid reduction (collapsing the subpersonal and first-person perspectives), individualism (society is just an aggregate of individual subjects), and strict structuralism (subjective actions and experiences are mere consequences of one's social position). Political philosophy of mind doubly modifies standard philosophy of mind, which is the philosophical treatment—that is, the conceptual development and clarification—of psychological and brain science. It does so both by the "political" modifier and by changing what is thought of as "mind."

What Do We Mean by "Mind"?

Let us first consider the notion of "mind." Here I can present only the barest outline.[2] The standard schools of thought in cognitive science see cognition as a kind of information processing—the middle slice in what Susan Hurley called the "classical sandwich": from sensory input to processing of representations to motor output (Hurley 1998, 21). Such "cognitivism" uses a computer model for the brain–mind connection: Brains, like computers, are physical systems, and minds are the "software" that runs on those computers. Computationalism sees cognition as the rule-bound manipulation of discrete symbols in a serial or Von Neumann architecture that passes through a central processing unit, or CPU. Connectionism, the second standard approach, is based upon another computer model, but it has a different, allegedly more biologically realistic architecture: parallel distributed processing. In connectionism's "neural nets," learning is a change in network properties—that is, in the strength and number of connections.

By contrast, the past thirty years has seen the development of a "4EA" (embodied, embedded, enactive, extended, affective) approach to cognition that modifies the notion of "mind." It sees "mind" not as that which represents an independent environment but as that which enables the navigation of an organism in its world. The 4EA approach challenges the traditional emphasis on an individualist, representational, and brain-bound or "neurocentric" model of mind (Varela, Thompson, and Rosch 1991). I will concentrate here on the "enactive" branch of the 4EA approach, as elaborated in Di Paolo and Thompson (2014). Enactivists define cognition as the direction of action of an organism in its environment. Enactivists reject the linearity of the standard model, as well as the allegedly central role in cognition of "representation," in which a model of the world is built up inside the cognitive agent. Rather, they see most cognitive processes as the real-time interaction of a distributed and differential system composed of brain, body, and world, in which perception and action are mutually looped: We move to perceive, and our perception guides our action.[3]

A base concept in enaction is "autopoiesis," developed by Humberto Maturana and Francisco Varela in the 1970s (Varela, Maturana, and Uribe 1974). The research focus of autopoiesis ("self-making") is on identifying an essence of life, but it also, in so doing, insists on preserving a first-person viewpoint for all living beings. Not only do autopoietic cells make themselves, but they also make a "self" by establishing and maintaining a recursive process between a cell's membrane and its metabolism; the metabolism produces the membrane, which enables metabolic functioning by providing it shelter and concentrating its loops; this is known as "organizational closure." Varela writes in explaining his work that "autopoiesis is a particular case of a larger class of organizations that can be called *organizationally* closed—that is, defined through indefinite recursion of component relations" (Varela 1981, 37–38). An autopoietic cell creates a self in distinguishing itself from an environment with which it exchanges matter; they are hence said to be autonomous, although "structurally coupled" with the environment. Their internal complexity is such that either such "coupling" with their environment, or endogenous fluctuations of their states, are merely "triggers" of internally directed action. This means that only those external environmental differences capable of being sensed and made sense of by an autonomous system can be said to exist for that system, can be said to make up the world of that system.

In a groundbreaking work, Ezequiel Di Paolo (2005) showed that for a full picture of organismic cognition, "adaptivity" must be added to autopoiesis, as the latter cannot explain sense making—directed action responding to environmental change relevant to the organism—precisely because it is all-or-nothing. Di Paolo writes, "But what makes bacteria *swim up* the gradient? What makes *them* distinguish and prefer higher sugar concentrations? As defined, structural coupling is a conservative, not an improving[,] process; it admits no possible gradation" (437). Instead of the autopoietic binary of survival and death, then, adaptivity adds a graded discrimination of tendencies to the capacity of organisms. Evan Thompson sums up Di Paolo's contribution thus: "A distinct capacity for 'adaptivity' needs to be added to the minimal autopoietic organization so that the system can actively regulate itself with respect to its conditions of viability and thereby modify its milieu according to the internal norms of its activity" (Thompson 2007, 148). Autopoiesis and adaptivity establish a first-person perspective, which in the "mind in life" school is found with suitable adjustment throughout the living world.

To find a political philosophy of mind, we must now find ways to connect to second- and third-person perspectives. A decisive step occurs with an enactive analysis of second-person cognition as "participatory sensemaking" (De Jaegher and Di Paolo 2007), a move that breaks with the focus on individual organisms to look at groups of interacting people. De Jaegher and Di Paolo begin by pointing to the well-known phenomenon of people coordinating movements while walking together or coordinating speaking in conversation. The crucial move is to posit that the interaction can itself become autonomous: We can identify the dynamics of a conversation over and above individual utterances, as the conversation enables and constrains the interactions that unfold within it and make it up. In other words, meaning can be seen as being generated in the very process by which the conversation unfolds (see also Di Paolo, De Jaegher, and Cuffari 2018).

From the first-person perspective of the organizationally closed and structurally coupled sense making of individuals, then, we have moved to second-person participatory sense making. The key for enactivists has always been to engage with neuroscience while resisting a reduction of that experience to an explanation based solely on subpersonal neurochemical processes. Varela's "neurophenomenological" proposal was to use subjects trained in either a rigorous phenomenological practice or in Buddhist meditation practice to allow access to first-person direct experience that would not be introspective guesswork or caught in an infinite regress of objectifying self-reflection; descriptions of experience by such trained subjects could then be put into a dialogue of "mutual constraints" with findings of correlated neural activity in a way that would preserve the first-person experience while still bringing third-person neuroscience to bear (Varela 1996, 1999).

We are now closing in on how we can use enactive insights in political analyses. First, we should note that a straightforward application of the concept of autopoiesis to social systems was vigorously contested by Varela, who sees autopoiesis as only an instance of a general mode of being, organizational closure; he restricts autopoiesis to cellular production—that is, to living systems bound by a physical membrane—and warns against its use as a model of social being (Maturana and Varela 1980, 118). After insisting on some concrete sense of "production" to define autopoiesis, Varela drives home his point in a contemporaneous essay: "Frankly, I do not see how the definition of autopoiesis can be *directly* transposed to a variety of other situations, social systems for example" (Varela 1981, 37–38).

Development of the Notion of Political Philosophy of Mind

With the question of which enactive concepts we should use to think of social systems now on the table, let me pause for a moment. We are trying to make sense of the notion of "political philosophy of mind." A recap of the development of the concept may help. The phrase "political philosophy of mind" was coined in Slaby (2016). Among the first steps in the field can be said to be Shaun Gallagher's discussion of the "socially extended mind."[4] In his early pieces, Gallagher looks at "enactive processes (e.g., social affordances)," which for him move beyond second-person relations to consider "institutional structures, norms, and practices" (Gallagher 2013, 4). Pursuing this critical turn, Gallagher asks us to "take a closer and critical look at how social and cultural practices either productively extend or, in some cases, curtail mental processes" (Gallagher and Crisafi 2009; Gallagher 2013). In his recent work, Gallagher goes on to cite Iris Marion Young on oppression and Charles Mills's critique of ideal theory to support his call to "give cognitive science a critical twist" (Gallagher 2020, 226–27).

A second important figure here is Jan Slaby. Slaby and Gallagher (2015) take up the notion of institutional extension: "The rational human subject is not an exclusively biological entity—it is an entity coupled to other biological individuals and various cognition-enabling institutions, tools, procedures and practices" (Slaby and Gallagher 2015, 53). The political edge comes when we realize that such extension is not always enabling for certain individuals; in the paper in which he coins the term "political philosophy of mind," Slaby (2016) points out that many social embeddings produce affective reactions that inhibit rather than expand human potentials:

> we can . . . distinguish enabling from disabling social structures,
> we can assess the extent to which social domains work to establish
> mental patterns that, in the long run, are enabling, conducive to
> individual and collective flourishing, or whether they instead create
> unhealthy dependencies, bind us to oppressive routines, maintain

inequality, destroy community ties, or lead to emotional and mental habits that are harmful to us or our loved ones. (Slaby 2016, 11)

In *The Mind–Body Politic* (2019), Michelle Maiese and Robert Hanna develop further the move that calls for a political philosophy of mind.[5] Maiese and Hanna have a deep-embodiment thesis (we are "essentially embodied minds," they write on page 2; on page 41 they speak of "minded human animals") in which social and material encounters shape the minds and bodies of humans, so their first-person experience and second-person interaction, while not determined politically, are nonetheless conditioned, as our inherent neural and somatic plasticity is molded by our cultural niches. In pursuing a political philosophy of mind, Maiese and Hanna criticize overly cognitive or belief-centered notions of ideology and call for the inclusion of affect and emotion in considering the frames of reference that condition our engagement with the world (Maiese and Hanna 2019, 260ff). Hence, instead of belief-centered ideology, they propose "affective frames" as a more effective way of analyzing the experiences and interactions of deeply embodied and socialized minds. In other words, for Maiese and Hanna, affect in its aspects of salience (importance relative to the background) and valence (impulsion to approach or avoid) is the key to understanding how essentially embodied minds operate in their physical and social worlds.

Drawing on the work of Slaby (2016), Maiese and Hanna describe "affective frames" as "spontaneous, non-inferential, and pre-reflective way of discriminating, filtering, and selecting information" (Maiese and Hanna 2019, 41). This filtering is accomplished in terms of the salience or importance of the environmental element for an organism's value systems: "Affect draws our attention to specific features of our surroundings and implies a 'dynamic gestalt or figure-ground structure' whereby 'some objects emerge into affective prominence, while others become unnoticeable'" (Maiese and Hanna 2019, 41; internal quotations from Thompson 2007, 374). Continuing with an enactivist approach, Maiese and Hanna insist that affective framing is distributed rather than brain-centered: "Affective framing is best understood as distributed over a complex network of brain and bodily processes . . . [including] metabolic systems, endocrine system, the musculoskeletal system, and the cardiovascular system" (Maiese and Hanna 2019, 41–42). Such a distributed somatic system is in essential interaction with the environment, which for humans very often has crucial social dimensions. Hence, an affective frame can be instantiated in a social institution that makes some affective stances more likely: "A social institution thereby significantly modulates affective framings, substantively molds overall bodily comportment, and literally shapes the minded bodily habits of the subjects involved" (Maiese and Hanna 2019, 56). As we can see, an affective frame is doubly distributed, spread across the social institutions and bodily systems that make it up. The episodes of our lives, then, are individuations of those distributed systems, which, unfortunately, may become out-of-sync with our well-being. Thus, one can all too often find "autonomous, self-sustaining structures of affective framing or habit that are actually *in essential conflict* with basic values associated with fundamental human needs and overall well-being" (Maiese and Hanna 2019, 59; italics in original).

Enactive Political Philosophy of Mind

We have noted Varela's prohibition on using the term "autopoiesis" to analyze social systems, and we have sketched the historical development of the notion of a political philosophy of mind. Our final step is to consider how one could do a political analysis using insights from the expanded enactive perspective. We want to take a final step to a *political* notion of nonreductive third-person analyses. Rather than going only "below" the subject to neurons, can we also go "above" and "beside" the subject to social and political structures? The key here, parallel to not reducing experience to neurons, is not reducing first- and second-person experience to a mere extrusion of a structure, but also without a naïve existentialist championing of raw "agency."

In my opinion, a political philosophy of mind fits well with the enactive approach. For the enactivists, cognition is rooted in organismic maintenance, which occurs in a political context for humans; as the title of Part I says, we live politically. While there must be some minimal meshing of organismic needs and institutional context to ensure the viability of a society for some time, sometimes the social norms (what keep social systems functioning) are incompatible with individual flourishing for many social positions.[6] For individuals to flourish, they need to be in mutually empowering relations at multiple scales. That's just what domination and exploitation prevent; they funnel material and symbolic surplus from bottom to top. This is accomplished by the manipulation of artificial scarcity producing coercive generational poverty (which can include deprivation of respect or mutual recognition of worth as well as material supports).

When enactivists talk about bringing forth worlds, we must remember that this isn't *de novo*. We have discrepancies in timescales with our social lives in built environments. I can produce significant changes in small-scale patterns of daily life: If having the window open provides too noisy an environment because of cars and trucks and taxis and ambulances and so on, I can shut the window, but I cannot do anything about road construction that accommodates heavy traffic of internal combustion vehicles, other than move to another zone with a different transportation system. But the patterns move and change much more slowly than closing a window or finding a new house. It takes long-scale political action to change an urban environment's car-centric design. Varela touches on this problem of discordant timescales when he shows, in an implicit critique of Durkheim, the way in which bottom-up causality allows the emergence of social regularities from the series of actions undertaken by individuals; these always risk being reified, their constitutive processes erased, so they confront us as transcendent and fixed (Varela 1999, 62). In pursuing a political philosophy of mind, I would like to enrich the Varelian perspective of upward social emergence—from individuals to social pattern—with an analysis of the downward causality of individual skill and habit formation, from social pattern to individual disposition. Hence, we need to analyze a differential social field channeling perception, action, and affect along lines of social roles. Varela has shown that laws, rules, institutions, and the like are produced emergently by bottom-up causation in a social emergence; what we want to look at are broad lines of top-down causation operated on a slow "socio-ontogenetic" scale by those regularities that guide the development of the individual person.

To have a political philosophy of mind, therefore, it is necessary to think of a pre-personal social field of the formations, of the apprenticeships, of the training programs, of which the individual bodies are resolutions—crystallizations or actualizations—of the interacting processes that form the cognitive-affective topology of the person, their affective ideology.

What Is Ideology Supposed to Explain?

Ideology is supposed to explain noncoerced social reproduction—that is, production and reproduction of "bodies politic." It's too often limited to cognitive errors that distort the perception of social reality in unequal societies by masking exploitation, but I'd like to expand it in two directions: (1) to cover shared ways of life in equal societies, and (2) to include the affective as well as the cognitive.

Bodies Politic

In the terms I develop in Protevi (2009), "bodies politic" imbricate the social and the somatic: The reproduction of social systems requires the production of certain types of "somatic bodies politic" (those whose affective–cognitive patterns and triggers fit the functional needs of the system) which enable social systems or "civic bodies politic" that are themselves bodily in the sense of directing material flows. I think this allows both an emergence perspective (social systems are emergent from constituents but are immanent to the system they form with them, although they can create an "objective illusion" of transcendent, pre-existing patterns into which we are parachuted as children charged with conforming to the way things are done) and a concretion perspective (most individuals are crystallizations of systems; we grow up in systems that form most of us but never determine all of us). The key to work out the consistency of emergence and concretion is to distinguish compositional and temporal scales for bodies politic, as well as to adopt a population perspective. Compositionally, we can distinguish first- ("personal"—though produced) and second-order ("civic") bodies politic. Temporally, we can distinguish the short-term or "punctual event" scale, the midterm or habit / training / developmental scale, and the long-term historical scale. It must be remembered, however, that these scales are analytical rather than concrete; all concrete bodies politic are imbrications of all compositional and temporal scales.

The "individuality" of a first-order body politic is produced rather than given. On a relatively short timescale, a first-order body politic is a dynamic system whose operations are experienced as background affects, as sharp or diffuse feelings of well-being, unease, or any of a variety of intermediate states. Events on the fast / personal scale are seen neurologically as the formation of "resonant cell assemblies," to use a term of Francisco Varela's (1995). On a relatively slow midterm / habituation or long-term / developmental timescale, system patterns gradually crystallize or actualize as intensive processes disrupt previous patterns. Psychologically, the first-order body politic engages in affective cognitive "sense-making." This making sense is embodied; on a fast timescale, the body subject opens a sphere of competence within which things show up as "affordances," as opportunities for engagement; and other people show up as occasions for social interaction, as invitations, repulsions, or a neutral "live and let live." Diachronically, we can see changes at critical points as intensive processes disrupt actual sets of habits.

A second-order body politic is composed of "individuals" who are themselves first-order bodies politic. A second-order body politic has a physiology, as it regulates material flows (1) among its members (the first-order bodies politic as the components of its body) and (2) between itself (its soma as marked by its functional border) and its milieu. A second-order body politic can also be studied psychologically, as it regulates intersomatic affective cognition, the emotional and meaningful interchanges (1) among its members and (2) between their collective affective cognition and that of other bodies politic, at either personal, group, or civic compositional scales. A short-term event for a second-order body politic is an encounter of first-order bodies politic. In the midterm, we see repeated patterns of such encounters or subjectification practices, and in the long term, we see the becoming-custom of such practices, their deep social embedding.

Ideology

"Ideology" has a psychological and a functional sense. Psychologically, ideology is the process that produces a rough coincidence of body political affective–cognitive patterns of an entire society. What is shared is an orientation to the world such that objects appear with characteristic affective tones: A bioenculturated person will not experience just "this action," but "this beautiful and graceful action that everyone should admire," or "this grotesque and shameful action that should be punished."[7] Functionally, the sharing of affective–cognitive orientation we call "ideology" contributes to the stability and reproducibility of social patterns of thought and practice on daily, lifespan, and generational scales. Ideological social reproduction is noncoercive, but no one thinks social reproduction happens by shared affective–cognitive patterns alone; all societies have regimes of violence that occasionally license practices of physical and social violence; these can, at least in theory and when properly applied, punish or eliminate those prone to system-disrupting behavior. Call that coercive social pattern reproduction. So, we want to be able to see the relation of the psychological and functional senses of ideology to one another and the relation of that pair to coercive reproduction.

In egalitarian societies, sharing affective–cognitive patterns via enculturation supports shared productive and reproductive labor via shared intentionality; hence we see the psychological and functional senses of ideology as noncoercive social reproduction.[8] Furthermore, as a result of mostly transparent shared production, the identification of the few cases of free-riders and bullies allows coercive social reproduction via punishment via ridicule, ostracism, exile, or execution (Boehm 2012; Sterelny 2016). In societies with unequal distributions of goods beyond a certain threshold of inequality, we see, alongside interest-concordant behavior, the appearance of interest-discordant behavior (assuming that the inequality in question is such that those on the short end are deprived of a level of goods necessary for their interests as human beings capable of flourishing). Deleuze and Guattari call the puzzle of interest-discordant behavior "Reich's question": Why aren't theft and strikes the general, rather than the exceptional, responses to poverty and exploitation? Allied to that is Spinoza's question: "Why do men fight for their servitude as fiercely as for their freedom?"

In unequal societies, ideology entails the spread, throughout the society, of affective–cognitive patterns proclaiming the system to be just and thus for the elites to have been justly rewarded (psychological sense) so that this coincidence contributes to the reproduction of the system (functional sense). The ideology of elite superiority (whether gained by merit or "blood") helps reproduce the system by epistemic and emotional processes. Elites do not see the injustice of the system and thereby feel justified in their success, thus protecting interest-concordant behavior from interference by guilt feelings should their benefits appear to have been unjust. For oppressed people who internalize their oppression—if such people exist—there is an epistemic effect of hiding the systematic sources of their social position and an emotional effect of resistance-inhibiting "justified" feelings of inferiority, thus protecting interest-discordant behavior from interference by feelings of righteous indignation (Jost et al. 2004).

Coercive reproduction works by punishment that produces expectations of the same for future deviations. We will focus on the role of ideology in enabling the internal discipline of the punishment forces deployed in coercive reproduction. Are police, army, and workplace personnel (from security guards to slave overseers) kept in place merely by practices of external rewards (raises, promotions, and esteem of their fellows for good behavior) and punishments (fines, demotions, dismissal, execution for deviation)? That is, are there effective collective action problems (Rosen 1996) produced by coercive reproduction practices targeting them, the enforcers? Call that lateral coercive reproduction. Or does that system of lateral coercive reproduction itself require an ideological buy-in on the part of at least some portion of the enforcers for them to do their work of disciplining the other enforcers for the successful operation of the punishment practices contributing to—or wholly responsible for—large-scale social reproduction? And finally, does that notion of ideological buy-in on the part of (some portion of) the enforcers not have to include an affective dimension?

Deleuze and Guattari's Treatment of Ideology

Deleuze and Guattari present their thought on ideology via a confrontation with Wilhelm Reich (1946), whom they credit with having linked fascism with desire rather than with simply false beliefs.

> Reich is at his profoundest as a thinker when he refuses to accept ignorance or illusion on the part of the masses as an explanation of fascism, and demands an explanation that will take their desires into account, an explanation formulated in terms of desire: no, the masses were not innocent dupes; at a certain point, under a certain set of conditions, they wanted fascism, and it is this perversion of the desire of the masses that needs to be accounted for. (Deleuze and Guattari 1977, 29–30)

In these pages of *Anti-Oedipus*, "ideology" is criticized because it focuses on the cognitive and neglects the affective–cognitive, or "desire," the direct libidinal investment of social structures. As they see it, ideology critique seeks to correct the irrationality that masks a vision of what rational social production would and should look like. But for Deleuze and Guattari that sort of being fooled as to social reality is not where the action is; what they say we need to explain are not cognitive errors but perverse desires. Hence, interest-contrary behavior is "not a question of ideology." Rather it is a question of desire, of an "unconscious libidinal investment of the social field." It's this libidinal investment that explains counter-interest behavior:

"it's not enough to say: they have been fooled, the masses have been fooled. It's not an ideological problem of misrecognition and illusion, it's a problem of desire, *and desire is part of the infrastructure*" (104; italics in original).

Despite his breakthrough, Deleuze and Guattari claim that Reich falls short in his analysis of fascist desires. "Yet Reich himself never manages to provide a satisfactory explanation of this phenomenon, because at a certain point he reintroduces precisely the line of argument that he was in the process of demolishing, by creating a distinction between rationality as it is or ought to be in the process of social production, and the irrational element in desire, and by regarding only this latter as a suitable subject for psychoanalytic investigation" (29–30). So, Reich's problem is reinstalling a distinction between rational social production (e.g., government provision of infrastructure through political decisions arrived at after deliberation in a system of rationally justified social structures) and irrational fantasies ("We're being swamped by a flood of immigrants, so we need a strong leader!"). He should have pushed through to "discover *the common denominator or the coextension of the social field and desire.* In order to establish the basis for a genuinely materialistic psychiatry, there was a category of which Reich was sorely in need: that of desiring production, which would apply to the real in both its so-called rational and irrational forms" (30).

Even though Deleuze and Guattari allow that Reich had insisted that the real question is "under which socio-political conditions did the masses come to desire fascism?" (345) he still pushes the old split between desire as irrational fantasy and production as rational reality, instead of seeing desiring production. Thus, psychoanalysis can find in social desire only what is negative and inhibited, not what is positively produced. To this concern with socio-political conditions I'd add that we need to pay attention to their concretion in affective conditions of transindividual "bodies politic"—rates and intensities and waves of anxiety, fear, depression, rage passing through the population. The "direct libidinal investment in flow-breaks" we saw above is a technical term for Deleuze and Guattari. It means that, for example, foragers can be joyous when meat circulates, imperial subjects feel awe or hate as they see the palace of the emperor (negative investment is still investment), and Christian subjects can feel rapture as the icon circulates. For Deleuze and Guattari, capitalist libidinal investment occurs through the double structure of money: The same units are used for the "giant mutant flow" of generated credit and in the paychecks of employees and the collection cups of beggars. This duplicity "is enough, however, to ensure that the Desire of the most disadvantaged creature will invest with all its strength, irrespective of any economic understanding or lack of it, the capitalist social field as a whole" (229).

In *A Thousand Plateaus*, Reich drops out, but Deleuze and Guattari produce their own complex account of microfascism, a particular formation of desire, as that which explains the way desire can desire its own repression:

> What makes fascism dangerous is its molecular or micropolitical power, for it is a mass movement: a cancerous body rather than a totalitarian organism. American film has often depicted these molecular focal points; band, gang, sect, family, town, neighborhood, vehicle fascisms spare no one. Only microfascism provides an answer to the global question: Why does desire desire its own repression; how can it desire its own repression? The masses certainly do not passively submit to power; nor do they "want" to be repressed, in a kind of masochistic hysteria; nor are they tricked by an ideological lure. (Deleuze and Guattari 1987, 215)

As a desiring formation, fascism is traceable to particular enculturation practices.[9] We live politically, and those political practices invest our bodies, minds, and lifeworlds: "Desire is never separable from complex assemblages that necessarily tie into molecular levels, from microformations already shaping postures, attitudes, perceptions, expectations, semiotic systems, etc." (215). Hence, we can see that while some people desire fascism, that is never some primordial desire to live in a domination-saturated society that would at least, so the promise goes, save us from a state of nature where anything goes: "Desire is never an undifferentiated instinctual energy, but itself results from a highly developed, engineered setup rich in interactions: a whole supple segmentarity that processes molecular energies and potentially gives desire a fascist determination" (215). And your beliefs, no matter how fervent, won't protect you from fascism if you neglect the orientation of your desire: "Leftist organizations will not be the last to secrete microfascisms. It's too easy to be antifascist on the molar level, and not even see the fascist inside you, the fascist you yourself sustain and nourish and cherish with molecules both personal and collective" (215). Thus, to understand fascism, you must understand desire. Belief-oriented ideology won't get you to the heart of the matter. To do that, we need a notion of affective ideology.

Affective Ideology

We have noted the need to account for the capacity to participate in punishment practices that constitute coercive reproduction. And that aspect
needs to have an account of affect constitutive of concrete mental states
because torture and killing (by nonpsychopaths) requires overriding at
least some level of inhibition produced by empathic identification with a
subject in pain, even given attenuation of empathy across group lines. The
relations among empathy, arousal, and violence are complex, and the literature discussing them is massive and constantly evolving. Nonetheless,
some outlines can be observed: Increasing in-group empathy increases the
violence of punishment of out-group members for threats to in-group, and
the targets of that violence receive less empathic resonance with the punishers, resulting in lower estimations of the pain dealt out. However, there
must still be some recognition of pain in the targets, or else the notion of
punishment loses its sense: You don't torture a wall, even if you bang on it
out of frustration. So, despite the attenuation of empathy toward out-group
members, consistent testimony from combatants shows the strong emotional surge necessary for almost all people to engage in violent confrontation.[10] The tension of the group faceoff characteristic of much combat,
however, once broken, can result in routs and torture of the enemy, especially in a situation in which a helpless enemy faces a group; in this case,
the conquering group members can escalate the atrocities in a lateral display to their comrades.[11] The heavy racial inflection of the use of torture of
enslaved people in the United States as elements of coercive social reproduction would require some modification of this basic schema, because
incidents of torture of those subjected to enslavement didn't always follow
outright combat but were routinely employed for work productivity or for
reasons of psychological dominance (Baptist 2013). Nonetheless, I think
it's clear that a strong affective component is necessary for torture, even if
that takes the form of a longstanding inferiorization or subhumanization,
rather than it always being a hotheaded rage state.

To get to a notion of affective ideology, we have to distinguish between
belief-desire psychology as a philosophical explanation of behavior and
the psychological processes involved in the encoding of experiential regularities. This absorption or enculturation mode of ideology transmission
accords with research done on unconscious transmission of racial bias via
body comportment independent of the semantic content of accompanying

words (Castelli et al. 2008). We could also note here Susanna Siegel's work on perception, in which gaze following indicates confidence, thus indicating a pattern of social valuation (cited in Stanley 2015, 249).

Jason Stanley's Notion of Ideology

Turning now to a recent noteworthy work that treats ideology among its other topics, Jason Stanley's *How Propaganda Works* holds that behavior-explanatory beliefs are generated from regularities of experience. I take it to be a widely accepted psychological fact that the experiential encoding of regularities is going to encode the affective tone of the situation along with representations of the state of the world. From the perspective of experiential encoding, emotions aren't separate mental states that bind beliefs to agents; they are an inherent part of the experience and become associated with the representational content.

Hence the emotions produced in the scenes of daily life are part of what is transmitted by the identity-constituting practices: The reproduction of the practice of white supremacy for a slaveholding family (to use Stanley's example) is not simply accounted for by instilling in children some beliefs with the propositional content of racial superiority and inferiority and binding them to those identities by love for friends and parents who participate in that practice. The reproduction of the practice of white supremacy is also constituted by an affective structure of white pride and vengeance motivated by white vulnerability, as well as by hatred of, fear of, and contempt for Black people that is encoded along with the representational content of the scenes of humiliation, torture, and death that constitute the daily practices of the coercive reproduction side of plantation white supremacy. The affective disposition allowing gruesome torture has to be part of the ideological transmission.

However, in the latter cases, emotion is exterior to belief; it is that which binds beliefs to agents engaged in identity-constituting practices. Although the emotion-generating desire for good self-image and positive connection with friends and family is left unaccounted for by Stanley, I do not think the psychological mechanisms and their implicit anthropology are all that controversial. But there is a risk that keeping beliefs at the center of an account of ideology focuses one on the puzzle of evidence-resistant belief. While that notion points to a certain aspect of social reproduction, it misses another aspect—that is, punishment practices that constitute coercive reproduction. And that aspect needs to have an account of affect constitutive of concrete mental states, instead of merely externally binding beliefs to agents, because torture and killing (by nonpsychopaths) require overriding at least some level of inhibition produced by empathic identification with a subject in pain, even given the attenuation of empathy across group lines.

Recall Stanley's discussion of a slaveholding family:

> One might expect the ideology to lead the members of the planta-
> tion family to believe that Blacks are inherently lazy . . . One might
> expect their ideology to lead them to believe that Blacks . . . are not
> capable of self-governance. One might expect them to believe that
> Blacks are inherently violent and dangerous and require harsh
> punishment and control to keep them from posing a threat to
> civil society. (194)

The first two sentences entail that the practice-generated ideology (expectations from regularities of having daily work done by slaves) is separate
from these other beliefs, which are consequences of the ideology. These
seem to be explicit narrative beliefs that we can expect the family to hold
on the basis of their social position. From that ideology other beliefs about
characteristics of Black people (laziness, incorrigibility, primitiveness, violence, and thus danger to whites) can be expected to be derived; these
serve to explain the behavior of Black people to the family and justify the
punishment dealt out. If we keep the parallel structure for the third sentence, then attributing violence and danger to Black people is an additional
belief, not included in the practice-generated belief set but derived later,
serving to justify the family's punishment and control practices—that is,
coercive reproduction (whether or not the agents of the violent punishment are family members or overseers).

But "laziness," "incapacity for self-governance," and "inherent" violence
and danger are theory of mind inferences—that is, beliefs held by the family that refer to supposed behavior-explanatory properties of Black people.
They are not observables, but inferences whose objects are character traits.
However, the coercive reproduction practices of the plantation—torture and
humiliation—are daily events, and the beliefs on the part of the punishers
(family members and overseers) in the laziness, incorrigibility, and danger
of Black people have to be able to account for that punishment behavior.
Are ideological beliefs up to the task of accounting for the practices of

coercive reproduction on the plantation? Only when paired with an emotional state capable of motivating the punishers to tear into the flesh of the enslaved. Hence there is a theory of motivation, latent in Stanley's account, that I'm trying to expand with the notion of affective ideology. As the actions constituting the punishment practices have heavy affective components, both for active, immediate participants and for family members who experience the scenes of torture, the notion of "aliefs" (Gendler 2008a and 2008b)—that is, psychological states that are at once perceptual, affective, and dispositional to behavior, such that their content would be something like "blacks are disgusting and frightening; we must torture them to set examples"—which seems to be a fuller explanation of the psychological state of the torturers (which is then transmitted to others experiencing the scene, preparing the children for their turn holding the whip) than simple Stanley-style belief in self-legitimating propositions, even when it is anchored by love of others. The affective disposition allowing gruesome torture has to be part of the ideological transmission.

Let us turn to the question of ideological buy-in on the part of the enforcers of coercive reproduction. This necessity of discussion of an affectively expansive ideological buy-in comes out in the passage from Hume cited by Stanley: "The soldan of EGYPT, or the emperor of ROME, might drive his harmless subjects, like brute beasts, against their sentiments and inclination: But he must, at least, have led his *mamalukes* or *praetorian bands*, like men, by their opinion" (232). The question here is whether a simple appeal to self-interest is enough to satisfy Hume as an explanation of the behavior of the enforcers, or whether there needs to be ideological buy-in for the enforcers to perform their coercive reproduction practices. Why do the rank-and-file of the police and the army, or the overseers of a slave society, drawn from the popular classes, act in ways that promote the interests of the elite? Is there any room here for ideology, or is discipline in the forces of order itself the product of interest-concordance (the cops, soldiers, and overseers get paid, after all) and collective action problems (the lone cop, soldier, or overseer who in the name of popular resistance steps out of line gets punished)? At least on the plantation, self-interest and lateral coercive reproduction practices do not seem sufficient to explain the behavior of the torturers. There has to be ideological buy-in, but only if we have an affect-inclusive notion of ideology. If simple beliefs are too pallid to explain the ability to participate in the terror-inducing torture regime of violence that is a big part of social reproduction of white supremacy in slavery and beyond, then I'd say the affective structure enabling terrorizing torture and class solidarity of the planters (they can be counted on to hunt runaways and return or kill them) is essential beyond the mere "belief" as cognitive stance holding a proposition to be true, even the proposition that Black people are dangerous.

I have claimed that if we restrict ideology critique to identifying cognitive errors, we risk missing the emotional commitments that accompany those putatively false beliefs and that allow for the punishment as part of coercive social reproduction. But if we push too far into the affective at the expense of the cognitive, are we really talking about "ideology" anymore? Throwing away the cognitive component of ideology critique seems too much; some people, sometimes, do respond to a cognitively oriented ideology critique: They are open to persuasion via exhibition of their cognitive errors; their beliefs become rationally revisable. However, that seems to happen only after a change in social identities—a move to a new location, the gaining of new friends—and that change has an affective component. So, in sum, I think we should retain the term "ideology" but broaden its scope to include the affective as well as the cognitive. Our concrete lives as "bodies politic" integrate the cognitive and the affective; that integration is needed to account for both coercive reproduction and for the occasionally successful rational revision of beliefs via ideology critique.

Part II

Political Psychology

3

Berserkers

In Part II, "Political Psychology," I provide case studies in political philoso-phy of mind. In this chapter I examine instances of the berserker rage in which violence is unleashed at the limit of, or exceeding, subjective con-trol.[1] I would say that this investigation falls into the realm of "political psychology," as some rages are prosocially motivated: They can be trig-gered by perceived threats to individual loved ones, and also by perceived threats to ways of life—that is, the social patterns in which our bodies politic have been shaped by enculturation practices that in their deep embodi-ment modulate the thresholds at which rages are triggered. Even in their full expression, past the point of subjective control, however, the berserker rage is encompassed in regimes of violence, whether they be state military forces or nonstate forces.[2] It is evoked in some warrior cultures by par-ticular rage-inducing practices (often including dance, music, and the use of drugs), while it is denigrated in others. When fighting is done at close range where fine muscle control is less important than muscular force and the ability to withstand injury, and where it can induce panic in adversar-ies, berserker rage can be prized as divine possession (e.g., possession by "Ares" in the Greek tradition). On the other hand, because of its uncon-trolled nature, it is unacceptable in what I will call the American imperial regime of violence, wherein infantry troops are used in peacekeeping mis-sions, urban warfare, and other circumstances requiring controlled action.[3]

The berserker rage is a fascinating phenomenon, awe-inspiring to those in some regimes of violence, repugnant to those in others. Despite the diver-sity of regimes of violence, such that there are cultural variations in its triggers, as well as diverse practices of breathing exercises and conscious attention-focusing practices that modulate its onset, its full expression seems to exhibit cross-cultural similarities: snarling, spitting, grimacing, scream-ing, along with prolonged and hyper-intense but not very precise no-holds-barred fighting, with a fairly sudden crash landing as the episode con-cludes, sometimes in the most intense cases bringing with it a "blackout" or impossibility in recalling the details of the episode. As we will see below, this profile leads some to posit its evolution as a result of selection for effective reaction of prey mammals. While predation is often conducted in a cool, stalking, manner until the final leap—which even then can have precise targeting of the vulnerable parts of the prey—prey behavior under extreme stress, when fight rather than flight or freeze occurs, is often a reactive lashing out at what moves in the attack zone to which the prey has access.

I follow the leading idea of an "inhuman gaze" to explore the perceptual-motor effects and possible episodic memory inhibition in extreme cases of the "berserker rage." I first locate berserker rages in a taxonomy of aggressive behavior as out-of-control reactive aggression triggered by blocked flight in a high-danger situation. I then sketch its military implications and present a plausible neurological substrate. I then zero in on the most extreme manifestations, the so-called blackout rages—or, in technical terms, "Transient Global Amnesia" (TGA)—in which episodic memory is inhibited or attenuated, even though there is retention of affective-charged sensory fragments. Here I have two objectives: First, I will present recent research on the neuropsychological mechanisms at work producing TGA; second, we will work out its phenomenological implications, using discourse analysis of the first-person reports of berserkers in interviews as well as the second- and third-person testimony of witnesses. In doing so we come upon the recurrent theme of an "inhuman gaze" in which the berserker seems to be transformed or even possessed, such that their eyes gleam or flash in compelling and disturbing ways. What, then, are we to say about an "experience" of which we have only a partial ability to reconstruct, and even then, "flipping a switch" or "automatic pilot" are prevalent terms in those reconstructions? We here face the paradox of a phenomenological report of an experience whose episodic details seem lost even if an affective tone is left behind to be available for voluntary recall or indeed to arise unbidden with sometimes debilitating effect in flashbacks.

Taxonomy of the Berserker Rage

The berserker rage is a highly intense reactive aggression behavior pattern eluding full conscious control. Hence the emotion term "rage" in "berserker rage" is tricky, as the extreme cases are blind or blackout behavior with no recall of a subjective experience. So, in this chapter "berserker rage" should not necessarily be taken to imply an emotional experience had on the spot, even though the feel of many violent episodes can be recalled. The berserker rage is a classical means for enabling close-range killing behavior; it is a close-to-automated state that unleashes extreme violence on almost anything, or anyone, in its path.[4] It can have both reactive, proactive, and redirected dimensions, insofar as it deals with immediate threats, but can then go out in search of threats to eliminate, or passive and helpless victims on which to vent. Its potential expression is a concern in all regimes of violence, whether to provoke it or suppress it. Within military regimes of violence, we find its most memorable invocation in Homer's description of Achilles in the *Iliad* (Cairns 2003). While some disinhibiting anger is needed in many close-range encounters by those who have not mastered the techniques of cold-blooded engagement, unleashing the berserker rage is associated with many problems in the contemporary American imperial military regime of violence (its "rules of engagement" in its formal expression). Its hyperactive threat processing fits poorly in counter-insurgency operations, both urban and rural, as it can lead to civilian atrocities (as in the case of Robert Bales [Vaughan 2015; Sherwell 2012]), and it is closely associated with PTSD (van der Kolk and Greenberg 1987).

We have many descriptions in historical accounts, scientific literature, and soldiers' memoirs of the experience of close combat in multiple regimes of violence where fear, anger, and aggression intersect in various dimensions and intensities (Keegan 1976; Shay 1994; Grossman 1996 and 2004; Kyle 2012). In the psychological literature, a threefold distinction among types of aggression is common: reactive, proactive, and instrumental. Although we have to beware of any simple models, in general, anger-mediated aggression depends on the surmounting of the first flash of fear and the avoidance of the final surrender of full-fledged freezing. Reactive aggression is a quick if not automatic attack on a close-range, inescapable threat that nonetheless offers the chance of being overcome by attack; the chance of winning is crucial here in avoiding freezing (Blair 2012; Siegel and Victoroff 2009). Proactive aggression is a consciously controlled attack made in order to eliminate a future threat (Siegel and Victoroff 2009; Wrangham 2019). Instrumental aggression is a consciously controlled attack on those that do not pose present or future threat in order to gain various rewards (Nelson and Trainor 2007, 536).

I propose the following links of these types of aggression to variations in anger. Appropriate anger is associated with reactive aggression that is calibrated accurately to the threat; contrast this with hyperbolic anger, which is associated with reactive aggression that comes from those with a low threshold of threat detection and poorly calibrated threat estimation, problems often acquired by previous trauma.[5] Instrumental aggression tends to be accomplished in cold blood; this can be associated with psychopaths (Nelson and Trainor 2007; Blair 2010, 2012; Hirstein and Sifferd 2014) but can also be produced by people who have undertaken various training procedures to control fear and anger and produce an emotional dominance over their victim (Collins 2008 discusses techniques employed by professional hit men). Proactive aggression, when subjects are not completely successful in using self-calming techniques, is intermediate in intensity between hot reaction and cold instrumentality. Proactive aggression often needs some angry arousal as one is attacking to eliminate a future threat to those in whom you are emotionally invested; thus, linking the image of the one to be protected and the image of the threat kicks up anger. In this way, proactive aggression is less intense than reactive aggression, but it is not cold-blooded instrumental aggression either. This is not the whole story, however, as Barash and Lipton distinguish reactive aggression or retaliation (attacks directed back at the aggressor) from redirected aggression, which sometimes targets the kin of the aggressor (2011, 39). Redirected aggression provides a costly, honest signal of continued potency that increases the chances of nonvictimization in the future. The proximate explanation of redirected aggression is relief from stress hormones released by the adrenals. Barash and Lipton hypothesize that prolonged stress, especially social subordination stress, burns out the pituitary–adrenal axis and produces lower testosterone and serotonin and higher cortisol. There is thus a hypothesized reduction in bad hormonal effects for those able to engage in redirected aggression when retaliation is not possible.

With this in mind, we can recognize a few basic dimensions to military anger, always keeping in mind two things: first, that anger is contrary to simple fear and to paralyzing freezing, and second, that both fear and anger are contrary to calm self-possession. Anger can be linked to quick reactive retaliation or self-motivated returned aggression; to quick or planned redirected aggression aiming to harm the kin or comrades of the enemy; to proactive or preventive aggression, either retaliatory or redirected, designed to protect self and others; and to vengeance or third-party mediated retaliatory or redirected aggression. Experiences of anger in each of these dimensions also vary in intensity, from white-hot flashes to the sort of simmering "baseline resentment" among U.S. soldiers in Iraq for wrongs ranging from 9/11 to Saddam Hussein's treatment of civilians (Sherman 2005, 90; cited in Flanagan 2016). This fluctuating background anger is amped up by the death or wounding of comrades; here there is a narrow temporal / spatial / attachment focus on wrongs done to the "band of brothers." There can also be resentment at the betrayal of a moral code by superiors (Shay 1994, 2003, 2014). Of course, there is also the hot flash of reactive anger at being trapped and in mortal danger yet with a chance of overcoming the foe.

Neuropsychology of Berserker Rage

While Panksepp (1999) invokes rage as a pan-mammalian "basic emotion" resulting from the triggering of subcortical neural circuits homologous between humans and other mammals, such that rage is triggered in us when we are put into the situation of a trapped prey animal, we have to nuance this picture. Human anger is dependent on situational analysis: For many soldiers, being trapped cuts off fear-mediated flight and thus pushes them toward rageful fighting, but often only when the situation is analyzed as winnable, even if dire, as otherwise panicked freezing might kick in or conscious surrender be chosen. To set the context for our investigation of the neuropsychology of the berserker rage we will first examine four paradigms for emotion. For Paul Griffiths, the concept of "affect program" is the key. Jaak Panksepp ties such affect programs to evolutionarily inherited "basic emotion" circuits. Departing from both Griffiths's and Panksepp's focus on specific modules or circuits are two "constructivist" accounts, Lisa Feldman Barrett's radical constructivism and Joseph LeDoux's moderate constructivism. We will adopt LeDoux's position.

From a cognitive psychology perspective, the berserker rage seems like a candidate for an "affect program," which for Griffiths (1997) is a modularized, automatic, behavior pattern (compare with the notion of "autopilot" that the recent American berserker Robert Bales mentioned [Vaughan 2015]). From this perspective, extreme cases of rage produce a modular agent or "affect program" that attenuates if not eliminates conscious control. "Affect program" draws on a computer metaphor in which the body is hardware and rage is the software, but with no pre-reflective self-awareness. Affect programs are emotional responses that are "complex, coordinated, and automated ... unfold[ing] in this coordinated fashion without the need for conscious direction" (Griffiths 1997, 77). They are more than reflexes, but they are triggered well before any cortical processing can take place (though later cortical appraisals can dampen or accelerate the affect program). Griffiths makes the case that affect programs should be seen in light of Fodor's notion of modularity, which calls for a module to be "mandatory . . . opaque [we are aware of outputs but not of the processes producing them] . . . and informationally encapsulated [the information in a module cannot access that in other modules]" (93).

From his "basic emotion" perspective, Panksepp cites studies of direct electrical stimulation of the brain and neurochemical manipulation as identifying homologous subcortical "rage" circuits in humans and other mammalian species (1999, 190). Panksepp proposes an adaptationist story for rage agents given their utility for prey, further sharpening the difference between rage and predatory aggression. While a hunting attack is an instance of proactive or instrumental aggression, rage reactions are a prey phenomenon, a vigorous reaction when pinned down by a predator. Initially a reflex, Panksepp claims, the rage action pattern developed into a full-fledged neural phenomenon with its own circuits (1999, 190). The evolutionary inheritance of rage is confirmed, for Panksepp, by the well-attested fact that infants can become enraged by having their arms pinned to their sides (1999, 189).

Lisa Feldman Barrett proposes a radical constructivism. Barrett (2017) insists on a strong neural globalism, which, with her insistence on holism, emergence, and degeneracy (same outcome from different mechanisms), results in a strong nominalism, such that no "fingerprint" of necessary circuits can be identified for either emotion instances or even emotion categories (2017, 35–41; see also Pessoa 2017 for a similar distributed network approach to emotions). For Barrett, an emotion instance (an "emotion concept" in her terms) is constructed via bottom-up summarizing of singular experiences, drawing on neural inputs from multiple brain sites mapping the body and other higher and lower intra-brain regions; each of these "core affect" experiences is tagged with a culturally specific emotion term. Hence there is a high-level, cortical, semantic component to emotion concepts, which are constructed from these multiple inputs. Such summarizing produces concepts as abstract but nonessential capacities that don't exist as enduring, locatable, actual firings but only as potentials for actualization. Given Barrett's strong holism (the brain works as a distributed network or differential field), acceptance of emergence (specific instances arise as integration of that differential field), and "degeneracy" (a technical term meaning that emotion instances can be produced by widely differing neural pathways), then for her, concept creation is the progressive construction of a virtual field (virtual, because emotion concepts do not exist as things do but inhere in the manner of potentials). For Barrett, then, an emotion episode is the actualization of the potential concept. It occurs as prediction, a top-down simulation that "unpacks" concepts, constructing an instance of the concept that assembles its components from occurrent inputs and checks the assemblage against the prediction. This actualization occurs in a degeneracy mode, such that no single set of neural firings is necessary for each instance of the concept. Hence the concept is a virtual diagram with multiple mechanisms for the actualization of instances. In Deleuzean terms, it is an "abstract machine" with multiple machinic assemblages for its actualization / individuation / integration / differenciation (Protevi 2013).

I classify Joseph LeDoux's work as moderate constructivism. *Contra* Barrett, he identifies specific neural circuits, so he is a moderate constructivist, but *contra* Panksepp's notion of pre-programmed basic emotional circuits, he is a constructivist, insofar as he says that there is a "recipe" for emotions constructed by a working memory agent—in LeDoux's terms, a *bricoleur*. For LeDoux, threat detection evokes nonconscious defense states, but not emotions. These states are produced from a "recipe" of nonconscious elements (senses, brain arousal, body feedback, and memory) assembled by a working memory *bricoleur* to produce conscious emotional feelings (LeDoux 2015, 228).

The neural circuitry of the rage reaction is recapitulated by LeDoux (93ff) in the following way. Sensory processing follows a fast "low" road and a slower "high" road. In the fast or low road, the lateral amygdala feeds the central amygdala and the basal amygdala. From the central amygdala, we get defensive behavior (initial freezing), physiological support in the autonomic nervous system, hormonal output via the pituitary, and brain arousal neuromodulators (norepinephrine, dopamine, serotonin, and others [LeDoux 2015, 90; see also Nelson and Trainor 2007]). For LeDoux, the slow or high road allows regulation of these first responses by the prefrontal cortex and hippocampus. Note that the first reaction is freezing (see also Blair 2012), so to activate learned responses, you have to inhibit freezing (LeDoux 2015, 101). LeDoux's full action model builds on the early reactions, adding connections from basal amygdala to the nucleus accumbens of the ventral

striatum in the pre-frontal cortex (2015, 102–3). At this point, past freezing, and when flight is unavailable or cognitively unacceptable, rage is the
last resort. The defensive circuit seems to be amygdala / hypothalamus /
periaqueductal gray (LeDoux 2015, 89; see also Blair 2012 and Siegel and
Victoroff 2007). Along with supporting physiology, the defensive rage reaction is an "innately programmed reaction pattern" (LeDoux 2015, 89).
Interestingly, the hippocampus, which is an important part of risk assess-
ment, creates environmental maps, especially of spatial relations (LeDoux
2015, 106). Might it be the case that overstimulation here accounts for the
very narrow focus or tunnel vision reported by some berserkers? LeDoux's
final suggestion relevant to us is that the BNST ("bed nucleus of the stria
terminalis") "sits at the crossroads between defensive circuits involving
the amygdala and accumbens and risk-assessment circuitry involving the
septohippocampal circuitry and pre-frontal cortex. It thus may coordinate
the two systems, balancing which dominates behavioral control, depend-
ing on the degree of uncertainty" (107). The berserker rage might then be
caused by a BNST-mediated lock-in of the defense circuits, outlasting or
overpowering controlled threat response and moving on to supercharged
hot reactive or redirected aggression-seeking behavior (as opposed to the
"warm" proactive or "cold" instrumental forms of aggression).

It's possible to bring together the perspectives of Griffiths, Panksepp,
and LeDoux, but not that of Barrett. We can say that a berserker rage is
a highly intense reactive aggression behavior provoked by culturally significant threat detection to the extent that conscious, subjective control is
severely attenuated, resulting in an automatically running of an "affect program" with the limit case being the inhibition of episodic memory, thus
earning the name "blackout" rages. (LeDoux 2015, 124, allows for use of
"affect program" terminology; on "redout" rages, see Swihart, Yuille, and
Porter 1999; clinical work with blackout rage is recapped in Potter-Efron
2007.)

Neuropsychology of Stress-Related Transient Global Amnesia

Normal threat memories occur with the encoding of pre-frontal cortex
(PFC) narrative consciousness of what happened, along with an affective
tagging performed by the amygdala's activating defensive motivational
states. Using LeDoux's moderate constructivism, we then see the constructed emotional state available for conscious recall: "I was angry when

that happened." However, in the "blackout rage," we speculate, very intense defensive motivational states will crowd out PFC encoding and hence prevent the formation of narrative memory. So, in these states there's nothing "there" to encode for episodic content.

There are a number of mechanisms proposed to account for stress-induced Transient Global Amnesia (TGA). A popular one is hippocampus damage in hyper-arousal states from stress-related cortisol exposure. A piece of evidence here is that the CA-1 region of the hippocampus has glutamate uptake blockage in stress episodes (Popoli, Yan, McEwen, and Sanacora 2012). So even if the PFC had encoded episodic detail, that content wouldn't be encoded in the hippocampus. However, critics of the hippocampus damage theory point out that the amygdala and the medial PFC play very important roles in stress. These critics call for a systems analysis of stress and hippocampus: "[I]t may be a time for stress research to shift its focus from the usual neurochemical emphasis to systems-level and neural computation approaches to capture the multifaceted nature of stress" (Kim, Pellman, and Kim 2015).

An example of such a systems-level analysis is the "temporal dynamics model" (Diamond et al. 2007). The key concept here is the distinction in phase in emotional memory encoding. In phase 1 we see that "plasticity in the hippocampus and amygdala are activated for a short time by a strong emotional learning experience" (1). In phase 2, however, the "induction of new plasticity [is then] suppressed" (11). Here we see a mechanism for a shift from narrative memories to flashbulb memories should an emotionally intense event occur during phase 2. With strong emotionality, the hippocampus shifts from a "configural/cognitive map" mode to a "flashbulb memory" mode (16). This "underlies the long-lasting, but fragmented, nature of traumatic memories" (1). The key idea here is that events occurring in phase 2 (post-stress) may not be well encoded; given that the PFC is weak under severe stress, it can be the case that narratives are not supplied. So, the shift from narrative to flashbulb memory encoding underlies the fragmentary nature of post-stress memories to the point of episodic memory failure or TGA but with retention of affective-charged sensory fragments. With flashbulb memories we see a strong emotional experience, sometimes accompanied by more or less coherent narrative memory, but sometimes not, if the experience is too intense. In these latter cases, only sense fragments tagged with amygdala-produced affect get through. Metaphorically, then, post-stress amnesia blackouts are when you look right at the flashbulb, so that all that is encoded for recall or flashback are "intense implicit components interwoven with fragmented declarative recollections" (8).

Phenomenology of the Blackout Rage

So far, we have classified berserker rage as an episode of hyper-intense pre-emptive aggression whose neurological profile includes a threat-activated defense state that attenuates conscious control. We then tied that to an account of the neurological basis for "blackout rages," or episodes of Transient Global Amnesia (TGA), using Diamond et al.'s (2007) "temporal dynamics" model. We now move to an account of the phenomenology of blackout, an endeavor that is made intrinsically difficult by the gaps in narrative memory shown in TGA cases.

Three Scales of Rage Episodes

Based on cases from his practice, the clinical psychologist Ronald Potter-Efron (2007) proposes three scales of rage episodes; we will re-order these from his presentation to move from least to most extreme. First, there is moderate rage, described as "losing control," in which the subject retains a feeling of ownership of action, even if they cannot control themselves. They are themselves, just behaving badly and unable to stop of their own accord. The second scale is something like "being possessed." There is still a subject, but it's a different one from one's normal self. You're not just out of control; you're someone else. The third and most extreme scale is the limit case of "blackout" rage or TGA as we have elucidated it above. The subject loses awareness of action and has no ability to construct spontaneously coherent memory narratives but must instead infer responsibility from testimony and evidence about what happened (Potter-Efron 2007, 157).

The first scale, "losing control," can be called, using terms from Shaun Gallagher (2005), ownership without agency—that is, the person can recall that they owned the experience, that it was they, but what is recalled is a lack of volition, in which they can't assume responsibility for stopping but can note only that a stoppage occurred. "When Ricky rages, he loses control over what he says and does. Notice however that even in the midst of this rage episode, he didn't lose total control ('I didn't even try to stop. I did stop, though')" (Potter-Efron 2007, 44). Here is another analysis of the attenuation of voluntary control such that the rage becomes the subject, as it were: "When Ricky rages, he becomes instantly furious, so angry that he cannot keep his rage from taking over control of his mind and body" (44). We claim that such a phenomenon of ownership without agency is the "automatic pilot" that the American berserker Robert Bales mentions. Potter-Efron continues, concerning what he calls a "mini-rage": "The 'I snapped' is a sign [of] a mini-rage. It felt to him, just for a moment, that he wasn't exactly himself. Not that he completely lost conscious awareness, nor did he lose his sense of his normal self. Yes, he was himself, but at the same time, he could sense right then that he was also not quite himself. He had an incomplete transformation" (45).

The next scales increase in intensity. The second scale is that of "becoming someone else" (the mundane expression for the Greek mythological trope of "possession by Ares"). Potter-Efron offers the following clinical evidence for this second state: Second-person observation shows that the body changes its appearance as the berserker shows an "inhuman gaze": "Friends tell Ricky when he is raging: 'It's your eyes,' they say. Ricky's eyes get weird when he rages, looking both glazed over and brilliant" (44). From the first-person perspective of second-scale episodes, we see the testimony of someone feeling they are no longer themselves. Not just themselves without normal control, but someone else: "Ricky admits that he feels like a different person when he rages, as if he were somebody else" (44). The "he feels like" and the "as if" mark this as still ownership; it's recognition of behaving in non-ordinary ways, poetically expressed as "becoming somebody else." There is still a "he," Ricky *qua* pre-reflective self, that feels like he—Ricky—is acting abnormally. So, there's still the ability to compare these actions to the expected actions as characteristic or not of Ricky.

The third scale is blackout rage. Potter-Efron writes of "Ricky" that "Sometimes he blacks out, unable later to remember much or all of what he has done" (44). Here we see the partial or full inhibition of episodic memory and the loss of a feeling of ownership, which we can attribute to either a disruption of pre-reflective self-awareness or an inability to reflectively access that pre-reflective state (Zahavi 2005; Gallagher and Zahavi 2019). To flesh out our account of blackout rage, we will turn to the case of Robert Bales we have previously mentioned.[6] Testifying in a notorious case of a violation of the American imperial regime of violence, while in the Afghanistan theater, Robert Bales claims he doesn't remember setting fires during his rampage. Nonetheless, in the trial, he admits, "I must have done it, it's the only thing that makes sense." So here there is a bivalence of the "I" as agent constituted after the fact by inferences, and the "I" as narrative self who now incorporates this action into the life story even without direct memory of it. Diamond et al. (2007) point to the role of later inferences: "[T]he reconstructed memory would therefore be a hybrid representation of information processed by the hippocampus (and amygdala) in a fragmented manner at the time of the experience, in conjunction with post-event reconstructions of the memory" (15).

From a long-form magazine story on Bales, with extensive interviews of him (Vaughan 2015) we read the following:

> The other soldiers wanted to simply haul the tree into a burn pit. To Bales, this would not do. He wanted to destroy the thing himself. Finally, on the morning of Saturday, March 10, 2012, after fixating on this symbol of failure for three days and mostly sleepless nights, Bales went at the tree with a hand axe. It took him eight hours— in full view of the entire base—but he eventually succeeded in chopping it to bits. "This tree was used to hurt my friends, man," Bales told me recently, recalling the episode in an odd, detached tone. "It was used by the enemy. I had to see it go, you know?"
>
> Later that evening, Bales would turn his rage to less symbolic targets. Shortly after midnight, under cover of a deep rural darkness, Bales slipped away from the base and walked to a nearby village, where he killed four Afghans, including a 3-year-old girl. Then, after returning to his base to reload and telling another soldier what he had done, Bales left again to murder 12 more in another village just down the road. Of the 16 people he killed, four were men, four were women, and eight were children. The youngest was 2. (Vaughan 2015, no pagination)

But Vaughan's phrase "turn his rage" makes the rage the possession of Bales. That's the deep logic in which actions are attributable to active subjects that being "possessed by Ares" calls into question. We can say in such extreme cases that the "subject" is split. It is both a seat of moral responsibility and a center of autobiographical narrative—"'I' did that" and a simple, abiding substance to which accidents can accrue—the rage belonged to Bales. So yes, in the history of the substance that is Bales, a rage episode occurred, so we can say "his rage." But it wasn't willed, which is what the first, moral and autobiographical, subject presupposes.

Five Selves of the Blacked-Out Berserker

From our discourse analysis of Bales's testimony I propose five "selves" of the blacked-out berserker: (1) a level of pre-reflective self-awareness allowing "ownership" of actions; (2) the body agent performing the behavior (recalled later by subjects as being on "automatic pilot"); (3) the abiding substance to which blackout rage happens as an event recounted in second- or third-person history ("you did it" / "he did it"); (4) the "I" as agent constituted after the fact by inferences ("it's the only thing that makes sense"); and (5) the "I" as narrative self who now incorporates this action into the life story even without direct memory of it ("I did it; I must have done it"). What's missing is the "true self," the "I" as classical subject: the seat of moral responsibility for actions consciously taken and able to be recalled in a first-person autobiographical narrative in which one directly "owns" one's actions, acknowledging them as products of their will. Here

Classical Self *Unified along five aspects*	Blacked-out Berserker *Five dispersed selves*
Pre-reflective self-awareness: that which allows ownership of action	A loss of prereflective self-awareness or an inability to reflectively access it.
Self-conscious agent: "I'm doing this"	Body-agent available in first person recall only as "automatic pilot" or "someone else"
Abiding substance to which self-conscious events accrue: "my life history"	Abiding substance to which events accrue via second- or third-person testimony: "you did that" or "he did that"
Agent continually self-constituting: "I recall doing this sequence at that time"	Agent constituted after the fact by inferences: "I must have done this: it's the only thing that makes sense of the evidence"
Narrative self: "I did that for the following reasons"	Narrative self who now incorporates this action into the life story even without direct memory of it ("I accept that I must have been the one to do this because of my rage")

Sense of "self" in blackout berserker rage.

events belong to the self, a unitary self that provides a focus for all five aspects that come apart in the blacked-out berserker. The phenomenology of such a dispersed subjectivity must then include, no matter its difficulties, reconstructing memories and forming integrated selves. This is for its subjects no mere philosophical exercise but the working through of trauma. Normal memory recall often has gap-filling inferences and third-party testimony. So, the post-stress amnesiac may assume ownership of the episode's contents at first by conscious inference, and then perhaps by reconstruction, so that they may "re-member" them.

Psychiatrist Jonathan Shay has extensive clinical experience with veterans of the U.S. armed forces suffering psychological trauma. Some of that is PTSD from being under continual stress; they are suffering from what was done to them and what they underwent. Some of Shay's patients, however, suffer from what Shay calls "moral injury," or psychological disturbance stemming from the soldier's actions. Shay feels that some of this damage can be ameliorated when soldiers can partake in self-narratives coupled to ritualized expiation, so that the soldier feels less isolated and recognizes that he was fulfilling a socially recognized role. As we have seen, however, some combat trauma experiences cannot be easily narrativized. When they can be reconstructed with the help of therapeutic intervention and guidance, by narratives that piece together fragmentary memories with the help of inference from other people's testimony, these narratives can help restore the connections among the "five selves" we discussed.

Severe trauma explodes the cohesion of consciousness. When a survivor creates a fully realized narrative that brings together the shattered knowledge of what happened, the emotions that were aroused by the meanings of the events, and the bodily sensations that the physical events created, the survivor pieces back together the fragmentation of consciousness that trauma has caused (Shay 1994, 191). Hence, for Shay, it's not simply isolated narratives inside the soldier's head that work; it's being able to share stories of the events that provides relief by what he calls the "communalization" of trauma, the recognition that it took place in our shared regime of violence. The "paradox that narrative temporality can never be completely true to the timeless experience of prolonged, severe trauma. . . . disappears when . . . narration is a step in the survivor's move to communalize the trauma by inducing others who were not there to feel what the victim felt when he or she was going through it" (Shay 1994, 191).

I have discussed the complexities of understanding how berserker rage is experienced by those who engage in it. When they assume the "inhuman gaze," who exactly is the subject of that gaze, who is looking outward? I don't wish to underplay the moral complexity of therapy for those who have performed atrocities; do we as a society really wish to make it easier for people to return to "normal lives" after showing an incidence or even a pattern of berserker rage? What are the limits of our regime of violence? What can we tolerate?

There are two things to say here: First, one can offer both deontological and utilitarian reasons for such therapy. Deontologically, contemporary military berserkers such as Bales are human beings, and they deserve the dignity of both care and help in understanding what they have done while participating in our American imperial regime of violence. And from a utilitarian perspective, the rates of domestic "collateral damage" in the form of violence and substance abuse that occur in untreated berserkers suffering from the physiological and psychological trauma of PTSD and "moral injury" might be mitigated by therapeutic intervention. We can't neatly enclose our regime of violence in the military; we have to reckon with spillover. Second, however, all our moral notions, to the extent they are tied up in notions of personal responsibility that rest on the capacity to keep agency and ownership together, are put to the test by cases of the transformed and sometimes dispersed "selves" we find in various scales of berserker rage episodes. The presence of a self that can take responsibility is not a given in these cases; it must be produced through processes of narrative construction trying to tie together affect-laden sensory fragments, second- and third-person testimony, and inferences.

It's an open question whether berserkers should feel themselves, at the end of those processes, to be guilty, or whether acknowledging the damage the "rage agent" has done and appreciating the dangers to self and others of allowing such states to recur is enough. While some berserkers avail themselves of "neurological exculpation," by referring to analyses of the "my brain made me do it" kind, others do feel guilty. We should remark upon the tenacity of retrospective guilt produced through passage from "I must have done that; it's the only thing that makes sense" to "My God, what have I done?" even when the practical agent of the act of killing can be acknowledged as a "rage agent." We can see a "centripetal power" to subject constitution, a power that draws to an abiding, conscious, directly memorialized and narratively accessible autobiographical self, responsibility for acts it never really committed, acts that were performed by another software program running their hardware, acts committed while "possessed," by "someone else," acts performed while the agent exhibits an "inhuman gaze."

Thus, it seems that some people who have experienced berserker rage episodes just cannot, paradoxically, help taking responsibility. In other words, to heighten the paradox, they are irresponsible in taking responsibility, in taking upon themselves moral agency, when practical agency lies elsewhere, in the "rage agent" that for a time "possessed" them. Questions for future research concern the genealogy of this powerful motivation for subject construction and the assumption of moral responsibility when seemingly exculpatory explanations based on deep neurological processes are at hand.

4

Esprit de Corps

In this chapter, I continue the investigation of "political psychology."[1]
In the preceding chapter we looked at the unleashed violence of the berserker rage, which violates the American imperial regime of violence by
its uncontrolled lashing out at the limit of subjective control. As opposed
to that breaking of a regime of violence, I will now look at the joyful form
of sports, which, with the obvious exception of combat sports (each with
their own carefully stated regimes of violence), are outside any regime of
violence. For instance, in the sport on which I will concentrate here, soccer,
fair play is the rule, and a player will be ejected for violent action. In contrast to the concern with joy in sharing food as an adaptation in chapter 1
(an honest signal of willingness to reciprocate), here I shift gears to focus
on nonutilitarian joy in shared bodily presence, especially resonant movement; you could say that here you don't give an object, but you give your
effort as teammate or even as a competitor—it's a shared, resonating, thrill
to drive down the homestretch neck and neck with a rival runner, each of
you pushing yourself and the other to dig even deeper.[2] I present a case
study in which we can see joy in playing and watching team sports, which
I will qualify as nonutilitarian "behavioral beauty," exemplified in a real-life
event: the Megan Rapinoe–Abby Wambach goal in the quarterfinals of the
Women's World Cup of 2011, one of the greatest in all World Cup history.[3]
They didn't just score a goal, they did so with such breathtaking grace and
skill that it was accompanied by a joy that went beyond mere happiness at
scoring.

In the case study, I will frame the event with evolutionary and political
context, then show how the concepts of relational autonomy and collective
intentionality provide an important perspective on team sports. I com-
plement those notions by bringing in some enactivist treatments of non-
reflective self-awareness that allow me to show the ontological status of
two key aspects of soccer, the linking of teammates by a pass and the emergence of the affective components of trust, joy, and *esprit de corps* from the

interactions of players. I conclude with a discourse analysis of Rapinoe's account of the goal, highlighting the aforementioned themes and culminating in the joy that enraptured her and the people in the stands and watching on television.

Evolutionary Aspects of Sport and Play

To ask about the origin and essence of sport is to ask the wrong question. Like everything else, sport is a multiplicity, an irreducibly diverse sheaf with resonances, feedback loops, and rhythms within a set of intersecting processes, rather than a unitary phenomenon. Turning now to the literature, we do indeed see that multiple sport origin theories have been advanced. From an interdisciplinary classical studies perspective, sport is ritual sacrifice of physical energy (Sansone 1992, 37).[4] From a psychological perspective, sport is related to interpersonal bonding (Davis, Taylor, and Cohen 2015). From an Evolutionary Psychology perspective, sport is an outgrowth of hunting and warfare skill development (Kniffin and Sugiyama 2018). You can also find talk about sports in terms of ritualized inter-group relations that provide prestige for those who facilitate the contests (Pisor and Surbeck 2019). There is furthermore a tradition of thinking of sport in terms of adaptationist sexual selection with male display, courtship rituals, and strength signaling (Miller 2011; Lombardo 2012).

Insofar as sport is regulated play, we should recall that play is a capacity displayed by the young of many mammalian species.[5] What is play? It too is a multiplicity; among its most important dimensions we can garner from classic accounts (Huizinga 1980 and Caillois 1981; see also Sutton-Smith 1997; Gray 2017; and Henricks 2020) are that play is autotelic or intrinsically rewarding but also functional-developmental. Play is also exploratory ("What are my limits?"), experimental ("Let me try this!"), and imitative ("Let *me* be Megan Rapinoe!"). In addition, play is often imaginative, placing us in new contexts (Mackenzie 2000); it also, in distinction to games and sports, makes up its regularities as it goes along. Finally, play, according to Caillois (1981), has two dimensions, *paidia* and *ludus*. *Paidia* is exuberant, exhilarating, rule-less or imbued with the free creation and re-creation of rules on the spot (think of the game of "Calvinball" in the Calvin and Hobbes comics). Its subdivisions are mimickry and "*ilinx*" (involving search for the experience of delirious vertigo). *Ludus* play is rule-bound; its subdivisions are *agon* (struggle) and *alea* (chance). While a soccer game is defined by rule-bound struggle, the shared joy spilling over into exuberance over a great goal to win the game involves *ilinx* on the part of both players and fans.

Play can be given an evolutionary reading. As one article put it, "Fun is functional: play is evolution's way of making sure animals acquire and perfect valuable skills in circumstances of relative safety" (Byrne 2015). A good bit of research has been done on play and neural development; play might have helped preserve plasticity so that our ancestors could adapt to complex eco-social environments. In this vein, play is said to refine the coordination of sensori-motor activity; Spinka, Newberry, and Bekoff (2001) see play as "training for the unexpected." However, while it's a necessary condition of our existence that all our ancestors did not starve, we need not conclude that mere survival was ever a sufficient motivation for continuing with human life. We should see exuberant, nonutilitarian play— "art" in an extended sense that includes sport—as an essential part of our humanity. That is to say, while adaptationist stories are all well and good, they just don't capture a full picture of human experience in its phenomenological richness or even capture life in its exuberant diversifying energy.[6]

We can, however, broaden our perspective on joy in line with Prum (2017), who links the mate-choice side of sexual selection to the evolution of nonutilitarian pleasure and beauty.[7] Here I want to propose thinking about joy in play and playful joy as "behavioral beauty," something desirable for itself that has broken free from an adaptationist paradigm. Prum (2017) writes that most current evolutionary biology sees the display of beautiful traits, morphological or behavioral, as "specific, honest information about the quality and condition of potential mates" (12). Here we see a utilitarian reductionism in which mating preferences are shaped by objective qualities, such that beauty is desired only because of its hoped-for side effects: the chance it gives you to have children with good health. In these cases, Prum says, sexual selection is seen as simply another form of natural selection. But for Prum, reading against the tradition that slights female mate choice in Darwin's *Descent of Man*, sexual selection is an independent force, such that "adaptation by natural selection is *not* synonymous with evolution itself" (italics in original). Hence, with a robustly independent notion of sexual selection, evolution is "far quirkier . . . than adaptation can explain" (13).

So, then, what if joy in play and playful joy were considered forms of "behavioral beauty"? What if they don't necessarily signal good health but are attractive because it's just fun to be around joyful people? In other words, can we liberate playing and watching sports from adaptationist accounts of honest signaling of healthy vigor? It's this aesthetic surplus of joyous sport that I'm after in this chapter. I want to distinguish sports from the idea that it's just a holdover from war training, or even that there's a historically verifiable linear development from war to some sports. Or worse, that sport is a sublimation of a natural violence drive that would otherwise be expressed in war. Sublimation assumes an original orientation to violence that is later diverted—that is, a culture-added-to-biology model, which I reject, as we recall from chapter 1. My position throughout this book is that violence is not an untrammeled natural drive that we deal with as we can. Rather, for me, since the being of humans is so deeply biocultural, violence occurs only in "regimes."

Now, obviously, some sports do have historical links to war practices (the javelin is a spear, after all) but I think sport takes a leap into another genre when it becomes aestheticized, to use Prum's term, when the desire for the object breaks free of adaptationist signaling. Prum (2017) writes that a "trait that was originally preferred for some adaptive reason has become a source of attraction in its own right. Once the trait is attractive, its attractiveness and popularity become ends in themselves" (56), free from the constraints of adaptiveness. Indeed, speaking ethically and politically, as beautiful as sports can sometimes be, we should also recall that not everyone benefits from our current sports institutions. To see what I'm saying here, De Block and Dewitte (2009) attempt an intermediate position of gene-culture coevolution or dual inheritance theory, following Boyd and Richerson (1985) and Richerson and Boyd (2005). In this line of thought, cultural evolution can separate culturally popular activities from those that are adaptive for the individuals involved in them. Thus, sports participation need not be adaptive for everyone involved because there's only a loose viability constraint to sport development at the population level: A sport can't kill everyone involved and be able to be transmitted. Furthermore, even though we stress a nonutilitarian perspective, we can't forget that adaptationist discourse has an immense capacity for capture: Even if dangerous to its participants, taking the risk of playing sports might be worth the adaptive reward if you succeed at them. Sport participation can be seen as adaptive because you might be attractive to others for your speed and strength as health signals, as well as for your teamwork as a signal of readiness to cooperate, and even for your exuberant joy as signaling an anti-depressive personality.

Stimulated by Prum's notion of the inherent link of beauty and desire, object and subject, I want to say that joy (in sports and elsewhere) is essentially a second-person affair—its infectious effects on others are part of what it means to be joyous. It's that inherent relationality that I think might distinguish joy *qua* "behavioral beauty" from mere contentment or happiness, which seems more like a private internal feeling. That might be what would be perceived if there were only honest signaling going on: "Ah, that smile, it means the person is in good health." Instead, there's no "observing" joy; there's only participation. Being in the presence of joy sweeps you up, closing down the distance between subject and object—I suppose at the ecstatic limit, eliminating that distinction. So, not even a curmudgeon "observes" joy: What a curmudgeon observes is someone displaying happiness. So, following the thread of joy, and echoing the "dynamic interactionist" dimension of human nature I proposed in the Introduction, we see the essentially social being of humans: In a closed-off first-person experience, alone by yourself, you can only be happy, albeit intensely, just as from an alienated third-person perspective you can only observe degrees of happiness. But being joyous entails being in second-person relation; in positive feedback situations of "collective effervescence," as Durkheim would say, but also, even in a zero-sum competition, you have that ignoble form of joy we call *Schadenfreude* by being in relation, by the uplift you feel in seeing the downfall of those on the other side suffering their losses.

We will pick up again on the theme of nonutilitarian joy below. To transition to the next section by one last point on the extra-survivalist theme, we see that, from a scientific standpoint, play is linked to surplus in multiple dimensions; it happens only above and beyond survival. Thomas Henricks, in his history of play theories, summarizes the "surplus resources" theory of play developed by Gordon Burghardt in these terms: "Animals are more likely to play when they have sufficient metabolic energy, when they are free from serious stress or food shortages, when they need stimulation to reach an optimal level of physical functioning, and when they follow a lifestyle that involves complex behaviors in varying environments" (Henricks 2020, 131). Let us turn now to the context in which the events of our case study took place.

The Bio-Socio-Political Context of the Women's World Cup

The year 2022 was the fiftieth anniversary of Title IX—the U.S. law mandating equal financial support for men's and women's scholastic sports—

and the forty-second anniversary of "Throwing Like a Girl" (Young 1980), a classic essay in what we can call feminine body construction. The Rapinoe–Wambach goal is historically determined; it could not have been enacted by Young's constricted body subjects and hence needed a world in which widespread young female sports participation was encouraged. There's a lot we could say about historically variable body constitution or, more precisely, the way in which being subjected to a constant stream of objectifying "gazes" can cause body image to impinge on body schema. Young's essay is inscribed in the "double consciousness" lineage of critical phenomenology of which DuBois, Beauvoir, and Fanon are notable names (Weiss, Salamon, and Murphy 2019). What we see here is the way third-person categorization preempts equitable second-person relations with negative effects on first-person experience. In other words, instead of being in a second-person relation, being a "you" for me to speak with, the person in front of me is instead just an example of a social category, one of "those people."

We should have a "bodies politic" analysis here, as described above, when talking about the social and political context of sports; we need population analysis and modest constructivism. Bioculturally speaking, we'd want to look at not just genetic variation but also at developmental plasticity, which, mediated by access to play and coaching, enables the formation of a repertoire of skills. Hence another sense of "body politic" would be a search of a population to detect youngsters with elite potential and select them for more intense training. Identification of those with potential to be elite soccer players in the United States runs through the youth soccer establishment; participation here often requires a substantial financial investment. Finally, we'd have to run the whole analysis through the lens of ableism and disability discourse, whereby access to equipment and training for wheelchair sports and electronic sports is part of the story.

Relational Autonomy

Classical Accounts

In Protevi (2013), I presented a theory of human nature as "dynamic interactionism" in which human beings develop in societies that vary across and within populations. In my view, human nature is quite deeply plastic, but with a prosocial bias; there are lots of different norms, but rarely are people indifferent to the norms that structure their lives. It's against that background that I now turn to discourses of relational autonomy, which are I think consistent with the hortatory ideal I propose in Protevi (2019): Act such that you nurture the capacity to enact repeatable active joyous encounters of positive sympathetic care and fair cooperation for self and others without qualification. In saying this, I'm wary of the naturalistic fallacy. I'm not saying we *should* act this way because we evolved this way; I'm just saying, in an anti-"biofatalistic" way (Barker 2015), that we *can* nurture that capacity when doing so receives the proper institutional support, which need not come at an unacceptable ethical and political price.

Mackenzie (2019) shows that two distinctions structure the relational autonomy discourse: causal versus constitutive and procedural versus substantive. In sports, diachronous causal relations of coach and player underlie the development of relational autonomy, which, when realized, allows the constitutive synchrony of relational autonomous play. I don't think the notion of content-neutral proceduralism (the way in which decisions are made) at stake in much of the relational autonomy literature is relevant here except in the minimal way that a player has a clear mind and isn't preoccupied with pleasing the coach rather than with making the right play. Regarding substantive relational autonomy, we can see direct relations to our athletes when we refer to Stoljar (2018). Weakly substantive accounts "do not place direct normative constraints on the contents of agents' preferences" but instead focus on self-relational attitudes; I think this is relevant in that players need self-confidence. As for strong substantive relational autonomy accounts, those that normatively constrain other-regarding attitudes, I also think this is relevant as you can be an autonomous playmaker only by empowering your teammates. Furthermore, Mackenzie (2019) posits that autonomy is multi-dimensional, involving self-determination (the practical power to accomplish goals), self-governance (competence to make decisions cohering with deep values), and self-authorization (self-respect attitude: You're worthy of making this decision). All this is accomplished by and through affirming relations with others. In its challenge to the cultural ideal of isolated autonomy, the development of the mainstream relational autonomy literature is a very important political engagement. Isolated autonomy often *de facto* hides homemaker labor, as in Judy Brady's (1971) American feminist classic: "I Want a Wife!" The relational autonomy discourse flows easily into a desire for positive liberty for others, which has its rebound effects on my flourishing. Hence "relational autonomy" means the more I foster the autonomy of others (freeing them from grinding survival-oriented work to allow them to pursue their capacities), the more autonomous I become, by virtue of living in a network of reciprocal positive feedback. That sounds like Spinoza's rational republic but also like a radicalized Kantian Kingdom of Ends (van den Linden 1988).

Rethinking Relational Autonomy

Di Paolo (2005) showed that autonomy for early autopoietic thinking was all or nothing, such that one needed to add adaptivity to the conceptual framework to account for the ways in which autonomous systems can be moving in good or bad directions. Hence, becoming autonomous can be thought of as an always ongoing, fragile process: It can lapse into heteronomy, being controlled by outside forces. Here we see why some recent enactivists appeal to Simondon's trans-individuation (Di Paolo 2021) because individuation—coming into your autonomy—is always in connection with a "pre-individual" relational field; such fields are not peopled with constructed individuals but are structured by individuating processes. That is to say, those with whom we are in relation—our families, friends, co-workers, etc.—are themselves never finished individuated products but are in ongoing processes of individuating themselves in relation to the never-finished others in their lives. They are always growing into their personalities, even when that growth slows to a crawl. We can see the connection of relational autonomy with trans-individual ontogenesis if we look at research in evolutionary anthropology intersecting child development psychology (for example, Hrdy 2009 and Tomasello 2016 and 2019). Here we see the ontogeny of primary intersubjectivity via practices of communicative musicality (turn-taking in exchanges between a baby's cooing and gurgling and a caretaker's "motherese") accounting for trust and joy, as the infant must have its own singularity to enter communication with another (Trevarthen 1999). For Hrdy and those like her who emphasize the interdependent sociality of humans, there is no original fusion of infant and caretaker because collaborative breeding has already rendered all caretakers multiple, even those who are individual people. That is, any one person assuming a caretaker role was also raised in a collaborative setting such that they are already radically relational (for a reading of the no-fusion concept from the perspective of ego relation psychoanalysis, see Benjamin 1988).

You gain autonomy through relations with others, but if we up the ontological ante a bit, we can also say that the relation has a consistency or autonomy, per the concept of "participatory sense-making" (Di Paolo and

De Jaegher 2021; Di Paolo 2021). Taking an enactive phenomenological perspective on soccer, then, a good pass is one that releases the teammate into a space in which their own relationally autonomous decision making takes over. And all that coordinated autonomy-supporting work of the teammates is enabled by coaching on a longer timescale, which empowers them to read and react by positing dynamic problems as the basis of skill development; skills are best seen not as simply body movements but as the ability to achieve solutions to dynamic problems posed by shifting relations of teammates and opponents (Hristovski et al. 2012; Woods et al. 2020). To concretize the experience in a dynamic systems theory spin on corporeal phenomenology: What the players experience is a shifting field of intensity and potential relations into which they intervene (Headrick et al. 2012). Hence, our enactive taking on board the concept of "relational autonomy" means paying attention not just to "social context," if that is modeled by two present-at-hand spheres of individual and a surrounding society, but by social affordances, what we can do with others (Rietveld et al. 2018; for more on affordances, see chapter 7). The question then becomes, If I make this move, what does this do for the options of others? If I'm constitutively related to others (if my autonomy is constituted by proper relations to others), my authentic or autonomous choices are going to take my relations with them into account. That's easy to see with a soccer pass—have I placed my teammate in a position to succeed? But this relationality is also what makes life transitions so difficult; if I want to change my way of life, I'll be affecting the way of life of others as well—what they might be comfortable with, what they might grudgingly accept, what they might lovingly affirm, etc. The "might be" here is the trans-individual, pre-personal, virtual field of relations. Such fields are differential: Changes in rates of change of one process will change rates of change of other processes. Affect is a sense of that, a feel for the game (in Protevi 2009 I present a case study of the Terri Schiavo court decision, a "right to death" matter).

Collective Intentionality

Classical Accounts

Tollefsen (2105) is my guide to the collective intentionality discussion. She explains that if collective intentionality is truly collective (rather than an aggregation of distributed individuated intentions), then there must be some emergent level, but positing such emergence conflicts with the widespread methodological individualism in philosophy of mind characterizing reductive physicalism and internalism. As Tollefsen reminds us, even if you say there's a commitment to others involved in collective intentionality, for many researchers that's still individuated on separate mind-brains. Thinking about collective intentionality is very difficult if you see intentionality as representational—as in the subject / content / propositional attitude trio—whether that is reduced to brain states or treated functionally as a state of a system with multiple individuals, as Tollefsen (2015) would have it. In the Conclusion to *Groups as Agents*, she writes:

> Even if one rejects the interpretivist framework, the basic insight that mental states are dispositional states of whole systems rather than internal, discrete states that carry informational content (as the neo-Cartesian would have it) provides a more easily extended account of propositional attitudes to groups. (137)

Interpretivism starts with the practice of attributing intentional states; if we can make sense of another being—if we can understand and predict their behavior using the folk psychology of beliefs and desires—it is an intentional agent. Here, cognition is still in the middle, connecting beliefs about the state of the world (beliefs are good when mind conforms to world) with desired outcomes by issuing motor commands to allow world-to-mind satisfaction (make it so that world conforms to mind). Tollefsen also spells out the rationality assumption in interpretivism: what a system ought to do to satisfy its desires in given circumstances. In her reconstruction of the debates, group attitudes are dispositional states of groups; hence they are "more akin to centers of gravity than to tables and chairs" (106). Here we encounter the notion of multiple realizability: Different types of groups have different realization mechanisms.

Rethinking Collective Intentionality

Problems in the collective intentionality discourse include both the "collective" and the "intentionality" aspect. In the former, we must consider how to think an emergent plural subject despite the objections of methodological individualism, and in the latter we must distinguish between representational and "operative" notions of intentionality (Gallagher 2017).

Concerning collectivity, Zahavi (2021) (see also Léon and Zahavi 2018) points out that much collective intentionality discourse (and much autonomy discourse) is individualist: The question is how to form a collectivity, which assumes pre-existent individuals. As we have seen above, this is what Simondon and the trans-individualists challenge (Read 2015). For them, the question is how to achieve autonomy without presupposing an original fusion, as that privileges a prior identity, either in a single person from whom one separates in development (typically a maternal figure) or a unified group from which one breaks free in asserting individuality. If you're stuck in this perspective that sees individuation from the perspective of a lost maternal or communal fusion, you can see why some fear crowds as masses of lonely atoms craving comforting or commanding leaders (Borch-Jacobsen 1988, analyzing the Le Bon–Freud connection; see also Gilbert 2014). To escape this trap, you must have communicative musicality, as each side of the infant–mother couple has to contribute even *in utero* (Martínez and De Jaegher 2020), even if infant singularity is larval and in need of scaffolding, even if the individual grows up to face what looks like Durkheim's social facts. Concerning intentionality, the supervenience of intentionality on brain states fails on an enactive model of the brain as a relational organ; for Fuchs (2018), brains are dynamically looped in brain / body / environment systems rather than cut off in linear and isolated command mode, as in Susan Hurley's "classical sandwich" jibe (Hurley 1998, 21) in which cognition is what happens between sensation and motor command. Rather, following Fuchs (2018), brains modulate ongoing organismic (brain and body dialogue) engagement with the environment. In enactive terms, structural coupling is ongoing.

Enactive Approaches

Emergent Effects of Passing and Teamwork

Examining the connection of relational autonomy and collective intentionality in our case study, using an enactively enhanced understanding of the terms, will display some important cognitive and affective aspects: *esprit de corps*, trust, joy, and love that occur when players strive together, reading and anticipating each other's moves and potentialities. Team sports show how relational autonomy and collective intentionality can fit together. You must be involved in multiple collective intentionality instances to exercise relational autonomy in team sports; as the name implies, you can't be relationally autonomous alone—you can do it only in relation, and team collaboration is a strong form of relation. In fact, there is even agreement between the teams to play the match and accept the referee's decisions (defeasibly—although it's rare, you can always quit the match in protest if you feel that the referee is being egregiously unfair). Furthermore, the collective intention of teams to win is best realized when the coach frees the players to incarnate relational autonomy in their play, especially in cases of a great pass, which releases teammates into a position to pass, dribble, or shoot.

Regarding our focus on team sports, the team is an emergent entity but not a collective fusional hive; rather, it is a network that produces an overall unifying effect in meshing intentions (Cooke et al. 2012). But team intentionality can't be representational. Another way to put it is that the problem with integrating the discourses of relational autonomy and collective intentionality is not trying to think "plural" as such but trying to think a plural subject when you assume a "subject" is a brain giving orders and a body that takes orders. What we need to do is to think collective intentionality as the meshing of operative intentions of a team of enactive organisms. You can say these are "mental states" only if you see that "mind" is an event accomplished in interaction with environment, as per the critique of the extended mind in Di Paolo (2008), who would say that mind isn't in space, even if that space stretches beyond the skin. Here I will refer to Gallagher (2017): "[O]perative intentionality is the real non-derived, primary intentionality" (80). Here, operative intentionality is nonrepresentational and action-oriented; it does not picture the world but enables a meshing of agents whose potential actions are revealed.

Changing perspectives a bit—but I hope they are ultimately compatible, or at least complementary—to something of a poststructuralist perspective that looks at subject positions as constituted out of a changeable network of real-world relations, I think we can say that the ontological status of the pass is that of a radical relational autonomy—what's autonomous here is the relation—as it is the pass that creates passer and receiver, rather than being a subsidiary event linking players conceived as already formed substances.[8] Building on this notion of a pass, we can look at the ontological status of the team from a dynamic systems perspective—which I think is compatible with poststructuralism given that structures, and the subject positions they create, are being formed and dissolved continuously via multi-scalar interactions, though not always with the same rhythm. Here I'll claim that a team is an emergent dynamic structure with downward causal effects via constraint of the dimensionality of individual players' movements (Varela 1991; Thompson and Varela 2001). In other words, you don't get a team unless you have players working together—the team emerges from component interactions—but you also don't get "players" without a team. Without a team, there's just folks knocking the ball around in a park.

Collective intentionality discourse typically examines the cognitive side of teamwork and competition—the teams integrate themselves via a collective intention to win, and the two teams together have a collective intention to play by the rules as judged by the referee. We must intend to play together. Is there a collective subject here? I think we can give a Spinozist reading to Margaret Gilbert's group subject or "body" (Gilbert 2003). A Spinozist turn to bodies in resonance undercuts overly intellectualist readings of collective intentionality just as attention to bodily development undercuts isolationist readings of autonomy. For Spinoza in the *Ethics* (1992), a new individual is formed whenever a composite body maintains a characteristic ratio of speed and slowness (see the section on body in E2P13Scholium). Kisner (2019) shows how Spinoza combines Cartesian extension (individuation by ratio of speeds and slowness) and Aristotelian individual essence in the concept of "conatus." In the Spinozist psychology of emotion, modulations of conatus are seen as affections and affects. (An affection is a change in a body by its encounter with another body; an affect is the change in the power of acting—which includes the power of enduring an encounter—of the body.) From this point of view, a team will be an emergent "body" insofar as it will have its individuation—what sets it apart from other teams—in its characteristic ratio of speed and slowness (its "style"). That is, the ratio of dribbles to passes, length and speed of runs relative to passes, types of shots (from what range, etc.). Team style is the characteristic actualization of a multiplicity of relations.

To follow this line of thought, teams achieve emergent effects via interdependent coordination. It's not coordination of independent beings; it's coordination that allows interdependence to work rather than hinder group efforts (Totterdell 2000). I must know what I can do on the field (I must have know-how) as well as what you can do and how our efforts affect each other; hence we have interdependent know-how (Williamson and Cox 2014). Some players have good "know that" capacities—good command of propositional knowledge so they talk a good game—but it's "know-how" that counts. And this is so even if sometimes "know that" verbal instructions frame practice or game action. The key in producing a team is to foster an internal structure of the composite body such that the subordinate individuals are not swallowed up but maintain their relational autonomy: The whole trick with teamwork is to allow the autonomous creativity of players, a creativity that is not simply a display of individual brilliance but one that sets up other players, gives them a space for their own autonomous creativity.

Socially emergent entities have degrees of coordination: Ant colonies are more ordered than soccer teams. Teams themselves are more or less coordinated at times, but a team does not have the unity of an organism or a super-organism. Players make judgments based on local information (Headrick et al. 2012), but when it is well functioning the team achieves effects over and above what's possible for any one player. To retain our focus on soccer, I'm going to say that the pass is the key move in creating a team effect. In principle, a player could dribble the length of the field to shoot and score but that's a limit case, approached only by a few solitary geniuses. In the overwhelming majority of cases, it's the pass onto the running line of another player that allows the emergence of a team effect.

At the limit, can you say that the teamwork relation reaches an autonomous status as well? If you can establish a strong emergence of a team, then the "we" of the team is not reducible to "me" or "you" but has enough autonomy to be the basis of normativity: Did you uphold your end of the bargain? Are you a team player? This can be another player who is criticizing you but also you when you are criticizing yourself. What the "we" expects survives counterfactual actualization: Even if you don't empirically live up to its demands, it's still there. There are some things you can't do, even if they are technically within the rules, without being derided as being someone who is not a team player. Hence the constraints on player action—what constitutes them as team players and allows the emergence of a team—are primarily affective: The players must reward the trust their teammates put in them as team players, or they risk criticism. Hence the affect here has two dimensions: a positive pull toward joy in togetherness and a negative push to avoid criticism.

Affect in Team Sports

Here are some of the components of the bodily, affective practices leading to pair and group bonding allowing the relational autonomy and collective intentionality interface in team sports.

1. Touching, such as high-fives, hugs, handshakes, pats on back (Kraus et al. 2010).

2. Resonant movement in drills (McNeill 1995).
3. Mutual effort to exhaustion (Cohen et al. 2010; Davis, Taylor, and Cohen 2015; Machin and Dunbar 2011).

Feedback loops are evident here: If you like one another, you want to touch your teammates to encourage them, which helps success, which helps liking one another, and helps you push your efforts to keep up with those of your teammates. Once you have created an emotional bond with teammates, that bond allows a better reading of body intentionality and shifting opportunities suited to the fast dynamics of play. It's not that unfriendly teammates can't read one another's potential moves, but it does seem to be conventional wisdom in team sports that friendship among teammates is desirable and often grows from the shared experience of touching, moving, and striving.

Esprit de corps

Collective intentionality in well-performing teams is accompanied by *esprit de corps*, which I define as trust that enduring pain will be worth it. (Miranda 2020 gives a genealogy of the term, noting its use in the military and in quasi-military corporate managerialism.) Even in a loss the effort is worth it for the togetherness, the love generated in mutual effort. There has been some interesting neuro-endocrinological work on sport and social bonding, focusing on synchrony and exertion (Cohen et al. 2010; Davis, Taylor, and Cohen 2015; Pepping and Timmermans 2012; De Dreu and Kret 2016). Given that soccer is resonant rather than strictly synchronous, we must be careful here, but there are moments of connection such as successful passes. And the game is soaked with effort. So, the bonding via shared exertion effect is there, and some "resonance" effect is plausible. Resonance is when you're "on the same wavelength"—that is, your timing allows successful passing. So, willingly undergoing exhausting effort with others produces bonds. The physiology seems to be that, upon binding to receptors, beta-endorphins release dopamine; you have positive team-building association of those with whom you share this state (Pilozzi et al. 2020; Machin and Dunbar 2011).

Trust

The team has an internally structured collective intentionality; teams have differentiated roles internal to their collective intentionality. Those roles cannot be rigid (i.e., only one player can fulfill the function, though that can be efficient as a limit tendency) but complete interchangeability (so-called total soccer as with the now-mythical Dutch teams of the 1970s) is a limit too. Coaches cannot control players; they must trust that players have relational autonomy to adapt to changing situations. Players show relational autonomy when they make decisions based on changes in relations; their job is to empower the others—to increase their ability to make a goal.

Trust must be there for relational autonomy in a collective intentionality context to be a human relation rather than a mechanistic exchange based on already achieved knowledge or a mere shot in the dark that isn't trusting so much as sheer guessing. Trust is reliance that another will fulfill expectations, expectations that can be implicit in the practice or mutually agreed upon in full-blown collective intentionality in the manner of Gilbert (2003). Now the fulfillment of this expectation can't be guaranteed, or it isn't trust. We could do a Derridean aporia here (Derrida 1995). Pure trust is impossible, but you still must act. If we are to trust, then we must have something to lose and we must make an informed decision based on knowledge of whom to trust. Fully blind trust isn't really trust but just guesswork; that's not trusting, as to trust you must have some reason to trust. But, on the other hand, if our trust decision is fully determined by this knowledge (of pure trustworthiness) then we seem to be thoughtless or mechanical in our trust and thus not trusting after all. Teamwork has a trust component: The playmaker must trust that their teammates will exercise relational autonomy in pursuit of their collective goal. The playmaker is the one who passes the ball, setting up others to score. The very best playmakers will also have the capacity to score, but they must also have the trust of teammates that if they work hard to be in position, the playmaker will deliver the ball if that's the best play, the best probability of team success.

Joyful Love

Following our discussion of joyful sport as nonutilitarian "behavioral beauty," we shouldn't think that even international sport eliminates the joy of play; we shouldn't limit joy to mere display to prospective mates, so we shouldn't overlook the sheer joy of togetherness in resonant motion. Hence, adaptationist accounts of play might not be the only way to go. Also, neurological research has been done on play and joy; perhaps play is also primitive and just fun, not just good for something (Pellis and Pellis 2010)? From this perspective, sport is autotelic, done for its own sake.[9]

Yes, team sports in a capitalist society can be a job, or it can be reduced to dutiful cardiovascular exercise. But beyond the "runner's high" of exertion there's the joy of connection in shared exertion (Cohen et al. 2010; Davis, Taylor, and Cohen 2015). I would argue that we should always keep in mind the irreducibility of joy as a deep intrinsic motivation in human affairs. As we have insisted in this chapter's autocritique of the adaptationist focus of chapter 1, the tenor of too much evolutionary thought conveys an ironic sort of glee in coming up with ultimate explanations that have the effect of grinding life down into survival and reproduction, eliminating talk of flourishing, and pushing art, sport, joy, and love into the realm of merely proximate psychological mechanisms that serve as advertising in the mating market. But love is not only biologically necessary to children's development; art, love, and joy make life worth living for symbolic and cultural creatures. We live only when we live politically. We shouldn't then be bashful when we say that teammates love one another, as they say it all the time. Love might be an adaptation, scientifically traceable to an evolutionary repurposing from parent–child bonding to pair-bonding to sibling affection to teammates, but it also breaks free into an autotelic status.[10] An excessive adaptationist focus on ultimate explanations, no matter how well intentioned, without appreciation for the autotelic nature of love, risks reducing the richness of human experience to a mere set of "proximate mechanisms" explicable by a cycle of production, consumption, and reproduction; such a reduction would be a root of nihilism.

Expert Performance: Thinking on and with Your Feet

John Sutton (2007), in a highly influential analysis, critiques the notion promulgated by Hubert Dreyfus that expert performance is done without subjective monitoring, but in a "zone" or "flow." Sutton writes:

> While starting from the prevalent view that thinking too much disrupts the practised, embodied skills involved in batting, the essay suggests that experts do in fact successfully learn mental techniques for how to influence themselves in action, and that the kinds of explicit thought and memory in question are themselves active, dynamic and context-sensitive. (763)

Using cricket batters as his example, Sutton continues, first calling into question the seriality of the traditional input–cognition–output view: "[T]he dynamic adaptability of successful batting under severe time constraints gives us reason to be sceptical about a distinct cognitive step mediating between perception and action" (770). But rejecting the applicability to sports of the traditional view of cognition as a discrete step between sensation and action does not mean we should go all the way to a "mindless" body flow: "[I]nstead, understanding of such flexible intelligent action in real time requires attention to the continuous coupling of perception and action, and the mutually modulatory dynamics operating between brain, body and world" (770). Sutton thereby upholds the notion of "thinking on your feet," which, in his account, means we should "not cut intellect and emotion off from our embodied, grooved performances, but to achieve and then access unusual flexibility in linking thought and action, knowledge and motion, conceptual memory and procedural memory" (779).

It's a truism of sports commentary that the game slows down for the expert: "[Y]ou can't speed them up" is a great compliment. In other words, experts can control their emotions, allowing their skill to show through, relative to opponents whose anxiety and panic cause them to lose fine motor control. For us, following Sutton, such slowing down is precisely not being "in the zone" in a Dreyfusian manner: the expert is self-present, though not of course reflectively self-objectizing; rather, it's a matter of inhabiting lightly, monitoring, and intervening in "pre-reflective self-awareness," as many phenomenologists would say (Gallagher and Zahavi 2021).

Phenomenology of the Play

Megan Rapinoe (2014) has produced a superb first-person recollection of the goal in which she took part. We will see present in her account many of the elements we describe above, including passing, teamwork, affective ties, and expert intelligent self-presence.

At the end of regulation, the Brazilians had the ball and were looking to control it until the end of the game. Rapinoe felt an extreme temporal distortion as she anticipated the end: "It felt like every second was a gift." Upon the U.S. team's regaining possession, there was a sea change of emotion as the Americans advanced the ball: "There was a wave of palpable energy that you could literally *feel.*"

As the ball was passed between teammates, Rapinoe timed her run, but the extreme emotional situation caused more temporal experiential distortion: "It felt like she had it at her feet for five hours." Rapinoe then says that despite the pressure, she was well aware of her relative position and that of her teammate and knew exactly what was going on, *contra* the Dreyfusian "in the zone" concept.

Here she displays the way in which players experience the field as dynamic areas of shifting intensity, as she knew that she had to "get the ball into a dangerous area." Looking toward the Brazilian goal, she saw action potentials rather than objective bodies in neutral space: "I had to pass the ball to an invisible teammate." Anticipation is key, as she admits she didn't know where Wambach was but only where she would be—in a "dangerous area."

Describing her strike of the ball, Rapinoe shows how the expert self-monitors and intervenes in real time into the motion; here we see body schema and body image intermixing, as Rapinoe has propositional knowledge of her capabilities and is able to use that knowledge to modulate effort in informed dynamic body schema modulation.

At the crucial moment, Rapinoe "didn't see the ball. I just saw a wave of bodies cresting near the net," a gorgeous description of the dynamic energy field that is a soccer match. After the goal, "the stadium shook." Here we see shared joy as much from the behavioral beauty of the goal as from the outcome; it wasn't just a goal, it was an amazing goal.

Retrospectively, she describes Wambach's brilliance of fitting into "an impossibly small window to head the ball into. The timing involved is like ballet." But the "dangerous area" is not just what is dangerous to the opponent's chances of winning but is physically dangerous, as Wambach had the "keeper's fists . . . flying right at her face. The concentration and precision involved, not to mention the raw courage, is unbelievable."

The conclusion of Rapinoe's narrative shows two forms of connection: the skilled connection of the pass and the joyous connection of her and Wambach's embrace: "When I finally got to Abby, I did a full-speed leap into her arms." Here we see full joy at the conclusion of a beautiful example of shared resonant movement; Rapinoe and Wambach give themselves to each other in effort and skill, enacting relational autonomy and collective intentions, and sharing with us the behavioral beauty that constitutes the aesthetic surplus of joyous sport.

Part III

Political Anthropology

5
_____

Statification

They come like fate, . . . too terrible, too convincing, too sudden, too
different even to be hated.

——Deleuze and Guattari, *Anti-Oedipus*, citing Nietzsche, *Genealogy of Morals*

In this first chapter of Part III, "Political Anthropology," I use the notion of
conflicting regimes of violence to examine the way Deleuze and Guattari
discuss processes of state-formation, what I will call here "statification."[1]
In pursuing the inquiry, I distinguish virtual patterns of social formation
(what Deleuze and Guattari call "pure abstract machines") from actual
societies formed by those processes (what they call "concrete assemblages").
Following this distinction, "the State"[2] is the limit of the processes of "overcoding" (Deleuze and Guattari 1977, 196, 1987, 223) and "capture" (1987,
437–48).[3] Overcoding involves processes of centralization, hierarchization, and "legibility" (Scott 1998, 2009, 2017); although most prominent in
states, they are inherent tendencies, actualized to a greater or a lesser degree,
in all concrete social assemblages. "Capture" means appropriation of surplus
labor, products of the land, and money. Thus, a state is a social formation
in which overcoding and capture predominate. Once flows of products and
peoples are overcoded, their qualitative differences erased and the underlying objects made amenable to quantitative comparison, an "apparatus of
capture" ensures that portions of those flows can be appropriated to the
state in the form of profit, rent, taxation, or conscription. Similarly, just as
the State is the limit of processes of overcoding and capture, there are tendencies in all concrete societies to primitive territoriality, nomadic mutability, and urbanity, each with their own regimes of violence.[4] In other words,
"the State" has never existed, any more than a purely urban, nomadic, or
primitive society has existed free of any admixture of other processes.[5] All
concrete social assemblages are mixtures of tendencies, though in the cases
of interest to us in this chapter, the statifying tendency to overcoding and
capture is so strong that we call them, empirically, "states."

I will focus on the way in which, in Deleuze and Guattari's discussions of statification, there are both endogenous and exogenous factors. Although Deleuze and Guattari insist on a qualitative difference between the abstract machines and regimes of violence of primitive societies and States, they nonetheless acknowledge "endogenous tendencies" toward centralized hierarchy in primitive societies as well as lines of flight that escape states; here I will discuss a social formation distinct from Deleuze and Guattari's pair of primitive and State societies. In these so-called trans-egalitarian societies (those with some measure of nonhereditary, earned, status-based authority), power centers organized by those with wealth, charisma, effective violence capacities, or ritual knowledge resonate to a degree that brings them close to the threshold of a society that deserves the term "state." As an exogenous factor, I will suggest an occasional role for nonstate or autonomous zone raiders, who are not always what Deleuze and Guattari call, using the Steppe nomads as their archetype, anti-State "war machines," but are nonstate peoples (often those who have fled states) who will sometimes extract goods (by theft, tribute, or trade) from neighboring societies, whether bands, chiefdoms, or indeed States. In effect, these violence entrepreneurs perform arbitrage by transporting a regime of violence from one social machine to another.

Current Research on Statification

It is important to note at the outset that Deleuze and Guattari do not discuss the deep history of the *Homo* genus, on which contemporary research still finds consensus in positing a predominant nomadic foraging social form (chapter 1; see also Flannery and Marcus 2012). Rather, in their writings on statification, Deleuze and Guattari restrict themselves to the archeological record of the past 10,000 years, where we do indeed find evidence of multiple changing social formations, of which the State is neither the telos nor even the dominant form (Scott 2017; Graeber and Wengrow 2021; Singh and Glowacki 2022). As we mentioned in chapter 1, on a long time-scale encompassing the entire *Homo* lineage, we can talk about the centralized, hierarchical, and "legible" agricultural State's becoming the hegemonic social form supplanting, though never eliminating, foragers, maroons, and other forms of nonstate life.[6] New research examining the establishment, growth, consolidation, and decay of early states shows that our picture of human life of the past 30,000 years has decisively moved away from any necessary link between urbanism, agriculture, slavery, militarism, and state-hood. This entails a temporal disarticulation of the concept of a "Neolithic Revolution" which saw those formations as a package deal, as well as abandoning any progressivism or "evolutionism" of social stages that posits an inevitable linear development of political economy forms from egalitarian immediate-consumption foragers through "storage foraging" societies with prestige gradients to command-structured hierarchical agricultural states.

Instead of linear development, then, in the current research on early economy one finds optional use of, and often seasonal rotation of, sedentary foraging, in which people let food come to them (e.g., fishing settlements); mixed systems of hunting, gathering, herding, horticulture, and non-intensive, multiple-crop agriculture; egalitarian urbanism;[7] and several other permutations, thousands of years before intensive mono-crop agriculture. One finds a similar repertoire of political forms, often with seasonal variation, from egalitarian bands (albeit with wide cultural networks permitting long-range travel); achievement-based status hierarchies with some command during special times; and full-blown top-down permanent and nepotistic command. New researchers also postulate several sources of political power that can be independently instantiated but coalesce in the State form, including personal charisma, accumulated prestige, advantageous position in debt networks, credible violence capacities, and control of rituals (this research is summarized in Scott 2017; Graeber and Wengrow 2021; and Singh and Glowacki 2022).

Despite the early diversity of Neolithic political economy, and keeping to the welcome dismissal of cultural evolutionism, we should still investigate the rise of the agricultural State form. We can't assume inevitability, as if the State were the telos of social development; nonetheless, empirical states are here, so we should investigate statification. Although early concrete states were fragile, states are now hegemonic, though that is not to say they are all-powerful and all-encompassing; indeed, *A Thousand Plateaus* is very helpful in theorizing the territorializing bands, mutation-engendering war machines, and ecumenical organizations that inhabit, outflank, and in general interact with contemporary states.

Deleuze and Guattari on Statification

From a wide-angle view, Deleuze and Guattari, especially in the section "Which Comes First?" in the Thirteenth Plateau, "Apparatus of Capture," of *A Thousand Plateaus*, are in accord with the picture given in the current research. They agree that we need to think of a range of social formations compatible with a range of political and economic practices. In Deleuzo-guattarian terms, there is a "social topology" of social formations defined by machinic processes in intrinsic and extrinsic coexistence; these formations are named primitive, nomadic, urban, ecumenical, and State, with their corresponding processes of anticipation-conjuring, war machines, polarization, linking of heterogeneity, and capture (Deleuze and Guattari 1987, 435).

Let us begin with a brief sketch of Deleuze and Guattari's relation of "primitive society" and the State. As it will become important later in our discussion of trans-egalitarian societies, note at the outset that Deleuze and Guattari's category of "primitive" doesn't distinguish nomadic foragers from sedentary horticulturalists, such as those studied by Clastres (1989, 1994); the importance of that distinction is insisted upon by Fry (2006). In their reading in *Anti-Oedipus*, which undertakes an interrogation of Lévi-Strauss (Viveiros de Castro 2014; Badaire 2023), the primitive society is inscriptive rather than exchangist. Primitive society initiation rites marked bodies of initiates in relation to the Earth as "socius" (source of all goods); such coding rendered their spatial location and their characteristic behaviors of transfer of goods and symbols ("mobile blocs of debt") predictable within the limits of their territories. Such coding was "overcoded" by imperial administrative mechanisms such as censuses, whereby people and their actions were inscribed in a centralized accounting system that transcends local codes. However, the calling up of a workforce to send to the sites of imperial *grands travaux* would entail "deterritorialization" to allow people to travel to the worksites and "decoding" to allow new behaviors (digging and hauling, let's say, as opposed to hunting, gathering, and craft work).

Deleuze and Guattari discuss the State form as *Urstaat*, modeled on the Marxist concept of the "Asiatic Mode of Production" (Sibertin-Blanc 2016; Badaire 2023). While any one actualization of the imperial agricultural State form was always precarious, with alternate tendencies toward other social formations winning out as empirical states fell apart, the *Urstaat* form abides as a limit condition, a fever-dream of total control (Sibertin-Blanc 2016) in which all material and semiotic flows are overcoded and captured by a threefold comparison and appropriation machine operating by profit, rent, and taxes (Smith 2018; Badaire 2023). Overcoding denotes the ability to make equivalences (what Scott 1999, 2009, 2017 calls "legibility") such that free activity is turned into comparable units of work enabling the capture of a portion in the extraction of profit; territories are turned into comparable units of land such that calculating the relative productivity of those units enables capture of a portion of the productivity by charging different rents; and exchange is tracked via the imposition of a currency that allows comparable units of money enabling the capture of a portion of the monetary flow by taxation (Deleuze and Guattari 1987, 437–48).

Deleuze and Guattari distinguish the abstract machine and concrete assemblages for both overcoding (and capture) and for mutation (223). Any one concrete instantiation of the State, a really functioning apparatus of capture operating on overcoded flows, is an always partial and tentative effectuation of the abstract machine of statification (sometimes called simply "overcoding" by Deleuze and Guattari). That is to say, concrete states tend to the limit of "the State." Hence, Deleuze and Guattari specify that the State is linked to but does not equal the abstract machine of overcoding, which "may be defined, for example, *more geometrico*, or under other conditions by an axiomatic, but the State apparatus . . . is only the assemblage of reterritorialization effectuating the overcoding machine within given limits and under given conditions. The most we can say is that the State apparatus tends increasingly to identify with the abstract machine it effectuates" (223).

How does this effectuation occur? What are the concrete mechanisms of statification? How do states come about in history? Deleuze and Guattari merely allude to the role of historical factors in statification without further ado. They write, "[A]ll history does is to translate a coexistence into a succession" (430). Thus, "[W]hat is contingent upon external circumstances is only the place where the apparatus is effectuated" (447). To remedy this abstraction, we will propose some concrete mechanisms of statification. To locate these processes of statification, we should note their opposing tendencies. For Deleuze and Guattari, statification is not the only social process; there is also the abstract machine of mutation operating by decoding and deterritorialization; it itself is a line of flight and erects war machines on its lines. Between the two poles of overcoding and mutation, there is "a whole realm of properly molecular negotiation, translation, and transduction" (223) that it is the "task of the historian" to investigate (221).

It is in that realm of negotiation, translation, and transduction that I will locate endogenous and exogenous factors in statification processes. For endogenous factors I will, without falling into the evolutionism Deleuze and Guattari rightfully condemn, look at "trans-egalitarian" societies (Sterelny 2021) to gain a full picture of endogenous processes of statification. In doing so, I will depart from the letter of Deleuze and Guattari's text. Although they are staunch critics of evolutionism, they do tend to concentrate on the relation of "primitive" territorial societies and imperial territorial states ("the State is established directly in a milieu of hunter-gatherers having no prior agriculture" [Deleuze and Guattari 1987, 428–29]). As an exogenous factor in statification, I will suggest an occasional role for nonstate "violence entrepreneurs." Here we will discuss differences in "regimes of violence." Deleuze and Guattari define the State form via its "machinic process" of "overcoding." This leads us to their analysis of the "apparatus of capture" in which the original violence of the State form makes resistance to statification into a "crime" that the police combat in secondary violence or lawful application of force. Nonstate raiders have their own regime of violence. Living in autonomous zones located in hills, swamps, and littorals, and often having fled from states as maroons, such raiders may return to install state apparatuses. Such a turn from raiding to administration is an example of the "transformation" social processes can undergo (see the analysis of "lines" whereby bands form empires [223]). I will connect this notion of violence entrepreneurs to two themes in Deleuze and Guattari: in *Anti-Oedipus*, the death of primitive territorial societies, the institution of the state form, "comes from outside" (Deleuze and Guattari 1977, 195); in *A Thousand Plateaus*, the warrior is exterior to the two heads of State sovereignty, the magician-emperor who binds by capture and the jurist-king who formalizes by law (1987, 351).

Endogenous Factors

Deleuze and Guattari's Refusal of a Development Narrative

Deleuze and Guattari refuse a development narrative for statification. For them, it is impossible to conceive of an internal mutation of the primitive economy leading the way, as primitives would have to desire to change, but following the notion of desiring production sketched in *Anti-Oedipus*, their whole way of life produces a different form of desire than that which funnels material surplus to the emperor and receives imperial command from a central point (Sibertin-Blanc 2016). For Deleuze and Guattari, "economics" in primitive society (production, distribution, and consumption) is not divorced from social relations. Nonstate peoples do not have jobs that are independent of family relations; rather, what one produces, distributes, and consumes is directed by one's family relations. Because "desire" for Deleuze and Guattari is not about lack but about flows and breaks, one desires that flows be produced and channeled in a particular pattern of "desiring-production"; in this case, those flows are coded by family relations or "overcoded" by the state, tied to the erection of an apparatus of capture (or, in another case, reterritorialized on the power of deterritorialization in the becoming-mutable of a "war machine" [Deleuze and Guattari 1987, 381]).

In theorizing statification Deleuze and Guattari are conflict theorists, to use the current term (Scheidel 2013); for them, there must be an external political force that imposes the transformation of primitives or nomads or cities to the State form. Thus, they do not see a state as a mere instrument of a pre-existing ruling and owning class. If there were a prior difference in force allowing an exploitative class, the logic goes, why bother constructing a state to wield force that already exists? Similarly, if the state protects pre-existing private property, how does that arise in primitive society dedicated to refusing private property? Sibertin-Blanc (2016, 33) puts this in terms of a commentary on the German political historian Karl Wittfogel: The state is not the instrument of a pre-existing dominant class; it is itself the direct organization of society enabling the surplus production that it then immediately appropriates. In other words, the primary violence of statification is that which produces the dominant and subordinate classes.

There's a qualitative difference (a difference in concept or in abstract machine) between primitive society and the States. With the dismissal of evolutionism, then, we should not look for the origin of "the State" even if historians can investigate the rise and fall of this or that empirical state. As we have seen, empirical states effectuate the abstract machine of overcoding (Deleuze and Guattari 1987, 223). That means the State, as an abstract machine of overcoding and capture, does not have an empirically assignable origin, for "the State" is a concept, idea, or abstract machine. All concrete assemblages are mixed; they are composed of tendencies from different machinic processes. Hence, there is no first time "the State" was effectuated, as no one concrete society is purely and solely "the State" in flesh and blood; rather, a concrete assemblage can only approach the limit of "the State," as it "is only the assemblage of reterritorialization effectuating the overcoding machine within given limits and under given conditions" (223).

Trying to identify the "first State" thus confuses the empirical order of events (the establishment of this or that concrete assemblage) with the abstract or qualitative distinction among machinic processes, for example, statifying overcoding versus primitivizing anticipation-conjuration warding off statification versus "war-machining" mutation that attacks legibility and appropriation, (i.e., what Steppe nomads do in reterritorialization on deterritorialization, they feel at home while on the move). Instead of an origin as a "first time," we should look for oft-repeated processes of statification as empirical states, concrete assemblages with greater or less affinity with the State form, emerge from interactions among concrete assemblages and machinic processes. That is to say, we should look at the becoming-state process, for the State is a limit of the processes of centralization, hierarchy, and "legible" comparison and appropriation that constitute overcoding and capture. By the same token, we should also look for concrete processes for the more or less intense effectuation of other social forms, such as, for instance, a becoming-forager, a becoming-nomad, a becoming-urban, a becoming-ecumenical, and, as I show in chapter 6, a becoming-maroon.

"Endogenous Tendencies" toward Statehood

Despite their refusal of a development narrative, Deleuze and Guattari do cite "endogenous tendencies" of primitive societies that prefigure the State. The death of the primitive machine comes from without, they say, but is prepared from within; there is a pre-figuration in primitive society of the despotic machine in the "general irreducibility of alliance to filiation, the independence of the alliance groups . . . mechanism of surplus value—all this already pre-figured despotic formations and caste hierarchies" (Deleuze and Guattari 1977, 195).

To explain this pre-figuration, the buildup of endogenous tendencies toward the limit that is Statehood, we have to distinguish, within Deleuze and Guattari's category of "primitives," acephalic nomadic foraging networks (see chapter 1's discussion of Bird et al. 2019), which are anti-state and anti-war, from chiefdoms. And within chiefdoms, we should distinguish between those with working anti-state mechanisms (among them, warfare, à la Clastres 1989 and 1994) and those that become a bit sclerotic, such that the distinction for their chiefs between charismatic war leadership and peacetime rhetorical persuasion starts to break down a bit, enabling some mundane peacetime social hierarchy and power. Adding in ritual control, you can get a priest–warrior coalition in which power centers start to "resonate" (Deleuze and Guattari 1987, 433). Hence, while Deleuze and Guattari distinguish primitive ranks from imperial castes and capitalist classes, they also say you can see "protoclasses" somewhat in primitive societies (Deleuze and Guattari 1977, 153). While primitive communities are on guard to prevent chiefs from becoming kings, nonetheless that wariness intimates their closeness to Statehood, the possibility that they themselves are always becoming-primitive in relation to a becoming-State. What else explains the way a primitive society "binds up the symbol . . . of a former despot who thrust himself upon the community from the outside long ago" (195)? Thus, when examining primitive societies, "it is not always easy to know if one is considering a primitive community that is repressing an endogenous tendency, or one that is regaining its cohesion as best it can after a terrible exogenous adventure" (195). On the same theme of the indiscernibility of the temporal ordering of concrete primitive societies and states, they add "in the end one no longer really knows what comes first, and whether the territorial machine does not in fact pre-suppose a despotic machine from which it extracts the bricks or that it segments in its turn" (219).

In *A Thousand Plateaus*, Deleuze and Guattari couple their distinction of limit and threshold (a limit is the last move in a series that still maintains a given social form, while a threshold indicates the leap into a new system [Deleuze and Guattari 1987, 432, 438]), with a physical language of waves and resonance when it comes to the leap into Statehood (431–35).[8] Primitive societies are traversed by waves (endogenous tendencies to centralization, hierarchy, and command) that their mechanisms of anticipation-conjuration prevent from converging at a central point where they "resonate" (223, 415, 433). When those damping mechanisms fail, the leap to a state *qua* overcoding apparatus of capture becomes possible— that is, the society reaches the threshold of "intraconsistency" in which all power centers resonate in a point of convergence (433). At that point of convergence, the imperial center, there is a convergence of material flows and an "inversion of signs," such that signs, instead of saturating the primitive society in multiple directions following mobile blocs of debt, now radiate out from an imperial center (431).

If we take seriously the physics behind Deleuze and Guattari's use of the term "resonance," we notice that resonance is a graded concept; it is not all or nothing; a system can experience amplitude gain in its waves without reaching its optimum resonance frequency. Is there not then a thick threshold, a sensitive zone where resonating tendencies fight it out with damping mechanisms, with a qualitative leap to a different form, at stake? It is to the study of these societies we now turn.

Trans-Egalitarian Societies

In effect, we have to disarticulate the large category of "primitive society" into different forms: nonsegmented forager bands and sedentary mixed economy segmented societies with clan structures, and within that latter category, communities whose damping mechanisms of "anticipation-conjuration" keep chiefs in line and, those that are close to the threshold of Statehood, societies with clan rankings via sclerotic debt economies. Where debt is scrupulously counted and payment rigorously enforced, we are close to a tribute or tax system, *Anti-Oedipus* tells us (Deleuze and Guattari 1977, 194–95). Strong chiefdoms are not small states, for state versus chiefdom is not a qualitative but rather a qualitative distinction. Nonetheless, they have strong tendencies to Statehood.

Let us turn to our new anthropological research to sketch trans-egalitarian societies. We will use Flannery and Marcus (2012) and Sterelny (2021) for an analysis of their political form.[9] These scholars have a roughly Rousseauian outlook, asking how we are to explain inequality from a beginning with egalitarian forager bands deep in the *Homo* lineage. They explain that egalitarianism by appealing to the "reverse dominance hierarchy" thesis of Boehm (2012a and 2012b), an equality-protecting system employing ridicule, exile, and execution when needed. The key change in social logic within nonstate societies for Flannery and Marcus is that from acquired status (gained via achievement in wealth, valor, and ritual knowledge) to hereditary power. They propose several conditions for identifying the trans-egalitarian chiefdom: surplus, debt, and closely guarded ritual. Stocked material surplus is important because it allows inequality beyond mere personal charisma. As Sterelny (2021) puts it, storage makes inequality possible, perhaps even likely, because its presence tends to undermine sharing norms, establish property rights and the coercion of labor, amplify intercommunal violence, and lead to increases in social scale (125–33).

Flannery and Marcus (2012, 195–200) have a long discussion of Edmund Leach (1970), who showed that the Kachin of early-twentieth-century

Burma alternated between a society with achievement leadership and autonomous villages (*gumlao*) and a rank society with hereditary chiefs controlling up to sixty subordinate villages (*gumsa*). As Leach figures in Deleuze and Guattari's criticism of Lévi-Strauss in *Anti-Oedipus* (for details, see Badaire 2023), we will spend some time here on Flannery and Marcus's account of his work, specifically on the question of the transition to rank society. Flannery and Marcus look at three scenarios for this transition. Each is interesting in its own right; the first concerns contact with complex society neighbors and the second, rivalry of clans over claims to divine favors. We will concentrate on the third, however, as it connects with Deleuze and Guattari's concentration on debt. Flannery and Marcus describe the genesis of ranked society via accumulated and generational debt servitude, whereby some grooms had to go into debt to pay bride-price, which fluctuated as a result of the estimation by the bride's family of what the groom could pay. As prominent men were asked to pay more and more, sometimes they might go into debt because the bride's family would set an inordinately high price. Although debts could go unpaid for a while, eventually some debtors went into bondage to pay off debts. Given the logic of clan responsibility, a debtor's lineage was held accountable, swelling the number of lines whose members lived as debt servitors. While such servitude isn't chattel slavery, it did diminish the prestige of the chronic debtor lineages.

Let us pause and recall the resonance damping mechanisms of primitive society. Those are its "anticipation-conjuration" processes that prevent centralization of command and funneling to a center of material flows. From *Anti-Oedipus*, we know these as "mobile blocs of debt" that allow stockage of surplus value of code only up to a certain point, at which point prestige is gained by producing the consumption of surplus in a feast (Deleuze and Guattari 1977, 150; Badaire 2023). Drawing at this point on Leach, Deleuze and Guattari claim that the always empirically negotiated circulation of surplus value of code is part of how the system works in disequilibrium, works by breaking down, works by local political alliances. But with the debt servitude scenario sketched above, the surplus value of code can become stocked and produce permanent debt status and "protoclasses" in "pre-capitalist societies" (Deleuze and Guattari 1977, 153). I don't wish to claim that all rank societies are generated by debt slavery; nonetheless, the possibility of such a genesis shows that, despite being on the "primitive" side of the statehood threshold, trans-egalitarian societies are in a sensitive zone, within which there is more or less resonance, more or less central control, more or less inherited hierarchical positions, more or less counting of the "legible" portion of their surplus value of code (stocking of goods given up in bride-price negotiations) such that minor fluctuations in empirical conditions (climate, personalities, competing societies) might flip them past the threshold into a new system deserving the term "state." This is not to say that states don't sometimes produce feasts or more mundane infrastructure projects to prevent too much grumbling and insubordination (per the "managerial" theories examined by Scheidel 2013) but simply to distinguish conceptually the transcendent despot as entrepreneur of *grands travaux* from the still-immanent chief who produces feasts from his advantageous position in debt networks.

Implicit in both Flannery and Marcus (2012) and in Sterelny (2021) is a shift in regimes of violence: Egalitarian foragers and trans-egalitarian societies might raid for revenge or prestige, but not for population transfer and coerced labor, as do states. This is our transition to a discussion of exogenous factors in statification, where we introduce the concept of arbitrage by violence entrepreneurs of differences in regimes and economies of violence.

Exogenous Factors

Although endogenous tendencies toward statehood prepare it from within, the death of primitive societies "comes from without," via the violence of the "founders of the State" (Deleuze and Guattari 1977, 192). These Nietzschean "artists" and "organizers" bind all the disparate social processes of the territorial machine into a whole (Deleuze and Guattari 1977, 191). In the mainstream terms of Scheidel's typology (2013), this puts Deleuze and Guattari in the conflict theory camp (production and perpetuation of inequality) rather than in the managerial camp (benefits of provision of public goods).[10]

Statification as a Regime of Violence

In Plateau 5 of *A Thousand Plateaus*, Deleuze and Guattari produce an analysis of regimes of signs; here I will analyze regimes of violence. They are related, as certain signs indicate acceptable and unacceptable targets of violence in a social system. The key phrase for us is: "Violence is found everywhere, but under different regimes and economies" (Deleuze and Guattari 1987, 425). So, if all societies have a regime of violence, each must fit the practices of their installation and maintenance: Steppe nomads fight states, fighting in primitive society is part of their anticipation-conjuration processes, cities fight to protect trade networks, and so on. Statification, then, in the sense of the putting into state form of nonstate societies, involves a shift in the regime of violence.

Let us then consider the regime of violence for states. When it comes to statification, Deleuze and Guattari belong to those who see force rather than contract at the origin of historical states (Scheidel 2013; e.g., Carneiro 1970). The erection of an apparatus of capture entails removal of independent access to the Earth as means of production. Thus, Deleuze and Guattari widen the application of the Marxist notion of primitive accumulation (Sibertin-Blanc 2016; Alliez and Lazzarato 2016; Smith 2018; Protevi 2019; Badaire 2023):

> as a general rule, there is primitive accumulation whenever an apparatus of capture is mounted, with that very particular kind of violence that creates or contributes to the creation of that which it is directed against, and thus presupposes itself. The problem then becomes one of distinguishing between regimes of violence. (Deleuze and Guattari 1987, 447)

In their analysis of state-formation as the installation of an apparatus of capture, Deleuze and Guattari see statification as political and economic. Forceful administration of a state apparatus can vary with space from the center, as the time it takes for forces to arrive to quell rebellion or to measure and appropriate via rent, profit, and taxes will vary when one considers the relation of terrain to modes of transport (what is called "friction of terrain" in Scott 2009). There's thus a geopolitical space-time appropriate for state administration, and other space-times better fit for other geopolitical systems. In statification, there is a (political) "originary violence" enabling (economic) primitive accumulation; by destroying nonstate autonomous territoriality with their qualitative flows, states create the measurable and comparable stock they capture. The violence of the apparatus of capture contributes to the creation of that which it is directed against; such violence thus presupposes itself. This means that in statification the autonomy of nonstate peoples must be destroyed (primary violence of conquest) to turn them into the primary producers (whether taxed peasants, debt bondsman, or chattel slaves) whom the tax collection / army / security forces (secondary violence of policing) can target as cheater, delinquent, criminal, heretic, or runaway when they fail to stay put and pay up. Such force in imposing capture is rendered invisible; it seems as if in establishing itself the state is establishing peace in nonstate life, which is, in the very act of statification, figured as a no-holds-barred free-for-all, a state of nature equivalent to or perilously close to a state of war.

Having said that, the regime of violence of the operation of the empirical state apparatus is not necessarily that which imposes the State form. To see that, I will eventually introduce the notion of "violence entrepreneurs" as the "founders of the State" described in *Anti-Oedipus* (Deleuze and Guattari 1977, 151). Before that final part of the chapter, however, let me introduce political actors whom Deleuze and Guattari neglect, maroons, or those who escape empirical states.

Supplementing Deleuze and Guattari's Topology: Maroons

The space-time or control zone that is appropriate for empirical state administration reaches as far as it can, until it comes upon sensitive zones where marginal state subjects can consider the option of flight versus staying put. Too much attempted control in a sensitive zone with tenuous links to the imperial center, as a result of the cost of moving state administration forces, tempts flight (Scott 2009; Sterelny 2021). Let us then turn to consider those who flee states. To do so, we need to add to Deleuze and Guattari's social topology. The additional figure needed here is the maroon, the enslaved person who escapes captivity (see chapter 6 for more detail than I provide here, as well as for extensive references).[11] Deleuze and Guattari talk a few times about freed slaves, but they don't say too much about runaway slaves.

We have already seen that Deleuze and Guattari speak of a "social topology" of machinic processes in intrinsic and extrinsic coexistence; these formations are primitive, nomadic, urban, ecumenical, and State, with their corresponding processes of anticipation-conjuring, war machines, polarization, linking of heterogeneity, and capture (Deleuze and Guattari 1987, 435). The next sentence will be our concern in this section: "But precisely because these processes are variables of coexistence that are the object of a social topology, the various corresponding formations are coexistent. And they coexist in two fashions, extrinsically and intrinsically" (435). "Social topology" means that machinic processes can interact, both in real-world systems ("concrete assemblages") and in being taken up in different proportions by systems other than those where they are the defining element.

Assemblages are defined by what escapes them, what flees from them. (We should take that literally in thinking of marronage as flight from states.) Extrinsic coexistence means interactive existence side-by-side: "States cannot effect a capture unless what is captured coexists, resists in primitive societies, or escapes under new forms, as towns or war machines" (435)—or as maroon societies. Intrinsic coexistence means that machinic processes are at work in social systems that are not those with which they are most associated. For instance, the "power of metamorphosis" of the anti-order mutation-supporting "war machine" (its capacity to change habits, to make a habit of changing habits) can be tamed by its transformation into a state military apparatus, but it can also resist such taming and be reborn in other forms, perhaps as revolution (436). To this example of intrinsic coexistence as transfer of machinic processes we can add the ability of state-establishing maroons to partake in the machinic process of overcoding.

To fully connect Deleuze and Guattari's account of state formation with the new anthropological research, we need to consider maroons in order to gain a fuller picture of concrete social formations and their machinic processes. Maroons want to be autonomous, but they don't shun interchanges with states when they can be conducted in freedom-preserving terms.[12] Maroon autonomy is neither a full-on nomad anti-state society nor is it a primitivism. It is a precise form of interaction with states, with trade, raid, tribute, and treaty as the main modes. Hence, I'm going to supplement Deleuze and Guattari's connection of geophilosophy and regime of violence, which poses two forms of nonstate peoples. The Steppe nomads or, more precisely, the becoming-nomad of people on a line of flight from states, are the most intense instantiation of a war machine that resists order and provokes mutation. And as we have seen, primitive people have their own relation to the State in "warding off" their own endogenous tendencies toward State ordering and their exogenous contact with existing states.

For maroons, however, states are not something that might happen to their societies; they are already there, in fact, as something from which to escape, to defend yourself against, and to find ways to deal with. Maroon geography relies on the "friction of terrain," as Scott says in *Art of Not Being Governed* (2009). Early state armies were based on infantry and cavalry, so maroons' getting into forests and hills frustrated state control attempts; maroons also improved the defensive capacities of their autonomous zones by fortification, booby traps, ambush points, and the like (Stennett 2020). The geopolitical regime of violence of nonstate raiders shows that they capture state surplus but retreat to hills, swamps, littoral spaces. To use the terms of the final section of *A Thousand Plateaus*, a maroon autonomous zone is neither "smooth" nor "striated"; rather, it is secluded or marginal: It enables hiding before and after raids; it imposes costs on pursuing state forces.

To conclude this all-too-brief treatment of maroons (I will expand on this sketch in chapter 6), let us note that borders between state and maroon spaces were two-way membranes, not one-way as a social contract narrative would have it. For the social contract tradition, the only rational move is to join a civil state to escape the state of nature (figured either as a state of war by Hobbes, or as easily risking degeneration into one by Locke). But civil states are a state of war between masters and slaves, so flight from the state is a rational option for slaves. And in fleeing, they needed to construct a regime of violence that would both protect them from states and enable predation upon them. Let us now consider one of the forms that predation might take, the maroon takeover of a state—that is, the operationalizing of a difference in regimes of violence that produces a capture of the apparatus of capture itself.

Violence Entrepreneurs

The state apparatus of capture provokes marronage, but some maroon raiders can turn around and take over state apparatuses in a transformation of regimes of violence. Maroons might trade with States or exact tribute from them, but they are not anti-State; they seek to be autonomous, which means resisting surrounding states, and, we might speculate, sometimes they take over a state.[13] Given the transformational powers inherent in the intrinsic coexistence of machinic processes in their social topology, Deleuze and Guattari allow that some state formation might be accomplished by maroons who erect their own state apparatus. There's no teleology, though, as we mustn't make states into the object of universal desire, even if sometimes some maroons establish them. As maroons don't have to construct a state, we could look at the counter-plantation system of post-revolutionary Haiti (Casimir 2020) as an example of a maroon society with territorial integrity and autonomous political power without an apparatus of capture but with dispersed autonomous production.

How might maroons go about establishing states, when they do? We can characterize state-establishing maroons as violence entrepreneurs. Maroons are those who have fled states to autonomous zones where they organize a regime of violence to protect themselves from re-capture by state forces.[14] Among their violence practices is raiding state production sites, either agriculture or trade routes. Now the maroon regime of violence connects with political economy, as recompense is often paid by raiders to targets in a prestige raid (Flannery and Marcus 2012). If that is repeated enough, the target group, I speculate, might switch to using part of previous raid-recompense ahead of time as tribute. Tribute can be solidified as taxes if the raiding group can annex the control of the target group's territory and take over a currency it can then demand (Badaire 2023).

Maroons as violence entrepreneurs who found states use a form of arbitrage. They organize their forces and travel to take advantages of difference in regimes of violence; they transport one regime of violence to another social machine that isn't prepared to handle it and, in so doing, transform their own regime of violence from raiding to state administration. I use the economic term "arbitrage" in keeping with Deleuze and Guattari's notion of talk about "regimes and economies" of violence. "Violence is found everywhere," they say, "but under different regimes and economies" (Deleuze and Guattari 1987, 425). The staggering differences activated by violence entrepreneurs' bringing their raid-based regime of violence to the state-based secondary violence of the police accords with Deleuze and Guattari's invocation of Nietzsche: "They come like fate, without reason, consideration, or pretext; they appear as lightning appears, too terrible, too convincing, too sudden, too different even to be hated" (Deleuze and Guattari 1977, 151–52, citing *Genealogy of Morals* 2.6).

To conclude, with what I hope is not too wild speculation, let me briefly allude to the analyses of chapter 3 of Protevi (2013) concerning the theory of Robert Drews (1993) of the 1200 BCE collapse that brought down Troy. Drews claims barbarian (hill-based nonstate) mercenaries "awoke to a truth that had been with them for some time: the chariot-based forces on which the Great Kingdoms relied could be overwhelmed by swarming infantries [. . .]" (Drews 1993, 104). Drews insists that before the 1200 BCE catastrophe foot soldiers recruited from nonstate "hill people" supported the chariots, performing the hand-to-hand combat in plains battles (141–42) and doing the fighting in the hills, where chariots couldn't go (147). For the skirmisher-runners, "Mobility rather than [phalanx] solidarity was essential" (152). What was the affect of the runners from the hills who made up the skirmishers of the imperial armies? Michael Speidel (2002) makes the argument that the hill people fought in berserker style as in a "swirling whirlwind" (Speidel 2002, 259).

Maroon violence entrepreneurs operationalizing a stunning difference in regimes of violence weren't always founders of states, but when they were, berserkers swarming down from the hills and fighting in a swirling whirlwind fit the description of those "too different to even be hated."

6

Marronage

I may run, but all the time that I am, I'll be looking for a stick! A defensible position!

—George Jackson, *Soledad Brother*

In this chapter, I continue my exploration of "political anthropology," examining the reciprocal relation of flight from states and state-formation.[1] As soon as states were formed, some people ran for the hills. This is intensely the case with those fleeing enslavement or other forms of severe domination and exploitation under states. States are formed by and maintain themselves with regimes of violence, as do those fleeing states, as they know they will be pursued by state forces.[2] I will concentrate on the plantation slavery system of the New World, though I believe that what I say, insofar as I incorporate work by James C. Scott on southeast Asia, will illuminate marronage in other circumstances. I will show in a materialist but not reductionist manner that the analysis of their regime of violence lets us see the social structure and geographical features of maroon communities through the lens of "marginality"—that is, the search for a form of life that best enables, though of course it doesn't guarantee, the independence of Atlantic system maroons faced with the massive violence capacities of the plantocracy. I don't want to say that my analysis is a total reduction, as I won't try to derive their art and music and religion and so on from their regime of violence, so I don't want to say that the cultural life of maroons was nothing but preparation for war, but I certainly think war is a central factor in their form of life.

Outline of the Multiplicity of Marronage

I hope what I say here will interest those familiar with Deleuze and Guattari's thought, as I will show that "mastery" and "marronage" have to be added to the list of "regimes of violence" they enumerate, and, because of the particular nature of the violence that shapes their form of life, marronage is a form of occupying space and time that, while certainly not "striated" as is plantation society (in which, at the limit, each movement and behavior is tracked and accounted for), is not purely "smooth" or "nomadic" either—that is, solely and always dedicated to mobility tactics bent on destroying the plantation system.[3] I also hope it will interest historians, anthropologists, political scientists, geographers, and others.

There is a large scholarly literature on marronage in the modern Atlantic system.[4] Reading a selection from that literature along with James C. Scott's work on nonstate peoples in southeast Asia, I propose the outlines of the multiplicity of marronage, a set of interlinking processes that trigger qualitative changes in the behavior of the concrete systems in which they are instantiated when thresholds in the relations of those processes are reached. This necessitates finding common structures motivating slave flight across different social forms, such as capitalist slavery (a form of chattel slavery in which the slave's entire person becomes a commodity bought on a market and the products of their labor are sold on a market) and other forms of slavery (for instance, noncapitalist chattel slavery, as in ancient Rome, or communal slavery in imperial systems, what Marxists used to call the Asiatic mode of production).

The multiplicity of marronage has a focus: In their flight, enslaved people search for a position of marginality to the state plantation system, where best to establish an autonomous zone with a regime of violence that will manage their relation to the state of war that slavery constitutes.[5] Here I use "war" in the sense of violence aiming at territorial control, population displacement, and enslavement, not in Deleuze and Guattari's specialized sense of the "war machine" as anti-state or, by extension, anti-regulatory violence. Most maroons looked to be free from, but close to—marginal to—the slave system from which they escaped. Most maroon communities were not anti-state in the sense of Deleuze and Guattari's nomads, bent on destroying states, as they often interacted with states in a regime of violence that included raid, war, and treaty, as well as trade when in relative security against the colonial system.[6]

Flight is itself multiple. I will follow Carolyn Fick's schema here (1992, 6–9). The classic sociological distinction, found in Debien (1976), is taken from planters' accounts, and is that between *petit marronage* (flight with short temporal extension, sometimes only a day or two) and *grand marronage* (flight with no intention to return). This sociological distinction is developed in a political dimension by Roberts (2015), who distinguishes, within *grand marronage*, between sovereign marronage, which looks to establish a state by a lawgiver, and sociogenic marronage, which looks to establish a new system wherein one finds "collective agency, non-sovereignty . . . cultivation of a community that aligns civil society with political society" (Roberts 2015, 11). Debates over the psychological dimensions of marronage noted by Fick in her literature review concern motivation, with some claiming that escape from cruelty was more important in the seventeenth and eighteenth centuries than a desire for freedom. A further socio-psychological distinction noted by Fick is that between "restorationist" marronage (seeking to escape from slavery to return to "African" subsistence) and revolutionary marronage (seeking to destroy the slave system). In a very helpful methodological remark, Fick cites Leslie Manigat, who distinguishes an empiricist descriptive stance, tending to dismiss the importance of marronage as a threat to the stability of the entire system (insofar as the system lasted hundreds of years), and a sociopolitical perspective that emphasizes the ongoing threat to the system represented by marronage (it motivated repeated expeditions, at considerable expense, on the part of planters against maroon communities).

A final distinction, which we could call geopolitical, in the multiplicity of marronage is that between wild and urban marronage. This distinction shows that maroon marginality is not solely geographical flight but is a social relation, a "becoming free" from slavery. Urban marronage is hiding in plain sight by blending into crowds of freed people of color in the city, often with the aid of forged papers (Price 1979, 24). Wild marronage entails finding—and improving (Stennett 2020)—a space outside state space but nonetheless close enough to states for the major forms of interaction that maroon communities have found with states: trade, raid, war, and treaty. Rather than a typology, from a Deleuzoguattarian perspective we should see these distinctions as representing tendencies; any concrete act of marronage will be composite, though one tendency might predominate. A nighttime escape might turn into *grand marronage* if the escapee meets the right companions. A *grand marronage* might dissolve into individual flights with quick return if conditions for sustained survival are not found. A flight from cruelty can turn revolutionary by circumstance, and so on.

Marronage is related to other social structures and movements. In Deleuze and Guattari's terms, as a set of potentials for a way of life (an "abstract machine," to use their technical term) the multiplicity of marronage forms connections with other multiplicities, other sets of processes with their own patterns and range of instantiation. Hence there are connections of modern Atlantic slavery to thermodynamics (global solar energy flows driving wind and ocean currents enabling the triangular trade system), to plant physiology (bio-available solar energy in sugar), to human physiology and the culturally inflected cravings of humans (sugar and other New World consumables such as tobacco and coffee), to other slavery systems (racialization leading to intergenerational slavery was more intense in transatlantic slavery reflected in lower rates of manumission and assimilation than those in other systems [Patterson 1989]), to other forms of flight (from peasantry, from genocides, from the drudgery of forced labor in general).

In examining marronage, we also find connections to other forms of resistance by enslaved peoples (slave ship rebellions, suicides, infanticide, killings, revolts, and revolutions). Revolts and revolutions that attack the slave system itself will involve the geographical heart of the slave system, the plantations, and cities, but Fick emphasizes the role of wild marronage in creating the basis for Mackandal's action in 1757 Saint Domingue. The events of 1791, Fick says, might have been called a maroon war elsewhere but in revolutionary Saint Domingue the process of maroons' turning revolutionaries became "irreversible." Small groups of maroons met others; "at this conjuncture that slave deserters, who in ordinary times were called maroons or fugitives . . . [,] become by the very nature of the circumstance, insurrectionaries, brigands, and rebels" (Fick 1990, 107). Fick cites Patterson, who says one may suggest that "all sustained slave revolts must acquire a Maroon dimension" (Patterson 1979, 279).

Deleuze and Guattari on Slavery and Capitalism

Deleuze and Guattari don't say anything directly about marronage in *Capitalism and Schizophrenia*, although deterritorialization and the line of flight (each term is roughly akin to changing the links of environmental features and habitual behaviors) are important concepts. They use the Black American radical George Jackson as a figure of the "regime of violence" often involved in a line of flight.[7]

What do Deleuze and Guattari say about slavery? They have both literal and figurative uses of the terms "slave" [*esclave*] and "slavery" [*esclavage*] in

Anti-Oedipus and *A Thousand Plateaus*. There's nothing too surprising about their figurative uses; they fit into what one might now consider an objectionable tradition of using a term whose primary extension for the past 500 years has been literal, real chattel slavery to which Africans were subjected to figure various other types of unfreedom. (There was real enslavement in the English workhouses used for vagabonds, as described by Marx in the primitive accumulation chapter of *Capital*, but I mean here the use of "slave" to figure European subjection to absolutism, as in Locke's *Second Treatise of Government*.) In *Anti-Oedipus*, we find *esclavage* as the self-subjugation of the bourgeoisie to capital (Deleuze and Guattari 1977, 254). We also see *esclavage* as voluntary servitude to fascism (29). And in *A Thousand Plateaus*, the term is used in discussing the self-command inherent in Kant's moral philosophy (Deleuze and Guattari 1987).[8] In the literal sense, many of their references are to "generalized slavery" in ancient empires—that is, of peasants subject to or conscripted into *corvée* labor for *grands travaux*—for example, monumental or utilitarian projects such as irrigation and flood control (1987, 448ff).[9] Again, in relation to ancient empires, Deleuze and Guattari discuss the figure of the freed slave (*esclave affranchi*) in terms of "deterritorialization" or the setting loose of flows of people to move from their traditional homes (1987, 448). In their terms, "primitive" society was "territorial" (although they mean this to include hunter-gatherers, their analysis is heavily weighted to the ethnography of sedentary chiefdoms [e.g., Clastres 1989, 1994; see also Viveiros de Castro 2014, 2019]).

In contrast to ancient slavery, transatlantic slavery of Africans is noted by Deleuze and Guattari only rarely, in passing and by implication. It is implied in contradistinction to generalized slavery: "Even slavery changes; it no longer defines the public availability of the communal worker but rather private property as applied to individual workers"—this would hold for both Greek and Roman slavery as well as for transatlantic slavery (1987, 451). It also appears in the discussion of the work model versus "free action": "[T]he Americans apparently imported so many blacks only because they could not use the Indians, who would rather die" (1987, 491).

While Deleuze and Guattari don't say anything about marronage in general, and hence nothing about it in relation to Atlantic slavery in the early phase of global capitalism, they do have a theory of capitalism as such. For them, capitalism is built on the surplus value of flow, as opposed to surplus value of code for "primitive" societies and the surplus value of overcoding for imperial systems. In a deliberatively provocative move, they will come up with a theory of "machinic surplus value" (surplus value generated through the emergent effects of cybernetic assemblages or human and machine couplings, as opposed to Marx's position that only human labor power produced surplus value [see Thoburn 2003, 96–99 for commentary]) but that would be for them a much later development, well after the abolition of gross forms of Atlantic chattel slavery.

The relation between slavery and capitalism is a highly technical and very much active debate. Noteworthy recent works focus on surplus value. For example, Foster et al. (2020) claim that Marx is best read as slaves' producing surplus value. Nesbitt (2022), on the other hand, shows how scholars who concentrate on the way slaves produced commodities for a global market see slavery as an integral part of capitalism, while those who concentrate on a definition of capitalism centered on the extraction of surplus value from wage labor see slavery as an antiquated holdover. For Nesbitt, both sides neglect the Marxian analysis of capitalism as a "social form." There is such a thing as capitalist slavery for Nesbitt, but despite its horrors, it does not involve extraction of surplus value. Slaves cannot be the source of surplus value as they have no labor power that can be sold as a commodity; rather than purchase labor power as do owners who employ wage laborers, owners of operations using slave labor purchase the person, not their labor power. Hence slaves are treated as constant capital, as sources of motive power, rather than as variable capital. On the other hand, slave labor does produce commodities that are sold on a global market, enabling slave owners to thereby capture a portion of the surplus value available in the global system, building up wealth for themselves. Nesbitt walks us through Marx's analyses in *Capital* volume 3 which show that the market price for commodities reflects an average rate of profit for the system as a whole, no matter the composition of capital in the production process for any one producer. (Although Nesbitt doesn't get into the details, Blackburn 1997 claims, in his support of Williams 1944, to be able to show that profits from West Indies slave labor plantations found their way into financial circuits in England, providing a catalytic effect in the form of easy credit for the burgeoning English industrial system.) Slavery gets squeezed out of the capitalist system by improvements to productivity of other forms of constant capital, which, when used along with wage labor, produces surplus value that producers using wage labor are able to capture as the market price of commodities falls. Nesbitt's case study is that of slave-produced cane sugar undercut by beet sugar produced by advanced machinery and proletarian wage labor.

Deleuze and Guattari are among those who see slavery as noncapitalist. By defining capitalism as the conjunction of flows of labor that is decoded (by people able to learn new habits) and deterritorialized (by people able to move in search of work) and flows of money that is decoded (made fungible between merchants, industry, and finance) and deterritorialized (through banking systems allowing investment and disinvestment on national and international scales), they see enslavement in terms of noncapitalist economies. Hence, they talk about the political economy of slave societies in distinction to capitalism in their "universal history" in *Anti-Oedipus*; in the case of Rome, "all the preconditions [of decoding] are present . . . without producing a capitalism properly speaking but rather a regime based on slavery [*régime esclavagiste*]" (Deleuze and Guattari 1977, 223).[10] Rome had chattel slavery, but production was dedicated to amassing concrete wealth via the profitable sale of commodities. Rich Romans pursued enjoyment from consumption of commodities; we do not see reinvestment, forced by competition in a market for the means of production, into accumulation of surplus value. For the most part, and speaking informally, to the extent that rich Romans sought to increase their wealth, they didn't search for ways to revolutionize the means of production (because they weren't compelled to do so by mobile capital investment). They found what worked and stayed with it, expanding quantitatively (more land, more slaves) but not qualitatively (new ways of mining or farming). In the Marxist formula, Roman production was commodity accumulation mediated by money (C-M-C) as opposed to money accumulation via commodity sale (M-C-M', the mature form of capitalism). A similar point is made in *A Thousand Plateaus* in discussing the conditions for capitalism: "[T]he flow of labor must no longer be determined as slavery or serfdom [*l'esclavage ou le servage*] but must become naked and free" (Deleuze and Guattari 1987, 452).

Although there is not too much on modern Atlantic slavery in *Capitalism and Schizophrenia*, a point of articulation to decolonial debates would be the references to Samir Amin in *Anti-Oedipus* 3 on the relation of periphery and center. For Deleuze and Guattari, although the tendency of the rate of profit to fall holds in the center (because of the replacement of variable capital by fixed capital via technologization of production), it is compensated for by continuing expansion of capitalism at the periphery (permanent primitive accumulation). Hence the periphery is not traditional or antiquated but is integrated into the global system. (See Weeks 2019 on Deleuze and Guattari as dependency theorists.)

Regimes of Violence in the Plantation System

As we recall, Deleuze and Guattari write, "Violence is found everywhere, but under different regimes and economies" (Deleuze and Guattari 1987, 425). In the Introduction, we established that a regime of violence is the pattern of approved and disapproved violent and peaceful (violence-avoiding, conflict-resolving and conflict-mitigating) acts and responses characteristic of a particular social system. Regimes of violence are an aspect of social systems, intertwined with political (decision making), cultural (sense making), and productive / distributive ("economic") patterns.

Let us examine the regimes of violence we find in the relation of maroons and states in the Atlantic slave system. Here we are defining states as do Deleuze and Guattari; states arise with the imposition of "an apparatus of capture," which, in emphasizing the removal of independent access to the Earth as a means of production, widens the application of the Marxist notion of primitive accumulation (for discussion, see Sibertin-Blanc 2016; Alliez and Lazzarato 2016; Smith 2018; Protevi 2019; Badaire 2023):

> as a general rule, there is primitive accumulation whenever an
> apparatus of capture is mounted, with that very particular kind of
> violence that creates or contributes to the creation of that which it
> is directed against, and thus presupposes itself. The problem then
> becomes one of distinguishing between regimes of violence.
> (Deleuze and Guattari 1987, 447)

As we saw in chapter 5, Deleuze and Guattari see statification as operating via a regime of violence. There is a (political) "originary violence" to (economic) primitive accumulation; states create that which they capture. The violence of the apparatus of capture creates or contributes to the creation of that which it is directed against; such violence thus presupposes itself. This means that in statification the autonomy of nonstate peoples must be eliminated (primary violence of conquest) to turn them into the primary producers whom the authorities can target when they fail in their newly installed duties (secondary violence of police). The violence in the apparatus of capture is rendered invisible; it seems as if in establishing itself the

state is establishing peace in nonstate life, which is, in the very act of statification, figured as a state of nature or state of war.

Let us reiterate that, like Scott (2019) and Clastres (1989, 1994), Deleuze
and Guattari reject any notion that the state evolves peacefully or contrac-
tually from pre-state conditions; rather, they insist, states are born by the
violent imposition of the state form or "apparatus of capture" (taxes, obligatory labor, and rent on land) on nonstate peoples. The state is then one
social form among others, not the telos of sociality. Such an apparatus of
capture, however, provokes flight or marronage. The first maroon societies
are thus contemporaneous with the first states; as soon as there were states,
people "ran for the hills." However, those fleeing the state could rarely simply ignore states, and they would sometimes wish to return either to settle
down or to trade with the state. In fact, nonstate people came to be necessary to states as supplying both nonhuman (raw materials) and human
(enslaved people) commodities. Thus, flight, while it is in one sense a mere
consequence of capture, is in another sense co-constitutive of states; without those who flee, the state would have no one to trade with and would
have to attempt primary resource extraction from hills, mountains, and
swamps on its own initiative and at its own expense. But such extension
would dangerously stretch the power of the state to extract taxes, labor,
and rent in its core. Much better, then, to manage the margins of the state
qua geographical border and deal with the outsiders as needed. At the
same time that states dealt with those on their geographical borders, internal population management was instantly set up, as states were in constant
need of importing new members whose differences in political status (free
versus slave, urban versus rural, and so on) needed to be regulated.

Mastery and Marronage as Regimes of Violence

Let us recall Deleuze and Guattari's list of regimes of violence before adding "mastery" and "marronage." They write, "We can draw a distinction between struggle, war, crime and policing as so many regimes of violence"
(Deleuze and Guattari 1987, 447). Struggle [*lutte*] is the form of violence
of primitive society, which Deleuze and Guattari gloss, in referring implic-
itly to Clastres, as coded, blow-by-blow violence: "a certain ritualization
of violence."[11] As we noted above, in Deleuze and Guattari's specialized
sense, "war" is the form of violence best exemplified in the Steppe nomad
"war machine" and its violence directed against the states they fell upon.

Crime is relative to states; it is the violence of illegality or capture without "right." State policing or lawful violence is capture constituting simultaneously the right to capture. But the state's peace is a regime of violence that disavows itself, that structurally hides the primary violence of the capture that denies access to the Earth to nonstate people, forcing them into peasantry or slavery, conditions that secondary state violence is then used to reinforce.

At the limit, each New World plantation was a state in Deleuze and Guattari's sense, in both the political violence and economic capture sense. Overcoding and capture are the imposition of a system of equivalence measurement and surplus appropriation, instantiated in labor discipline, bookkeeping practices (ability to measure individual productivity of workers), financial speculation (mortgages, credit, insurance), and so on (Thoburn 2003; Alliez and Lazzarato 2016; Weeks 2019). In its violence aspect, slavery is war, a system of terror. Mastery is the creation of a zone where lives can be taken or exposed to threat of torture and death with impunity.[12] It can be encapsulated in the notorious phrase of the *Fundamental Constitutions of Carolina* that "Every freeman of Carolina shall have absolute power and Authority over his Negro slaves."[13] There might be a slight ability for the metropolitan or colonial government to control the actions of planters (the LeJeune affair showed the inability of the Code Noir to be enforced [Fick 1990, 37–38]), but within each plantation the rule of the master was absolute, making "mastery" a regime of violence in Deleuze and Guattari's sense.

Hence, we can say that mastery is institutionalized terrorism; it is the ability to impose a regime of social death on people (Patterson 2018)—enslaved people are those who face utter insecurity about the present and future caused by a pattern of torture and killing at whim.[14] Further, mastery's regime of violence, although produced locally and individually, could, when faced by resistance or revolt masters, call upon reinforcements from government or other slaveholders when needed. The structure of planter society was thus also a factor in the regime of violence of mastery. Patterson makes the point that absenteeism increased the probability of marronage and revolt. Slavery-based planter colonialism had a limit case in which it was not a state in the sense of living under a centralized authority but was rather pockets of absolute autocracy of masters who had only economic and social relations with neighbors with very little overall government; the planters were just living side-by-side. As Patterson put it in the case of Jamaica, whites were "transients" hoping to grab their riches and flee: "a brittle, fragile travesty of a society which lingered during these years constantly on the brink of upheaval and anarchy" (Patterson 1979, 251).

Marronage has its own regime of violence. Dimensions of the maroon regime of violence in its interactions with surrounding states are predatory raiding, defensive war in the traditional sense of territorial control, and post-treaty capture and return of escaping slaves.[15] From the state perspective, maroon raiding is crime, though we can also see it as an alternate form of predation on primary producers as opposed to self-created "legitimate" state taxation. The political economy of maroon communities conformed to the regime of violence; hunting and swidden agriculture are adapted to the social environment, the risk of attack (Price 1979, 10; Scott 2009). All these relations are entangled and change with changing relations to the still-enslaved population and to autochthonous populations. Relations with those who were still enslaved were often friendly and co-conspiratorial but could turn antagonistic as treaties of maroon communities with states often required the maroons to assist in pursuit, capture, and return of still-enslaved populations. The Jamaican revolt known as Tacky's War was ended by maroon troops (Patterson 1979). This created enmity between maroons and the enslaved (Price 1979, 22), though that is now finessed in the installation of Queen Nanny as a symbol of resistance.

Maintaining the social structure of maroon communities required an initiation ritual to handle the situation of multiple African origins of their inhabitants (Price 1979; A. M. Johnson 2020). Ensuring loyalty was a constant preoccupation; deserters from a maroon community were executed (Thornton 2008, 780; Price 1979, 17). Maroons often distinguished captive slaves taken in raids from those enslaved people who escaped and found refuge in maroon communities. The former were held in bondage for a time to ensure acculturation (Price 1979, 17; Johnson 2020). In her study of Jamaica's Windward Maroons, A. M. Johnson (2020) concluded that their form of servitude was not that of chattel slavery:

Maroons navigated a middle ground between the traditions of their West African ancestors and the realities (and opportunities) of life on the sugar-producing island of Jamaica. . . . The relatively small size of the "slave" population, the stability of "slave" families, and the continuities in lines of ownership in Maroon towns intimate that masters saw their "slaves" as more than chattel. This was consistent

with the types of bondage practiced in other kin-based communities during the pre- and early colonial period. (A. M. Johnson 2020)

Relations with autochthonous peoples were also multiple, ranging from
alliance (Schwartz 1992, 1304), to neighboring coexistence, to mingling to
form a new people, to war, either spontaneous or by being hired by states.
Maroons and natives would also play off different European powers against
each other in shifting alliances.

Social Structures of Maroon Communities

There is a large and specialized scholarly literature on the social structure
of maroon communities. Among the most interesting and well-developed
debates is that over the social structure of the seventeenth-century Brazilian maroon community of Palmares, with Kent (1965), Schwartz (1992),
Anderson (1996), and Thornton (2008) seeing it as a kingdom and Freitas
(1990) seeing it as a "republic"—that is, as decentralized and egalitarian,
albeit with a centralized military defense system.

Let us see how Deleuze and Guattari's notion of a regime of violence
can illuminate the question of social structure of maroon communities.
As Deleuze and Guattari specify in *A Thousand Plateaus*, their work is not
an analysis of mode of production, of infrastructure and superstructure, but
an analysis of their "machinic processes" (characteristic means of arranging material and semiotic flows):

> We define social formations by machinic processes and not by modes
> of production (these on the contrary depend on the processes).
> Thus primitive societies are defined by mechanisms of prevention-
> anticipation; State societies are defined by apparatuses of capture;
> urban societies, by instruments of polarization; nomadic societies, by
> war machines; and finally international, or rather ecumenical, organi-
> zations are defined by the encompassment of heterogeneous social
> formations. But precisely because these processes are variables of
> coexistence that are the object of a social topology, the various cor-
> responding formations are coexistent. And they coexist in two fash-
> ions, extrinsically and intrinsically. (Deleuze and Guattari 1987, 435)

"Social topology" means that machinic processes can interact, both in real-
world systems ("concrete assemblages") and in being taken up in different

proportions by systems other than those of which they are the defining element. Assemblages are defined by what escape them, what flees from them. We should take that literally in thinking of marronage. Deleuze and Guattari write about what defines a society:

It is wrongly said (in Marxism in particular) that a society is defined by its contradictions. That is true only on the larger scale of things. From the viewpoint of micropolitics, a society is defined by its lines of flight, which are molecular. There is always something that flows or flees, that escapes the binary organizations, the resonance apparatus, and the overcoding machine. (216)

Extrinsic coexistence means interactive existence side-by-side: "States cannot effect a capture unless what is captured coexists, resists in primitive societies, or escapes under new forms, as towns or war machines" (435)—or as maroon societies. Intrinsic coexistence means that machinic processes can work in social systems that are not those with which they are most associated. For instance, the "power of metamorphosis" of the war machine (its capacity to change habits, to make a habit of changing habits) can be tamed by its transformation into a state military apparatus, but it can also resist such taming and be reborn in other forms, perhaps as revolution (436).

I'm going to speculate here that concrete maroon societies had a number of these machinic processes at work: (1) prevention-anticipation of state forms—to the extent that they were anti-hierarchical (again, that is a matter of debate with regard to Palmares); (2) war machines (power of metamorphosis)—though not nomadic, they did have to be able to organize to fight state invasion in mobile bands and to conduct raids without having predictable habits of fighting; (3) and perhaps ecumenical—they "encompassed heterogenous social formations" to achieve consistency, to have it all hang together for a time, in trading with the coastal settlements, in accepting people from all sorts of cultural backgrounds.

Geography of Marronage

Geography or, more precisely, topographical features, plays a key role in the regime of violence established in wild marronage (for a literature review and original analysis, see Wright 2020). State space is a space of enforceable regularities; state agents look to detect irregularities from the expected

location and behavior patterns of subjects. Spaces open to early statification are valleys and rivers allowing for military enforcement, administrative "legibility," and economic integration. Nonstate spaces in Scott (2009)
are mostly hills and mountains but include any region where state military reach is hampered, such as jungles, deserts, marshes, and so on (2009,
13). Deleuze and Guattari see the paradigmatic example of an anti-state
war machine in the Steppe nomads. Classical maroon societies, by contrast, are found in hills and mountains (Jamaica, Saint Domingue), in
swamps (the "Great Dismal Swamp" between North Carolina and Virginia), in littoral spaces (coves, offshore islands, and the like, as in coastal
South Carolina).

Let us look more closely at the intersection of economies of violence
with geographical features, specifically the "friction of terrain" that James C.
Scott thematizes (2009, 43, *et passim*; 2017, 116–49). Marronage is a spa-
tializing practice, as maroons improve the hiding, ambush, booby trap, and
raiding aspects of their territories (Stennet 2020). The space of marronage
differs from the "smooth space" of the nomadic war machine in its Steppe
incarnation. A smooth space is noncartographic; it allows movement within
it that would be unpredictable to those used to movement in a gridded
space from point A to point B. To their state adversaries, it seems as if the
forces of the nomadic war machine are able to "instantaneously" appear
here or there; it's as if the war machine operated by whirlwinds, vortices,
and other tactics hard to perceive by state-trained eyes. Maroon spatializ-
ing, by contrast, seeks to find and hold a space that is inaccessible to pursuing infantry but that allows multiple options for inter-relating with states:
raids on people and trade routes at times, but also commercial exchanges
when those are possible and desired.

Maroon attacks on pursuers are enabled by their choice of territory
and the improvements they have made to it, such as constructed vantage
points, escape routes, ambush points, barricades, booby traps, and the like
(Stennett 2020). Although the smooth versus striated distinction in *A Thousand Plateaus* 14 is too abstract to be useful in theorizing the space of marronage, even with the way Deleuze and Guattari say we should be thinking
about differing geosocial tendencies rather than different actual or physical spaces (smoothing or striating as practices versus smooth or striated
as a fixed space), Deleuze and Guattari do say that there are other spatial
practices to consider. Nonetheless, despite its specific adaptation to their
marginal geographic positions, maroon attacks have elements of "smooth

space"—they don't follow predetermined lines; they are experienced by state troops as coming from everywhere and nowhere.

The choice of a wild marronage geographical situation—mountains, forests / jungles, swamps, coastal zones—looks to impose a high cost on pursuing state agents. Rough terrain imposes a cost in time and money and physical effort on pursuers. Biotic elements encountered by the pursuers can impose disease or predation costs. All of that can lead to discipline problems among the pursuers and additional costs of reimposing order (punishment is never cost free; it distracts from pursuit at a minimum but risks slacking, desertion, or even mutiny). All of that was especially germane when pursuers relied on slaves as porters (Patterson 1979, 266). Then there are costs imposed by ambush, booby trap, and other forms of guerrilla warfare.

Contemporary Dimensions of Marronage

Marronage has become a generalized figure of resistance to the local and state power structures of global capitalism. We can cite only a very few instances here. In Caribbean letters, Edouard Glissant uses the figure of the maroon extensively in his literary (*The Fourth Century* [2001]) and theoretical works (*Poetics of Relation* [1997]), where he also refers to Deleuze and Guattari's line of flight.[16] The figure of the maroon as symbol of the resistance of African peoples to global white supremacy is also found in Sylvia Wynter. Greg Thomas (2016) analyzes the theme of marronage in Wynter's legendary manuscript "Black Metamorphosis" and provides multiple references to contemporary works where the notion of the maroon spreads out from the historical: "Maroonage can be mobile or urban; hydro or maritime; folkloric, cosmological, metaphysical, or supernatural; spiritual or religious as well as territorial and psychological, and so on" (72–73).

Within the social sciences, marronage has come to be investigated in the Black Geographies movement. For instance, Adam Bledsoe (2017) calls marronage "one of the most creative and emergent methods of life-building found in the modern world," while noting its relative absence in the U.S. Black resistance which is "more frequently associated with advocating inclusionary politics or nationalist separatism," with the exception of the Black Panther party. In that regard, Bledsoe cites James Tyner, "The Black Panther Party was consonant with other 'Black geographies' in rethinking the underpinnings of black oppressions," such that "the geopolitical thought of the Black Panthers . . . demonstrates a particular human geography that is predicated on the respatialization and repoliticization of urban space" (Tyner 2006, 116; cited in Bledsoe 2017, 41). Nonetheless, Bledsoe does find some resonance of maroon practice in "communities like the Gullah-Geechee of the Southeastern United States . . . which have preserved aspects of marronage in the present . . . as they evidence Black spatial self-affirmation and definition amidst an anti-Black society" (43–44), albeit amid challenges by capitalist "land development" practices.

Finally, we can note that marronage has come to figure in the Afropessimism tradition for escape from the fundamental anti-Blackness of the contemporary world. In "The Case of Blackness," Fred Moten (2008) writes, commenting on Fanon: "What's at stake is fugitive movement in and out of the frame, bar, or whatever externally imposed social logic— a movement of escape, the stealth of the stolen that can be said, since it inheres in every closed circle, to break every enclosure. This fugitive movement is stolen life, and its relation to law is reducible neither to simple interdiction nor bare transgression" (179). And in their analysis of the "undercommons" in American universities, Harney and Moten (2013) tell us that despite university disciplinary efforts,

> [there] stands the immanence of transcendence, the necessary deregulation and the possibilities of criminality and fugitivity that labor upon labor requires. Maroon communities of composition teachers, mentorless graduate students, adjunct Marxist historians, out or queer management professors, state college ethnic studies departments, closed-down film programs, visa-expired Yemeni student newspaper editors, historically black college sociologists, and feminist engineers. (30)

Such dispersal of the figure of the maroon is all the more necessary when we reckon with contemporary State geographical dominance. Scott (1998, 2009) analyzes contemporary state domination; despite failures of central planning, more modest administration can keep internal population management going very nicely in the core—going off the grid or creating police no-go zones in the cities notwithstanding. When we consider contemporary urban marronage, biopolitical and neoliberal state administration can keep internal population management going in the core: the middle and working classes that are registered, tracked, and managed, some with full disciplinary force, others with the more "dividualizing"

practices of "control" via databases and so on (Deleuze 1992). Nondocu-
mented people, or those who are dissatisfied citizens, go about trying to
live as squatters, as inhabitants of "no-go zones," as those who "go off
the grid," and other forms of evading state rule within state territories. On
the periphery, surveillance with Geographic Information System analyses
of data from satellites and drones, force projection with helicopters, and
brutality with automatic weapons can keep the peasantry in line and keep
nonstate people confined to the margins and ineffective in resisting resource
extraction when desired. This is not to say that sheer force is confined to
the periphery; what we see in so-called no-go zones is a sort of "shared
sovereignty" between nonstate actors—in Scott's terms, "barbarian" gangs—
and state police forces, who arrive in force when they want to and shoot
first and ask questions later.

One last turn of the screw. Scott agrees with Deleuze and Guattari on
the need to conceptually separate the primary or originary violence of
statification as capture and enslavement of nonstate peoples, and the ordinary, everyday, or secondary violence of policing, tax collection, and labor
coercion, which repeat and reinforce the originary violence by which tax
and labor become obligations and attempts to evade them and / or to appropriate surplus by private means become criminalized. Might it not be the
case, however, that in "no-go zones" that nonstate actors, often seen as
"criminal gangs" by the state, engage in a sort of "shared sovereignty" by
which they compete with states for appropriation of surplus ("protection"
rather than taxes being a form of regularizing plunder, hence requiring
punishment of those even gangs consider freelancers infringing on "their
people") and, sometimes, for provision of services (food handouts, hous-
ing via squatting or camping, and so on) for the marginal populations that
states show little interest in managing other than by intermittent raids for
deportation and camp dismantling purposes?

Part IV

Political Events

7

The Capitol Invasion

Here in Part IV, I provide case studies of political events in relation to their regimes of violence, which can be direct and physical, as in the current chapter, or indirect and social, entangled with racism, as will be the case in the following chapter. The object of our case study in this chapter is the invasion of the U.S. Capitol on January 6, 2021.[1] In the terms developed in the Introduction to this book, the patterns and triggers of the bioenculturated bodies and minds of Donald Trump's followers, their affective–cognitively structured bodies politic, were prepared by a carefully crafted affective ideology composed by years of fascist impugning of liberal institutions ("drain the swamp") and provocation of a cult of personality ("I alone can fix it" [Plumer 2016]). The followers were then stoked to fever pitch by months of exorbitant claims about the 2020 election, such as "fraud," "stop the steal," or as Trump reinforced it on January 6: "All of us here today do not want to see our election victory stolen by emboldened radical-left Democrats, which is what they're doing" (AP News 2021). Trump's words in his speech on the Washington Mall mobilized his forces: "We're going to walk down, and I'll be there with you, we're going to walk down, we're going to walk down . . . you'll never take back our country with weakness. You have to show strength and you have to be strong" (AP News 2021). And march they did, having been transformed from a mass of individuals to a crowd operating under the call of the leader, albeit one no longer physically present by the time they left the Mall (see Gilbert 2014 for comments on crowds and leaders in Canetti 1984; Freud 1989; and Le Bon 2002).

Using our terms from chapter 4's analysis of soccer, the march, although emergently identifiable as a march and not a collection of bodies, was not in complete resonance; nonetheless, there was some fellow feeling brought about by the common direction and purpose of the bodies politic in motion. In this vein, we also have to take into account the binding effect of the call-and-response of the speech and the shouted slogans on the march (Protevi 2011). In the mood of the march, we see the collective euphoria of passive joy, to use Spinozist terms we will discuss in the Conclusion. All this brought Trump's followers to the Capitol, where they enacted a regime of violence whose norms were left deliberately vague but were to be worked out on the spot in the transverse waves of confrontational energy with the Capitol police. Trump's injunction to the crowd left no doubt that violence was called for: "We fight like hell. And if you don't fight like hell, you're not going to have a country anymore" (AP News 2021).[2]

Now, many others have interpreted the meaning of the actions—among them, fighting, shitting, praying—so rather than simply repeat their efforts, I want to show how the events were not just provoked by Trump's words but also evoked by the political "affordances" of the Capitol, the way in which some actions were called forth by features of the built environment. Think of this, then, as a case study in ecological psychology, a Gibsonism (Gibson 1986; Radman 2012) of political actions, bodily affects, and architectural affordances in a politically charged built environment (Harrison 2020). In looking at the conditions of the event, I'll first reflect a bit on the methodology of case studies using the Deleuzean terminology of sense, dramatization, haecceity, and problem. I'll follow that with a recap of current work on the convergence of enactivism with Gibsonian ecological psychology. I'll end with a look at how features of the building solicited actions that are ordinarily mundane but were spectacularly out of place when performed by those people that day at the Capitol. In particular, I'll look at how the dais in the Senate chamber solicited prayers by Jacob Chansley, the "Q-Anon Shaman."[3] Chansley declaimed in the simultaneously grandiose and paranoid "Trumpian ecumenical" style (Jenkins 2021b); the contrast case to his speech is that many prayers in the American civil religion style (Bellah 1967) have been offered in the Senate chamber by the Senate chaplain.

The Events of January 6

Allow me to reflect a bit on the ontological ramifications of case studies. (I will consider their ethical implications in chapter 8.) Case studies are an underused tool in philosophy, as opposed to thought experiments such as brain transplants, brains-in-a-vat, zombies, and others. Case studies do not aim at identifying the necessary and sufficient conditions for an essential distinction, as do thought experiments. Instead, case studies reveal the outlines of concrete problems, which are the points of intersection of "multiplicities," a Deleuzean term of art that means a "problematic" field in which linked rates of change create conflicting pressures, so that any one move changes the conditions for future moves, and no one solution exhausts the potentials for future creatively different solutions. In other words, Deleuzean problems, the problems of life, cannot be "solved" once and for all; they can only be dealt with.[4]

The events of January 6 had a sense, "insurrection." In *Logic of Sense*, Deleuze (1990) provides a reading of Stoic philosophy in which sense lies at the surface separating the transcendence of words, concepts, and names and the depths of bodies, things, states of affairs. Sense is expressed in propositions and attributed to states of affairs, but it is neither height nor depth but surface. We can attribute the proper name "Capitol insurrection of January 6" to a particular state of affairs, but the insurrection itself is an incorporeal event (or sense) with no other reality than that of the expression of that proposition; what we find in the state of affairs are bodies mixing with one another—flagpoles stabbing flesh, bullets flying through the air, bear spray shot into faces, bodies being trampled—and the insurrection itself is the *effect* or the *result* of this intermingling of bodies. The insurrectionary events were dramatic in the ordinary sense, but they were also a "dramatization" in Deleuze's sense, a set of actions or "spatio-temporal dynamisms" that resolved tensions inherent in a problem, or network of intersecting processes. Dramatization is something like, though more dynamic than, a Kantian schematism, which is the rule for producing an object consistent with a concept (Deleuze 1994, 218; Deleuze 2004.) For Deleuze, problems cannot be solved once and for all, though they can be dealt with, or resolved, practically and temporarily in concrete situations by singular actions (Williams 2005, 130). As networks of intersecting processes, problems admit only tweaks to open-ended situations that produce another iteration of the problem. In other words, just as hurricanes only temporarily resolve the problem of global heat transfer, the insurrection was only a temporary resolution to the pressures built up by Trump's intransigence regarding the normal processes of certifying presidential elections.

Dramatizations can also be seen as immanent haecceities—that is, compositions of the movements and affects of bodies (Deleuze and Guattari 1987, 260–61).[5] In the concept of haecceity, an event is individuated in part by its temporal and spatial coordinates, its being situated. That is, the "block of space-time" that was January-6-at-the-Capitol provided some of the dimensions of the event of the insurrection. A haecceity is also defined by its "longitude"—the "speeds and slownesses" of its material motions—and by its "latitude"—its set of affects (Deleuze and Guattari 1987, 260–61). Following Spinoza, Deleuze and Guattari define affection as the change in the material relations defining a body by an encounter with another body, while affect is the change in the power of acting of the affected body due to the affection. Think of a haecceity as the temporary configuration of a kaleidoscope that constantly shifts its aspects as its components act on and react to one another, shuffling their affections and affects.

The multiple and interconnected pressures and consequences of open-ended and evolving problematic haecceities can be studied better in case studies than in experiments done in the armchair or even in the lab. There can be synergy here: An apprenticeship in case studies can help us identify key dimensions of situations that can be isolated from their real-world context and tested experimentally, and that very experimental knowledge helps us critique old case studies and produce new ones. For a case study itself involves the choice of what to include: a map that produces a 1-to-1 duplication of the territory, as in the Borges story, is no map at all. Hence my focus on the Q-Anon Shaman's prayer's being solicited by the Senate chamber dais.

Political Affordances

Ecological psychology, in which invariant structures of the "ambient optic array" or field of light in an environment allowed organisms to attend to these structures to guide their perception and action, gets its inspiration from Gibson (1986). While there was some tension between ecological psychology and early enactivists (Varela, Thompson, and Rosch 1991, 203), recent work shows a rapprochement of the two orientations (McGann et al. 2020). Kevin Ryan and Shaun Gallagher highlight some "resonances": "Orthodox ecological psychologists and enactivists agree that the best explanation for a large share of cognition is non-representational . . . instead of focusing solely on factors interior to an agent, a good part of cognition is to be found in the link or coupling between an agent and the external world. This link is fluid, dynamic, and active in a variety of ways" (Ryan and Gallagher 2020, 1147).

Enactivism had always conceded that only certain environments allowed world-enactment for certain organisms. The environment had to provide viability; but this requirement provided only loose constraints rather than incite adaptive optimization. As Varela, Thompson, and Rosch put it:

> The constraints of survival and reproduction are far too weak to provide an account of how structures develop and change. . . . The enormous diversity constantly generated at all levels in the genetic and evolutionary process both shapes and is shaped by the coupling with the environment. . . . Much of what an organism looks like and is "about" is completely underdetermined by the constraints of survival and reproduction. (Varela, Thompson, and Rosch 1991, 194–96)

For the enactive approach, the action came inside-out, as it were, from the side of the world-enacting organism, whose organizational closure allowed for structural coupling. Ecological psychology worked from outside in, specifying invariant structures in the ambient optic array, but it was never naïve realism or objectivism any more than enactivism was naïve subjectivism or constructivism. Affordances are not features of the environment but are relations between organism and environment. In other words, the ambient optic array is analogous to viability constraints for enactivism: It provides outer boundaries but under-determines the exact ways in which an organism engages its environment. (For the classic work in setting forth Gibsonian affordances in an approach to cognitive science, see Chemero 2009.)

For a closer look at affordances, let us turn to Chemero's work.[6] Chemero offers us a recap of what he calls "Affordances 1.1" in three claims: (1) "affordances are what we perceive; they are the content of experience"; (2) "affordances are relations between what animals can do and features of the environment"; (3) "the perception of affordances is also a relation; it is a relation between an animal and an affordance" (Chemero 2009, 200). We should note that in his discussion of Affordances 1.1, Chemero insists that abilities are not dispositions, which in Chemero's understanding are automatically triggered under the right circumstances (145). Thus, Chemero will claim that abilities are inherent not in animals (as are dispositions) but in animal-environment systems. Chemero continues with Affordances 2.0, a dynamic theory of affordances. In developing Affordances 2.0, he asks his readers to start with Affordances 1.1, "then consider the interaction over time between an animal's sensorimotor abilities and its niche, that is, the set of affordances available to it." Chemero specifies two timescales here. First, there is the developmental timescale, in which an "animal's sensorimotor abilities select its niche—the animal will become selectively sensitive to information relevant to the things it is able to do." Second, there is the behavioral timescale, in which "the animal's sensorimotor abilities manifest themselves in embodied action that causes changes in the layout of available affordances, and these affordances will change the way abilities are exercised in action. . . . Affordances and abilities causally interact in real time and are causally dependent on one another" (Chemero 2009, 150–54).

As I mentioned in chapter 2's discussion of a political philosophy of mind, enactivism has developed a branch that moves from a focus on the perceptual-motor linkage in individual organisms to second-person participatory sense making to third-person political philosophy of mind. Maiese and Hanna (2019) use the term "affective frame" (41–42) to indicate that bodies are in essential interaction with the environment, which for humans very often has crucial social dimensions. Hence, an affective frame can be instantiated in a social institution that makes some affective stances more likely: "A social institution thereby significantly modulates affective framings, substantively molds overall bodily comportment, and literally shapes the minded bodily habits of the subjects involved" (Maiese and Hanna 2019, 56). As we can see, an affective frame is doubly distributed, spread across the social institutions and bodily systems that make it up.

We can connect the notion of an affective frame with the ecological psychology notion "social scaffolding," environmental structures that enable or afford characteristic action of properly attuned agents. Hence, Erik Rietveld and Julian Kiverstein emphasize the difference between the landscape and the field of affordances. Affordances are said to be in a landscape when they are potentials that might be taken up, while they are said to be the field when they are currently in use by a particular organism. The next step toward the study of the political affordances of the Capitol riot is taken by Maxwell Ramstead and collaborators, who develop the claim that the full range of affordances for humans must include the social-cultural world. When an organism is engaged with features of the environment, these features are "experienced as 'solicitations,' in that they solicit (further) affective appraisal and [hence] act as perceptual and affective prompts for the organism to act on the affordance" (Ramstead, Veissière, and Kirmayer 2016, 5; for a radical enactivist take on the notion of "cultural affordance," see Hutto et al. 2020).

Finally, Segundo-Ortin (2024) writes of the "education of intention," which "occurs via the acquisition of habit-based preferences for particular actions" relating "socio-cultural norms" to habits of perception without need of specific mental representations (2). In our terms, affective ideology shapes the way certain circumstances call for certain actions, all the way down to how things appear to us. We will investigate how the perception of the Senate chamber by Jacob Chansley evoked his prayer. As Segundo-Ortin says (2024, 6–7), this insistence on affordances' soliciting politically meaningful action resonates with the manifesto of the "Skilled Intentionality Framework," in which the authors insist that "affordances always have to be understood in the context of an ecological niche that implies the form of life of a certain kind of animal" (Rietveld, Denys, and Van Westen 2018). In something of an existence proof for what we will attempt below, Simon Harrison (2020) provides a case study that links a social affordances analysis with an ethnographic study of consumers in a cosmetics pop-up store in Hong Kong, revealing "the affective and emotional experience of perceiving relevant affordances in the environment" (1). We will follow this thread in looking at the emotional attunement of the participants as their actions unfold.

Political Ontogenesis of Subjects

We are almost there, but a final discussion of difference and development is in order to complete our prolegomenon. Affordances appeal to subjects, but not all subjects are the same. In my own work paving the way for a political philosophy of mind, I've always striven to disabuse us of the customary focus on the already established characteristics of rational male adult subjects by focusing on the interplay of the supra-subjective, adjunct-subjective, and sub-subjective, following the slogan "above, below, and alongside the subject" (for more detail, see the Introduction to this book as well as Protevi 2009 and 2013). We go above the subject to the geopolitical, below the subject to the neurophysiological, and alongside the subject to the social-technical. But we have to do this using three temporal scales—the evolutionary, the developmental, and the behavioral—as well as three compositional scales for "bodies politic": the civic, the somatic, and the "evental." In doing so, we see that the patterns, triggers, and thresholds of affective–cognitive dispositions are produced via transgenerational subjectification practices that are the intensive individuation processes of a social-neural-somatic multiplicity. Thus, the social and the somatic are not synchronic opposites but are linked in a spiraling diachronic inter-weaving at three temporal scales, the long-term phylogenetic, the midterm ontogenetic, and the short-term behavioral.

The relation of the production of the large-scale patterns of con-sciousness (the development and triggering of affective–cognitive traits) by subjectification practices are themselves analyzable in terms of political economy. The question here is the "granularity problem": What is the level of specification of analysis that ecological psychology and enactivism should adopt when investigating concrete cases of political events? The question is, how can you avoid simply saying something about a generic human subject's capacity for interacting with other people and the accessing social affordances of built environments? Conversely, how far down can you go along the path of differenciation—the ontogenetic and behavioral scale—yet avoid being bogged down in the idiosyncrasies of singular situations? To have a political analysis of the subjectification processes that track the distribution of affective–cognitive traits in a population needed for mesh-ing with social affordances you need the right granularity, neither an un-marked generality nor a swarm of idiosyncratic singulars. In other words, there is no politics where each person has his or her own differenciated category, their own life story and "point of view." On the other hand, there is no politics either with the unmarked generic "subject" of too much cog-nitive science, which only limns the least differentiated dimensions of humanity, technology, and the built environment.

There are three aspects to consider to get the right granularity—between idiosyncrasy and unmarked generality—for discussions of social affordances: (1) synchronic variation, countering the tendency to think a generic "subjectivity" or "the" subject; (2) diachronic development, focus-ing on the embodied affective–cognitive development of a population of subjects in a field of multiple, overlapping, and resonating or clashing sub-jectification practices, countering the tendency to focus on adult subjectiv-ity; (3) properly granular political categorization, thematizing politically important categories such as race and gender lying between generic human subjectivity and idiosyncratic personality or subpersonality. Lacking a pop-ulation perspective on the development of affective–cognition capacities, we risk impoverishing a notion of "cultural scaffolding" by relegating the cul-tural to a storehouse of heuristic aids for an abstract problem-solver who just happens to be endowed with certain affective–cognition capacities that enable it to interact successfully with the people and cultural resources to which it just happens to have access. Positing an abstract or generic subject neglects the way in which culture is the very process of the construction of biosocial subjects, so that access to certain cultural resources and to the training necessary to acquire certain forms of affective–cognitive capacities are distributed along lines analyzable by political categories. This is not simply technical training for cognitive capacities in a restricted sense but also the training necessary for acquiring positive and empowering emotional patterns, thresholds, and triggers.

But this foregoing treatment is still too simple. It does no good to replace a single generic human subject with two abstractions, "the" feminized subject and "the" masculinized subject. We need to think in terms of a range of gendering practices that are distributed in a society at various sites (family, school, church, media, playground, sports field . . .) with variable goals, intensities, and efficacies. These multiply situated gendering practices resonate or clash with one another and with myriad other practices (racializing, "class-ing," "religionizing," "nationalizing," "neighborhoodizing" ["that's the way we roll"] . . .). We have to think a complex virtual field of these differential practices; in dynamic systems terms, we could think a complex phase space for the production of biosocial subjects—or, in my terminology, "bodies politic"—with shifting attractor layouts as the subjectification practices clash or resonate with one another. But even this is still too simple, as these gendering practices also enter into complex feedback relations with the singular body makeup of the people involved, in distinguishing fully differentiated multiplicities from singular individuation processes.

Prayer in the Senate Chamber

When I say I'm looking at political affordances of the Capitol as conditions of the insurrection, I don't want to avoid hermeneutic analyses altogether. Rather, I just want to see them anchored to the concrete experience of embodied and affective subjects, past and present. Some very useful readings of the Capitol insurrection, in a genre we might call Critical Race Architecture, in fact highlight the contradiction of a building that purports to represent democratic ideals of freedom and equality having been built by enslaved persons. Carolina Miranda puts it bluntly: "In the Capitol building, idealized narratives of liberty and democracy rest on brute force"

(Miranda 2021; see also Davidson 2021). Peter Minosh, in an essay written before the insurrection, puts it this way:

> The neoclassical design of the Capitol has been taken to represent the classical virtues of an American enlightenment. I argue that the proper subjects represented in this monument to representational democracy are not the citizens of the Republic, but the enslaved people excluded from political and architectural representation. By examining [William] Thornton's preliminary designs for the Capitol in consideration of the greater trajectory of his philosophical projects and political activities, we can discern in this neoclassical edifice the terms of an irresolvable crisis between the enlightened Republic and its foundation within a regime of chattel slavery. (Minosh 2020)

A case study must, however, narrow its focus, even as it keeps the big picture claims that the building itself embodies a conflict of democratic symbolism and the labor of enslaved persons in the background. We will focus on the Q-Anon Shaman's prayer in the Senate chamber, which, given the civil religion aspects of the chamber, was both in place and out of place.[7] Let's begin with a brief description of the of Senate chamber (Architect of the Capitol n.d.). The chamber is encircled by a balcony serving as the viewer's gallery. The entrance doors to the chamber open under the balcony onto a gently sloping floor lined with the senators' desks in a semicircular pattern. In the well of the chamber, we find first the clerk's desk, then, a small level up sits a long marble counter, and finally, another small level up we see the Senate president's desk, flanked by the U.S. flag and the U.S. Senate flag, serving as the focal point for the room.

I will use the Luke Mogelson video from *The New Yorker* to document a small subset of the events, culminating in the Q-Anon Shaman's prayer (Mogelson and Wolansky 2021). We first see Jacob Chansley, the Q-Anon Shaman, shouting and chanting from the balcony. It's something of a commonplace of political architectural analysis to note the penchant of authoritarians to deliver addresses from balconies, and in fact Trump's balcony appearance after being released from the hospital for Covid-19 in October 2020 sparked dozens of commentaries noting just that (Ben-Ghiat 2021). So, we can speculate that for Chansley, the balcony solicited a powerful urge to vocalize, not simply from being higher than others (but not neglecting that physical relation), but also with the resonances of balcony speaking by strongmen. The chants and howls were, however, more of a California-style Men's Rights, Iron John, back-to-nature performance, befitting Chansley's wild-man look, his bare torso and tattooed body (prominent among the tattoos is a depiction of Thor's hammer), and by now infamous horned helmet with cascading fur pieces framing his face.

We then see Chansley triumphantly striding down the aisle, face jubilant, chest expansive, feeling the power of strides aided by the slope, shouting, "Fucking A, man!" while carrying his bullhorn and spear wrapped in the American flag. He greets people already in the chamber, congratulating them, paternalistically, on their service. Shortly thereafter, a police officer enters the frame and asks if an injured man needs help. Having established his bona fides as a public servant, he asks if they could leave. The injured insurrectionist says, "I been making sure they ain't disrespecting the place." The policeman says, "Just want you to know, this is like *the* sacredest place." This exchange definitively primes the participants to recall the civil religion aspect of the Capitol as a "temple of democracy," further charging the affective space of the chamber for Chansley.

Chansley has soon mounted to the president's desk, where he puts his bullhorn down and takes off his backpack; he then sits in the president's chair. The police officer asks him to move, but Chansley replies that he's sitting there "'cause Mike Pence [the then-president of the Senate] is a fucking traitor." Sitting in a chair is the classic example of meshing action with an affordance, but this is not just "a" chair, for Chansley is taking possession of a chair whose occupant, he believes, has forfeited the right to control it. The police officer asks the people if they could leave. There is some agreement, but Chansley demurs, staying around to write a note, appropriating paper from the desk. The policeman objects to this, saying, "I feel you're pushing the line." The injured man further primes the scene as one resonant with civil religion: "C'mon, man. This is our Capitol, let's be respectful. There's 4 million people coming in . . . we love you guys, we love the cops." We now see a shot of Chansley's note: "It's only a matter of time. Justice is coming!" So, we've moved from the injured man's rootedness in the day (albeit rather hilariously exaggerated) to Chansley's apocalyptic channeling of what he thinks will be justice.

There are now four men at the dais, behind the president's desk. One raises his fist to the heavens in a power salute, arm at 90 degrees, and yells out, "Jesus Christ, we invoke your name, amen!" Chansley takes over, suggesting to the participants, "Let's say a prayer in this sacred space" (Jenkins

2021a). As Chansley begins, the man to his left doffs his MAGA hat as sign of respect. All the men at the dais follow suit, further cementing the dais as an altar and the men as responding to its solicitation as a place of prayer. During the prayer, Chansley's companions offer rhythmic gestures of affirmation and supplication (arms extended, palms up, then clenching in triumphant fists). Chansley's prayer finishes with a triumphant chorus of "Amen!" I will leave a full semantic analysis of the prayer to others,[8] but I did want to at least mention the way Chansley evoked the ambience of the chamber: "Thank you, divine, omniscient, omnipotent, and omnipresent creator God for filling this chamber with your white light and love, your white light of harmony." Is it going too far, or not far enough, to note the possible racialized overtones of a "white light" as part of "Trumpian ecumenicalism" (Jenkins 2021b)?

There's much more to be said about Chansley in terms of what we can call his being swept up in a stochastic manner by Trump's widespread call that brought him to the place where the dais could solicit his prayer. For instance, to recall our analysis of affective ideology in chapter 2, we can't deal with just Chansley's ideas without tackling his emotional investments. As for stochastic factors, we can't set up impossible demands for exact times in which Chansley imbibed one or another idea or resonated emotionally with Trump. Rather, we can look to the way in which increased political stresses will reveal those in a population with lowered thresholds for violent action. In this way, we can see Chansley as a "socially invaded mind" as opposed to the "socially extended mind" of 4EA cognition (Protevi 2013, chapter 5).

There's also much more to be said about other actions that day at the Capitol. What was the intersection of emotional investment and political affordance that led some to heed the call to climb walls, storm doors, and fight cops (Collins 2021)? Let us also ask ourselves if there was something about the cold, hard, shiny marble floors that called for shitting, for defilement? The *Daily News* writes, "They took a dump on American democracy—literally. Some of the unhinged pro-Trump rioters who stormed the U.S. Capitol on Wednesday defecated inside the historic building and 'tracked' their feces in several hallways, the *Daily News* has learned" (Somerfeldt 2021). It's unclear whether the insurrectionists defecated in the hallways on purpose or if the presence of fecal matter was just the result of a toilet overflow that was tracked about unintentionally. What is clear is that media attention assumed it was intentional because of its symbolic shock value.

But should it have been shocking? If you get cleanliness only by abjecting the accursed share, then shit defiling a clean Capitol could be shocking only to those whose good conscience is achieved by repressing the memory of the enslaved laborers who built the Capitol. Perhaps we should let the shit on the floors remind us that the Capitol was already defiled, from the start, by its very construction.[9]

8

Covid-19

In this final chapter of the book, I present a case study of the death of an "essential worker" from Covid-19. This is perhaps the most interdisciplinary of the chapters in this book, and while I can't promise that it brings everything together, I do feel that it resonates with the main conceptual themes of the book: regimes of violence, affective ideology, and loving caring. In May 2020, as Covid-19 swept through southern Louisiana, I read an article in my local newspaper that was both heartbreakingly concrete and illustrative of wider trends (DeRobertis 2020).[1] The article relayed the story of the life and death of Ms. Shenetta White-Ballard, a nurse at a senior care facility and, hence, an "essential worker," who died after exposure to Covid-19 at work. The powerful affective tenor of the reporting immediately pulled me in. Ms. White-Ballard was described by friends and family as "terrified" of the risks of contracting Covid at work, "responsible" for her family's financial viability, and as having a "beautiful heart" full of concern for her family and her patients. I would like this chapter to serve as a tribute to her courage as well as a critical account of the social forces that shaped the affective frame (affect-modulating institutional context; see chapter 2's discussion of "political philosophy of mind" for more on this term) within which she enacted her agency.

I will use an outside-in method so we can see the full dimensions of the situation in which Covid-19 served as an affective frame for Ms. White-Ballard's death. I begin with a reflection on the ethics of case studies, then move to a closer look at affective frames and embodied minds. From there I will provide a Foucauldian analysis of the long development of "biopower" regimes for public health and disease management, culminating in the development in the past forty years of a regime of neoliberalism, financialization of daily life, and risk management as we are subjectified as "self-entrepreneurs" responsible for health decisions for self and family. Moving still closer to the present, I will look at race and Covid-19 in the United

States, specifically the notion of "pre-existing conditions" or "comorbidities" and their relation to "weathering," the thesis that chronic stress in populations suffering anti-Black racism will accelerate aging as measured by telomere length (for the epigenetics of stress, see Turecki and Meaney 2014). As a result of the entanglement of racialization with financial and viral risk, those who are negatively racialized and precariously employed, deprived of a robust social safety net so that they are left as life-management agents responsible for both self and family, faced a double bind of choosing either financial ruin or viral exposure. Turning briefly to enactive accounts, we see that searching for epistemic solutions to such a no-win situation itself imposes a physiological cost that contributes to weathering. Finally, I will show how all these factors crystallize in the case of Shenetta White-Ballard, who, having strongly identified with the affective components of her roles as providing necessary care to her family and her patients, and who, when faced with the conflicting risks of family financial ruin by stopping work and contracting the virus by continuing to work, chose the latter and ultimately died of Covid-19 in May 2020.

The Ethics of Case Studies

In this chapter I will conduct a case study of a deleterious, socially instituted affective frame that, during the early days of the Covid-19 pandemic in the United States, produced individuated circumstances that came crashing down on "essential workers" who were forced into a double bind, a no-win situation with an unavoidable entanglement of financial and health risks. We saw here an untenable and ultimately fatal situation that forced a choice between, on the one hand, increasing the risk of their failing to provide financial support for their family if they quit their job or reduced their hours, and on the other, increasing their risk of contracting the virus by continuing to work. The case study will thus be itself an affective frame that will bring to the fore for its readers a nexus of harmful social practices of contemporary American society. Form is reinforced by content here, as this particular affective frame brings forth a further emphasis on affect when we focus on workers being simultaneously socialized into roles as breadwinners and as members of the caring professions. For those people, quitting work becomes even more difficult as they come to affirm their self-identity of being providers of affective labor for those in their care at work and of being the affective anchor of family life at home, the one who finan-cially helps keep a roof over the heads of their loved ones as well as being the emotional backbone of the family. Hence the affective frame in which "essential workers in Covid times" found themselves foregrounds their self-image as caring helpers of those in need, at home and at work.

In my view, case studies have epistemological benefits and ethical con-cerns. Epistemologically, they render concrete what is otherwise a study of patterns rather than an investigation of a particular event. This in turn implicates an ontological point about the way concrete lives are lived as the nexus of processes whose patterns can be treated statistically but which are concretized as a series of events that one experiences (Protevi 2009 con-tains several case studies). Alongside its epistemological benefits, a case study raises ethical concerns of privacy and social positioning of authors and their subjects. I don't think there's precisely a privacy concern here, as the case study relies on a published newspaper article; the people quoted therein presumably consented to have their words used and their names cited. However, there is a change from reporting a set of facts—Ms. White-Ballard's death and the comments made about it by the people quoted—to using the story of her death to render concrete the dilemma of "essential workers." I could anonymize the chapter by cutting out the case study entirely to talk just about the structural problems of juggling financial and viral exposure risks. But that would stay on the level of statistical patterns, which loses the emotional connection to a life cut short by the way those processes, whose patterns can be discussed statistically, came crashing down on a singular life, like that of Ms. White-Ballard.

Regarding social positioning, I'm conscious of being a white scholar writing on a Black subject. In treating the testimony surrounding Ms. White-Ballard's death, am I making a spectacle of Black suffering? Lindsey Stew-art's challenging new book, *The Politics of Black Joy* (Stewart 2021), calls attention to a "neo-abolitionist" focus on Black pain to the exclusion of Black joy. I don't believe we should take Stewart's challenge to mean that any focus on social structures that disproportionately harm Black people is to be avoided; in other words, "neo-abolitionism" is not off the table entirely. Rather, its focus on suffering should never be allowed to overwhelm our reverence for the entirety of the lives one discusses; in Ms. White-Ballard's case, the fullness of her humanity shows through in the beautiful tributes conveyed by her friends and family.

Affective Frames and Bodies Politic

Our next step in providing the theoretical context for our case study moves from a general metaphysical scheme to the incarnation in bodies of habits formed via social practices. In previous work, I have used the term "political affect" to denote ways "in which a body is patterned by the social system into which it is acculturated" (Protevi 2009, 32; quoted in Maiese and Hanna 2019, 43). Throughout this work, I have used "affective ideology." In the writing of the article on which this chapter is based, I used "affective frame," which I borrow from Maiese and Hanna (2019, 260ff; see also Slaby 2016). The terms are connected; "affective frame" emphasizes the institutional side of human experience (as "political living"), while "affective ideology" emphasizes the psychological side. Affect is both openness and feeling—being affected. Affect is the feeling for variation; it is the intensive as opening access to the virtual, to the differential field or multiplicity of the situation. The intuitions in the affective frame generated here are the integration of the differential situation.

In my view, humans aren't substances with properties but singular patterns of social and somatic interaction. The embodied and the embedded aspects of our being intersect—we are bodies whose capacities form in social interaction. That is, our biology, our nature, is to be so open to our nurture that it becomes second nature—that's the upshot of the intersection of plasticity and niche-construction. And it's in this intersection of the social and the somatic that subjectivity and selfhood emerge. In much simpler terms, "singular patterns of social and somatic interaction" means that we are what we can do with others—the way our embodied capacities, which develop in the history of the social interactions we have had up to the present, intersect with the similarly constituted embodied capacities of the others we now encounter and the social affordances of the environment. The complexity and creative potential of these encounters is such that we don't know who we are until we experiment with what we can do.

My analyses so far in this section have been abstract. In other works, I have always insisted that when cognitive science looks at the extended and embedded mind, it needs to have a political analysis of the subjectification processes in a population (Protevi 2009, 2013). Without a population variation perspective, we risk relegating the cultural to a storehouse of heuristic aids for an abstract problem-solver who just happens to be able to interact successfully with the people and cultural resources to which it just happens to have access. So, we need to analyze not simply technical training for cognitive capacities in a restricted sense, but also the training necessary for acquiring positive and empowering emotional patterns, thresholds, and triggers. Hence, we need to think in terms of a range of subjectification practices that are distributed in a society at various sites (family, school, place of worship, media, playground, sports field, and so on) with variable goals, intensities, and efficacies. These multiply situated practices resonate or clash with one another and with myriad other practices (gendering, racializing, and so on). But even this is still too simple, as these subjectification practices also enter complex feedback relations with the singular body makeup (genetic and epigenetic) of the people involved. All the way down, we are biological and social; we are "bodies politic."

To keep contact with the experiential dimension, we should turn to "critical phenomenology" (among the classics are Beauvoir 2012 and Fanon 2008; for further developments see Ahmed 2007; Weiss, Murphy, and Salamon 2019; Guenther 2019). A classic in that field is Iris Marion Young's "Throwing Like a Girl" essay, which reveals an unstated masculinist (or at least nonfeminized) and ableist body subjectivity in Merleau-Ponty, one that enjoys its competence in navigating the world. In noting that classical phenomenological analyses of embodiment, temporality, intentionality, perception, intersubjectivity, and historicity by Husserl and Merleau-Ponty, echoed in Noë and other enactivists, presuppose a neutral or unmarked, socially unsituated, body-subject, critical phenomenology that loops us back to the first-person experience of individuals subject to politically analyzable, socially denigrated subjectification practices. Critical phenomenology shows us the necessity of a move from the unmarked abstract subject to a differential field of embodying practices being actualized in a differentiated field of concrete embodied subjects.

In reflecting on the early days of phenomenology, critical phenomenology thinkers show that the unmarked subject had a hidden content of white, male, able-bodied, and economically secure subjects moving in a world fitted to their actions such that whiteness, maleness, able-bodiedness, and economic security were rendered invisible. I often use the following image: For me, with my subject position, the opening to a subway is a call to adventure. The city opens up for me, allowing me to travel where I will. (Of course I have my fears of "bad neighborhoods at night," but we can at least say that I have a wider range of anxiety-free travel spots open up for me than those with other subject positions, for whom subways are sites of surveillance, harassment, and general uneasiness.) Similarly, for the most part, police officers appear to me as potential aids should I call on them (even though I know intellectually that they have no duty to intervene in an ongoing assault on me, the effects of fifty years of copaganda are such that I still feel they would help me if I needed them to).

It is only in tracing the movement from Sartre's gaze of the Other to Beauvoir's male gaze to Fanon's white gaze and other such phenomena of "sociogeny" (Fanon 2008, xv) that we see racializing, gendering, "able-ing," and securitizing as practices producing whiteness as well as blackness, masculinity as well as femininity, able-bodiedness as well as disability, and security as well as precarity.

Biopower

Previously known mostly among academics, Michel Foucault's term "biopower" achieved new public prominence in the Covid pandemic as commenters reacted to governments' enacting public-health measures beyond those already in place, which had become with the passage of time naturalized or invisible. For Foucault, the terms "biopower" and "biopolitics" referred to long historical modifications of regimes of power-knowledge or, roughly speaking, theoretically guided practice. In his middle period works of 1975–78 (*Discipline and Punish,* "*Society Must Be Defended,*" *History of Sexuality, Volume 1,* and *Security, Territory, Population*), Foucault distinguished several overlapping and intersecting forms of power-knowledge; any one historical era institutionalizes a different blend of these forms, rather than simply replacing one with another.

When operating in a sovereign power modality, governments deduct taxes and compel obedience of law by force; the slogan of sovereign power is "take life or let live." Disciplinary power operates in institutional settings and aims to increase productive obedience by individualizing examination, establishing norms, and implementing exercises to reduce deviation from those norms. Sexuality is a form of power-knowledge that, rather than operate by sovereign command or by disciplinary asymmetrical orders, instead induces people into acts of reflective self-subjectification, asking them to find their truth in their sexual desires. Foucault locates sexuality at the intersection of individualized discipline and population-level biopower, our final concern. Biopower regimes manage the biological realities of a population in its environment; the slogan here inverts that of sovereignty, whose "take life or let life" is transformed into biopower's "foster life or let die" (Cisney and Morar 2016).

While a transitive, externally directed, and adversarial "war" frame for power fit the transition from sovereign power to disciplinary power in *Discipline and Punish,* power relations became more subtle in *History of Sexuality, Volume 1,* as instead of highly constrained transitive commands of discipline ("take this test, perform these exercises") the practices making up the sexuality framework (*dispositif*) very often "induced" a self-subjectification in which subjects are constituted in and by the search for personal truth in sexual desires. At this time, then, Foucault introduced "governmentality" as a frame for reading intransitive, nonadversarial, self-subjectifying power relations (Lemke 2019). In governmentality situations, third-person-directed and second-person-instantiated practices condition the way in which I relate to myself in first-person lived experience. Governmentality is defined as "conduct of conduct"—that is, leading people to govern themselves, to self-subjectify in a particular way. Foucault's genealogy of governmentality in *Security, Territory, Population* and *Birth of Biopower* disentangled several strands: religious self-subjectification as led by "pastoral power"; sexual self-subjectification as an agent searching for truth in sexual desires; liberal self-subjectification as an agent in pursuit of self-interest; and, finally, neoliberal self-subjectification as a "self-entrepreneur" (Lemm and Vater 2014).

It will be germane to our study, then, to see the way in which a further concretion of the practice of being a self-entrepreneur comes from the inducement to self-subjectify as the agent of your and your family's health choices by being an active partner with healthcare providers. A further twist then comes when your financial situation depends on and is entwined with your work in the healthcare wing of "the caring professions." Here we allude to a self-subjectifying practice, unmentioned by Foucault but later developed by theoreticians of "emotional labor," in which some are led to identify with the caring practices they perform at work, as if one were to say, "This job comes easily to me, as I am a caring person at heart" (Hochschild 1983; Ashforth and Humphrey 1993; Johnson 2015, 113, explicating Hochschild, warns of "the mismeasurement of emotional labour as a natural disposition with its own intrinsic rewards").[2]

Risk, Financialization, and Neoliberalism

The core of my analysis is that contemporary workers deemed "essential" during Covid-19 and hence unable to work from home were caught in a double bind of navigating increased risk of viral exposure at work to mitigate their exposure to financial risk incurred by taking on debt in a world of stagnating wages. Here I will briefly treat the intertwining of risk and financialization in the neoliberal system.

Risk has been a popular social theory topic for the past forty years or so; Jacob Hacker's *The Great Risk Shift* (2006) is a noteworthy treatment of the destruction of the social safety net focused on the Fordist bargain and its "family wage." Melinda Cooper's *Family Values* (2019) refuses any leftist nostalgia for Fordism and instead provides detailed case studies of the way in which, during the neoliberal restructuring of society, "instead of trying to revive the family form of the New Deal, they [neoliberal policy makers] tried to revive the much older poor law tradition of family responsibility, which identified marital and kinship relations as the proper source of economic security and a suitable alternative to the welfare state" (Cooper 2018). Debt, risk, and Covid all come together, then, in an affective framing that pushed "essential workers" to accept increased Covid risk exposure by continuing to work due to their need to service financial debt. The major sociological work on risk is Ulrich Beck, *Risk Society* (1992). For Beck, modern society is faced with managing risks that the very operation of the system has created. Mitchell Dean (1998), from a Foucauldian perspective, demurs. For Dean, rather than being system-wide, risk is best thought of as managed in rational calculation in small assemblages. Curran (2013a, 2013b, 2016), for his part, criticizes Beck's lack of class analysis. Curran calls for "critical risk analyses" such that "differentials in economic power constitute a key form of social power for avoiding certain risk positions and rendering others exposed to the worst of the emerging damages" (Curran 2013b, 75). Beyond Curran's work, we also see further research that looks at risk in intersectional terms, adding race and gender to class (Luft 2016; Olofsson et al. 2021; cited by Zinn 2018).

"Financialization" refers to the way cost–benefit analyses saturate society at all levels, from individual to household to city, state, federal, and international (Martin 2002 is an early classic on individual and household-level financialization). A recent noteworthy analysis of the literature on debt, risk, and financialization is Adkins (2018), who shows that credit is no longer extended with a view to full repayment of the debt. Rather, creditors seek monthly revenue streams that can be securitized and sold on various secondary markets. Faced with declining purchasing power, workers now commonly leverage salary to take on the debt (credit cards, car loans, mortgages) that allows them to make ends meet. You don't work hand-to-mouth anymore; you work hand-to-check-to-credit-application. Cooper comments on these developments in neoliberal policies, the results of which produce private debt:

> We can also observe multiple ways in which cuts to public funding in healthcare, education, and welfare have pushed people back toward kinship-based forms of self-care and mutual support and how the expansion of consumer credit has turned household deficit-spending into a substitute for state deficit-spending. Today, family responsibility very often takes the form of intergenerational debt where parents and other family members are actively enrolled in the debt obligations of children, signed up as guarantors or required to post their housing wealth as collateral to fund the social mobility (or simply stasis) of younger generations. (Cooper and Mable 2018)

"Neoliberalism" is sometimes said to have degenerated into an empty epithet, just a term for critics of contemporary capitalism to use to sound sophisticated. (See Mirowski 2018 for a superb rebuttal to those claims.) For the purposes of this chapter, I follow Foucault's analysis, laid out in *The Birth of Biopolitics* (2008). Foucault writes that neoliberals reject the classical liberal notion that humans have a natural propensity to truck and barter, such that governments should step back to allow this natural process to take place. They rather assume, Foucault writes, that competition is fragile and needs state intervention to set up its conditions. *Contra* Maiese and Hanna (2019, 103), I don't think that neoliberalism is Hobbesian individualism (i.e., a social contract based on the need for government to allow personal security and economic collaboration via securing stock and enforcing contracts that people naturally desire in order to produce a social and business environment that protects against the ravages of exorbitant competition). Rather, neoliberalism does not trust that competition will last, as it fears that competition is always on the brink of falling into cooperation, and individualism into collectivism. Hence neoliberalism is the inverse of Hobbes; for the neoliberals, competition is fragile and needs state oversight to guarantee that it does not break down.

Furthermore, the classical political economy standpoint in which labor power is a commodity for purchase (e.g., Harvey 2007, 20) cannot be reconciled with Foucault's treatment of Gary Becker's human-capital theory. Becker undercuts the (Marxist) treatment of commodified labor power by treating individuals as firms. Salaries become returns on investment in skills; education becomes development of "human capital." Picking up on Becker enables Foucault to develop the notion of individuals as "self-entrepreneurs" for whom each action is either investment or return on human capital. In this way, Foucault can inscribe neoliberal governmentality in his history of subjectification practices. In other words, for Foucault, neoliberal governmentality conducts our conduct by inducing us to subjectify ourselves as self-entrepreneurs concerned with obtaining a return on our human capital (Foucault 2008, 221–26).

Racial "Weathering"

Governmentality practices that induce self-subjectification as a self-(health)-entrepreneur would start with contemporary American mandates for individual health insurance packages purchased from government-subsidized insurance markets but extend to such matters as legalizing direct-to-consumer medical advertising ("ask your doctor if X is good for you!"), state support of medical research, laws and regulations for reproductive health, and on and on. Insofar as producing the conditions for self-entrepreneurship allows for management of an individualized population, American biopower practices depend on analyzing rates in a vast multiplicity of myriad dimensions. Just to begin, multiple agencies at local, state, and federal levels analyze the way in which citizens with such-and-such a demographic profile (income, occupation, residence, gender, race . . .) consume such-and-such a level of health care (number of office visits, rate of prescription refills . . .) and have such-and-such health outcomes (sickness leading to days missed at work, life expectancy, cost of end-of-life care).

Insofar as the American biopower multiplicity includes dimensions affected by political practices of racialization, gendering, and other forms of "deep embodiment," we see here a biopolitics of "differential vulnerability" (Lorenzini 2020). Recall that the slogan of biopower is "foster life and let die." Lorenzini shows that Foucault's position in *Society Must Be Defended*" (Foucault 2003) amounts to racism as "a way of introducing a break into the domain of life taken over by power: the break between what must live and what must die." In biopolitics, racism "fragments the bio-logical continuum" (we all are living beings with biological needs) to create hierarchies between different human groups and thus differences in the way in which some are exposed to increased risk of death. Here we see biopower as "letting die" as opposed to sovereign execution; however, see Mbembe (2003) on contemporary sovereignty and "necropolitics," the construction of geographical and social zones where racialized bodies are marked not just for withdrawal of biopower support but also for killing with impunity.

Hence, we must not think that biopower is the only form of govern-mental action on biological processes going on today. Nonetheless, follow-ing Lorenzini, we can say that the differential exposure of human beings to health and social risks is, per Foucault, a salient feature of biopolitical governmentality.[3] The "deep embodiment" biological effects of the racial-izing subjectification practices analyzed by critical phenomenology links racial discrimination to "weathering" or premature aging, which must be considered in discussing Covid as affective frame. Fanon had already talked about the impingement of body image on body schema (Fanon 2008, 90–91). With weathering, we find an instance of "political physiology" that fits with the mind-shaping and body-shaping theses of Maiese and Hanna.

"Weathering" figures into the Covid analysis by Chowkwanyun and Reed (2020). It is already a classic in its insistence on warning against sim-ple ascription of Covid vulnerability to race without adequate context: "[D]isparity figures without explanatory context can perpetuate harmful myths and misunderstandings that actually undermine the goal of elimi-nating health inequities." Chowkwanyun and Reed cite three main dangers to sheer racial ascriptions. First, we risk ascribing inherent biological dif-ferences to what is a biosocial event. (The saying "there is no such thing as a natural disaster" was made popular during Hurricane Katrina; the same thing holds for Covid.) Similar warnings hold against ascribing Covid racial discrepancies to behavior or to sheer residential patterns. The latter risks the psychological phenomenon of "place-based stigma," when in fact we should be looking at "place-based risk"—that is, material factors respon-sible for poor health outcomes in the location. Neighborhoods with high Black population are not "bad neighborhoods" as if the mere presence of Black people hurts their reputation; some of them are literally poisoned by air pollution contributing to high respiratory disease rates and related high Covid rates (Wu et al. 2020; cited in Olumhense 2020). To fight this,

Chowkwanyun and Reed insist, we need socioeconomic status (SES) data to contextualize disease rates. "Complementary SES information will clarify how racial and class forces are intertwined—and when they are not—in the case of Covid-19. In general, members of minority populations are disproportionately likely to have low SES and are likely to have the most undesirable health outcomes."

Most interestingly for us, however, the authors now turn to the concept of "weathering" for cases when SES does *not* explain Covid-19 racial disparities:

> One possible explanation is the role of stress and what public health researcher Arline Geronimus has termed "weathering," or advanced aging caused by bodily wear and tear from fight-or-flight responses to external stressors, especially racial discrimination [internal citation to Geronimus et al. 2006]. Weathering has been linked, in turn, to cardiovascular disease and diabetes, two conditions that have been associated, in preliminary research, with elevated risk for severe Covid-19. (Chowkwanyun and Reed 2020)

Chowkwanyun and Reed conclude, "In sum, to mitigate myths of racial biology, behavioral explanations predicated on racial stereotypes and territorial stigmatization, Covid-19 disparities should be situated in the context of material resource deprivation caused by low SES, chronic stress brought on by racial discrimination, or place-based risk" (Chowkwanyun and Reed 2020).

Let us now turn to the concept of "weathering" laid out by Geronimus in numerous publications. First, let us note that one aspect of weathering is measured by telomere length. Telomeres are repetitive sequences of noncoding DNA that, during repeated episodes of cell division, protect coding DNA on the chromosome from degradation. However, each time a cell divides, the telomeres become shorter so that, eventually, the telomeres become so short that the cell can no longer divide. Geronimus et al. (2010) studied U.S. Black women and telomere shortening; note the importance they place on "perceived stress" in their abstract:

> We hypothesize that black women experience accelerated biological aging in response to repeated or prolonged adaptation to subjective and objective stressors. . . . We also perform a first population-based test of its plausibility, focusing on telomere length, a biomeasure of

aging that may be shortened by stressors. Analyzing data from the Study of Women's Health Across the Nation (SWAN), we estimate that at ages 49–55, black women are 7.5 years biologically "older" than white women. Indicators of perceived stress and poverty account for 27% of this difference. (19)

Following up on her early research, Geronimus (2013) calls for a "deep integration" approach to public health, linking epigenetics to weathering, for it's not just intrauterine or very early childhood that is corporeally inscribed. Rather, lifelong chronic stress can result in an accumulated "allostatic load" (described as "cumulative burden of chronic stress and life events" by Guidi et al. 2021); the concept of weathering then claims that racial discrimination is a cause of heightened allostatic load compared with other segments of the population.

Predictive Processing and Chronic Stress

With the notion of allostatic load, we come across an interesting connection with the currently prominent cognitive science school of "predictive processing." Predictive processing says that the brain seeks to minimize the gap between predictions of the environment and arriving sensory information that serves as error correction to those predictions. Current work looks at exteroceptive (from environment), proprioceptive (from musculoskeletal sensations), and interoceptive (internal milieu) prediction and sensation (Seth and Friston 2016). Error correction occurs as perceptual inference or active inference. Perceptual inference is changing beliefs to fit incoming sensation, thus reducing prediction errors from the previous cycle. Active inference is action to change sensation to fit beliefs. This could take the form of changing head position to hear or see better, or it could be dynamic anticipatory control of interoception. In unpredictable and dangerous environments, we should note, such error correction carries a heavy physiological cost, resulting in allostatic load.

Peters et al. (2017) is a very thought-provoking article that examines such physiological costs. The authors examine the "mathematical, neurobiological, and medical aspects of uncertainty." In other words, they bring together the Bayesian Brain, the Selfish Brain, and what we could call the Stressed Body. The Bayesian Brain concept looks at how brains minimize "free energy" in its information theory aspect as uncertainty in strategy choice for perceptual or active inference that would reduce prediction errors, while the Selfish Brain concept looks at the physiology of the stress response that provides cerebral energy via increased metabolic mechanisms enabling perceptual and active inference. The Stressed Body concept looks at the deleterious effects of unresolved uncertainty: in simple terms, somatic wear and tear or weathering in continual active inference in no-win situations. The authors outline three aspects of stress: First, stress is evoked by situations with novelty, unpredictability, and uncontrollability; second, there must be a sense of threat; and third, there must be multiple options for potentially uncertainty-resolving behavior. They then invoke three processes to resolve uncertainty: attention, learning, and habituation. In brief, information-hungry Bayesian Brains become hypervigilant to reduce uncertainty about strategy selection (information), and they selfishly need extra energy (thermodynamics) that is provided by the stress response.

Long-term stress, however, wears you out; you accumulate allostatic load. To alleviate uncertainty, goal-directed decision making is seen as active inference—that is, changing the probability distribution of relations of three types of states: (1) the current states of body or world; (2) attainable states (repertoire of actions/what you can do); and (3) goal states (where you would like to be). If you're confident that your actions will work, then you produce motor output. If you're uncertain, then you initiate an "emergency program" to get information to update beliefs and get inferences back in good shape. That is, stress reaction will sharpen senses/attention and increase learning via release of cortisol and catecholamines.

The upshot is that living through a no-win situation requires a juggling of multiple future scenarios, a cognitive load that has both affective and physiological consequences. The affective angle of irresolvable anxiety is matched by a physiological cost, per the "Selfish Brain" hypothesis, as fruitlessly searching to resolve uncertainty in choice of action in an essentially indeterminate future is itself a source of physiologically significant chronic stress. That is to say, in a no-win situation, if you don't revise down your expectations in "adaptive preference" (crudely speaking, being resigned to your fate), if you keep fighting to find a solution, if you stay "resilient" in the face of change, as we are endlessly told to do, then you become trapped in a hypervigilant, cortisol-soaked state to consume and process as much information as possible. But—and here is why the enactive interpretation of predictive processing to which we will shortly turn is important—the situation is ultimately political and material rather than epistemic; your problem is lack of power, not lack of information, so continuing an information search to refine your risk probabilities doesn't get you anywhere and in fact actually wears out your body, setting you up for an even worse case of Covid should you catch it.

Enaction and Chronic Stress

The enactive approach to cognition (Varela, Thompson, and Rosch 1991; Thompson 2007; Gallagher 2017) sees cognition and action linked in brain-body-world coupled dynamic systems. For the enactivists, the boundaries of the cognitive agent extend not only beyond the brain but also beyond the skin; body, brain, and world are structurally coupled or mutually co-determining, to use the enactivist terminology. The overall enactive complaint is that for restricted or classically neurocentric processing models, the body is there only as a support (it provides energy to the brain or modulates attention and learning by glucocorticoids), and the world is only a brake on perception as controlled hallucination (what predictive processing would be without feedback). In other words, for neurocentrists, the brain is in central command mode, rather than being part of an overall system (Hutto et al. 2020). Kirchhoff and Kiverstein (2019) adopt Hurley's (1998) notion of "extended dynamic singularity" or nexus of brain-body-world coupled dynamic systems. Kirchhoff and Kiverstein provide an account of the realization base of phenomenal consciousness extended by social and cultural practices; in Fanon's critical phenomenological terms, this would be a matter of sociogenic lived experience: "What it is like" to be a Black man cannot be divorced from its social setting, as being Black in a world of anti-Black racial colonialism is different from such experience in a differently racialized social setting.

Autonomous systems have self-production and self-distinction; enactive sense making is historical (path-dependent) as experience locks in habits and is extended sometimes to include active engagement with other agents that produce participatory sense making in which coupled dynamics have a life of their own (Thompson, Di Paolo, and Beer 2021). So intersubjectivity for enactivists is not just mindreading—that is, inferring hidden mental states to predict action, but entering dynamics with other agents whose emotions affect you. For our purposes, the enactivist challenge amounts to insisting that some problems are political rather than (purely) epistemic. You act to change the world to improve the flourishing of those with whom you interact, not just to change sensory inputs to better fit predictions.

When it comes to consciously accessible pondering of options, it's intuitively clear, I believe, that you can get worn out consciously "ruminating," or endlessly going over options in a no-win situation. There is a physiological cost even to subpersonal, offline simulations in conditional mode ("What would happen if I adopted this strategy?"). In high-stakes situations, with high-risk scenarios abounding on all sides, you get some allostatic load even before you act; predictive processing is supposed to save you from risks of damage involved with action in the world, but in these cases you are being damaged already. People in vulnerable social positions—that is, deleterious affective frames—then, are doubly punished, especially in double-bind or no-win situations: Even thinking about your options can exert a physiologically inscribed emotional cost, and then you must absorb the cost of the real-world feedback on top of that. In other words, in traditionally conceived allostatic action you're trying to change the world to restore a stable environment fit to habitual predictions. But if the world is recalcitrant, if the deck is stacked against you, then you get a double dose of allostatic load: not just a high cost to those allostatic actions that are swimming upstream in a racialized world, but there's even a high cost to simple internal scenario generation.

The Death of an "Essential Worker"

Shenetta White-Ballard lost her life while serving as an "essential worker" in her job as a nurse in a senior care facility. Naming people as "essential workers," and thereby changing their attendant risk profiles, differs across political jurisdictions. In the case at hand, Louisiana had a fairly standard "Stay at Home" order (Office of the Governor of Louisiana 2020) that included healthcare workers at the top of the list of "Essential Worker Functions," citing the Cybersecurity and Infrastructure Security Agency (CISA) guidelines of March 19 (Cybersecurity 2020). DeRobertis (2020; see also Guardian 2020) notes that Ms. White-Ballard suffered from a pre-existing condition: "A severe case of bronchitis followed by pneumonia had left the forty-four-year-old with chronic respiratory issues two years ago, so relying on oxygen to go about her daily life was a relatively new normal." We don't know the contribution of "weathering" here, but its presence should be a plausible hypothesis.

As might be expected, White-Ballard's employer reduced the situation to "choice" and willing assumption of risk on behalf of patients, thus naturalizing and individualizing the affective frame. DeRobertis reports, "Legacy representatives say White-Ballard made 'a personal choice' to continue working in an environment with Covid-19 positive patients." Nothing is said about financial circumstances or forced choices. "Mrs. White, like many healthcare professionals across the country, chose to continue serving her resident population," said Myles Holyfield, a Legacy spokesperson. "She did so with honor and professionalism. Shenetta is an example of risk that healthcare workers are willing to take while caring [for] the most vulnerable of our citizens." A bit later in the article the mealy-mouthed abnegation of corporate responsibility in the name of "choice" is made even more clear:

> A Legacy representative said White-Ballard was aware of her options. Some employees chose not to work in the facility because of Covid-19 positive residents. Others took a short leave of absence and have since returned to work, while others have chosen to not return at all. "These choices are very personal to health care workers across the industry," Holyfield said. "We, at Legacy, support those choices, whichever direction they may lead."

The reporter followed up with a better, more concrete analysis than sheer "choice" of the affective frame that produced the entangled individuation of self-image as caring worker and financial and viral risk management facing White-Ballard: "Yet friends and family said she was terrified. As the member of her household with more secure financial footing, she felt a responsibility to keep working." Here we see the affective term "terrified" linked to the status of the breadwinner responsible for the family; in the destruction of the social safety net—that is, the Great Risk Shift—the family becomes the locus of private debt's substituting for public policy, as we saw with Cooper. Another analysis from DeRobertis shows the double bind: "White-Ballard's experience on the front lines of the coronavirus battle highlights the plight of many essential workers these past few months: continue to work at a job that places an employee at risk of infection, or walk away and face serious financial challenges." Here we also see the predictive processing stress-load of constant risk calculation of viral and financial risk scenarios.

The conclusion of the article is gutwrenching. First, we read of those left behind: "Eddie Ballard, Shenetta White-Ballard's husband of eleven years, knows all too well the struggles of being 'essential' right now. He works at Walmart and has been given a two-week period to mourn his wife's death. His grief has debilitated him, he said, leaving him feeling aimless and unable to think clearly." DeRobertis quotes Ballard:

> "The only thing I'm doing right now is trying to hide it—I'm holding it down inside," Ballard said. "I know I have to release it, but I can't right now. I have too many things to do." Now, he has to both raise and provide for their 14-year-old son alone. For this reason, Ballard said he "can't completely break down" from his sadness. "I wish I could," he said.

Turning again for the last time to White-Ballard's situation, we see that self-subjectification as caring worker cannot ultimately be divorced from financial and viral risks. DeRobertis reports,

> A coworker of White-Ballard, who did not wish to be named to protect her job, said she feels it is not a mystery why her colleague returned day after day to a place that put her in danger. "The same reason as to why she was willing to go to work is the reason a lot of people are still going to work," she said. "They don't have anyone else to do [the job]. It has to get done."

At the very end of the article, DeRobertis reestablishes the double bind of affective workers who identify strongly with their caring for others: "Her husband said she never told him she dealt with Covid-19 patients; had he known, he would have demanded she find a way to stay home. Friends said she didn't feel financially stable enough to walk away, but also that she loved her patients and cared for them deeply." DeRobertis continues by quoting White-Ballard's husband as saying that she had "a beautiful heart" and that her husband wishes her "to be known for her sacrifice."

It's a truism of critical social theory that there's no such thing as a natural disaster. In Latourian terms, the SARS-CoV-2 virus is an actant in an Actor Network including social practices and individual human bodies as they have been shaped by social systems (Hanson 2020). The very genesis of contemporary zoonotic diseases, to say nothing of their rapid spread, is connected to practices of financialization and globalization that collapse distances between wildlife and humans on the one hand and enable mass air travel on the other (Wallace et al. 2020). One could say that with Covid-19 we are in a period that is globalizing and intensifying the "domus" theorized by James C. Scott (2017; Protevi 2019). Hence, to return to our Deleuzean framework, any one case of Covid-19 would be an individuation of the entire planetary disease system, including social, political, economic, and geographical aspects contributing to zoonotic origin, species transfer, propagation across nations, and then on a smaller scale the multiplicity of transmission, including factors of ventilation, distance, time, activity, and immune systems.

We must remember that biopower did not begin in March 2020 with Covid "lockdowns." Hence the desire to return to the "normal" rates for flu, asthma, COPD, and so on tempts us to overlook the multiple biopower dimensions that established the very same baseline rates to which we want to return. Furthermore, even keeping such a denaturalizing genealogy of the pre-Covid "normal" in mind as we scrutinize government Covid actions, we need to remember that not all "lockdowns" are the same, as different levels of government support are going to influence the fallout that takes the form of increased rates of depression, anxiety, domestic violence, substance abuse, and so on.

As we have seen with Chowkwanyun and Reed, Covid illness factors are all subject to gender, race, class, and other analyses. A more fine-grained analysis would add to those factors status as "essential workers," transport modes, intergenerational living, pre-existing conditions, and, as we have seen, personal and familial financial risk management. Following Adkins (2018), we have seen that underpaid essential healthcare workers faced increased virus risks to leverage their wages to take on the debt necessary to make ends meet. Many such people end up working for monthly payments to service their debt, which is no longer issued in view of repaying the total, but of providing a securitizable revenue stream. So, we have a multidimensional regime of risk on viral, physiological, domestic, and institutional levels. All these levels intersect governmental risk management in the naming of "essential workers" as those whose increased exposure to the Covid virus was an acceptable cost in implementing lockdowns: masks for all; remote work for some; in-person work for "essential workers." A final dimension to the multiplicity that individuated in White-Ballard's last days: As we noted above, emotional labor has a way of becoming a self-subjectifying practice, as many come to identify themselves with the caring aspects of a job. This only deepens the double bind: Not only must you work for your family's financial security, but you must also live up to your self-image as a caring health professional on the job, as well as provide emotional in addition to financial support to those at home.

In the reporting on White-Ballard's death we see all the dimensions of this case study of Covid as an affective frame: distributed biosocial systems individuated as "bodies politic"; the neoliberal self-family-health-entrepreneur juggling risks in our epoch of biopower; the corporealization of racism in weathering as a subset of "political physiology"; and essential worker status forcing a complex juggling of financial and health risks in a no-win situation; and finally, an affective-cognitive "allostatic load" from that risk juggling that we can speculate exacerbated weathering-enabled pre-existing conditions and "comorbidities" and contributed to the tragic death of Ms. White-Ballard.

Conclusion

A Politics of Joy

This book intervenes into a politically saturated discursive field. To be explicit about my motivations, I felt called to uphold an anti-fascist position. I am not, to be clear, accusing my colleagues who uphold the war-focused account of the evolution of prosociality of anything like fascism. I am, however, saying that the inter-group conflict story of human evolution is often taken up in the crudest way possible by fascist ideologues, so having alternate accounts on hand is useful, rather than just showing the mistakes made by fascist readings of the universal war literature (as necessary as such critique is).

I hope all of my work is anti-fascist. I have tried to sketch a view of human nature such that being anti-fascist is not swimming against the tide of an essentially violent human nature that needs a transcendent leader to keep the masses in check, to give them order and purpose more than squabbling, grubby, and ultimately nihilistic self-interest. In thinking of how to pursue an anti-fascist life, we are used to re-reading Foucault's Preface to the English translation of *Anti-Oedipus*, which gives it the alternate title of *Introduction to the Non-Fascist Life*—an "art of living counter to all forms of fascism"—and its equally famous, and frightening, invocation of the "fascism in us all." The question is how we can construct a notion of human nature such that we are not condemned to be forever fighting a deep drive to micro-fascism as the desire to have all human relations be those of command.

Writing in 1982, Foucault explains how, for a certain time in France (he specifies 1945–65) critical social thought had Marx and Freud as its obligatory reference points, along with "the greatest respect" for sign-systems. This conceptual field was then also the underlying borders of the usual readings of late 1960s social movements: "A war fought on two fronts: against social exploitation and psychic repression . . . had returned and set fire to reality itself: Marx and Freud in the same incandescent light" (Deleuze and Guattari 1977, xi–xii). While these two thinkers are certainly present, *Anti-Oedipus* is not a new Marx–Freud synthesis, Foucault continues; it's not a new system of thought, a "flashy Hegel." Rather, *Anti-Oedipus* is an "art," a guidebook helping us address the following: "How does one introduce desire into thought, into discourse, into action?" (xii). But "desire" has two valences in *Anti-Oedipus*, fascist and revolutionary, paranoid and schizophrenic, molar and molecular. To activate the kind of desire described by the latter term in each couple, we must defeat those desires described by the former terms, which lives as "the fascism in us all, in our heads and our everyday behavior, the fascism that causes us to love power, to desire the very thing that dominates and exploits us" (xiii). We must insist, however, that this "fascism in us all," if we are to be faithful to Foucault and to Deleuze and Guattari, must not be an ineradicable part of human nature but must instead be a historical artifact, an "assemblage." Hence some of Foucault's suggestions: Be multiple, not totalizing; never "terrorize" your readers, never claim to have found "the pure order"; be joyous, "Do not think one has to be sad to be militant"; above all, "Do not become enamored of power" (xiii). These last two are connected: Never be sad in that specifically Spinozist sense of bringing yourself and other people down, of sapping their horizontal power of friendship and cooperation in favor of a vertical power of command. These are memorable suggestions, well worth revisiting, pondering, and implementing.

The politics of joy is not straightforward, however. For those in the Spinoza–Deleuze line, joy arrives when you join an assemblage that increases your power. To live well, however, we must distinguish between active and passive joy: active joy comes when you have an adequate idea and are an adequate cause of the increase in power in an encounter—that is, when you understand how your singular essence is positively contributing to the increased power, as opposed to simply being passively uplifted by external forces. Our capacity for mutually active joyous encounters gives us the potential to resolve the conflict of egoism and altruism as in those cases' increasing my power increases yours.

Here we need the distinction between *pouvoir* and *puissance*. *Pouvoir* is transcendent power: It comes from above. It is hylomorphic, imposing form on the chaotic or passive material of the emotions or the mob. In its most extreme manifestation, it is fascistic: It is expressed not simply as the desire to rule but more insidiously as the longing for the strong leader to rescue us from the chaos into which our bodies politic have descended. Note that "bodies politic" here are both social and somatic. Fascists are obsessed with what they see as the inadequate security provided by liberal society (hence the vigilantism of action movies, wherein the tough guy rescues those innocents whom the feckless judges and conniving lawyers leave at the mercy of the bad guys) and by the corporeal decadence of "sexual deviants," "groomers," and the like (those being also enabled by the alleged laxity of liberal mores). *Puissance*, on the other hand, is immanent self-organization. It is the power of people working together to generate the structures of their social life. The difference between *pouvoir* and *puissance* allows us to nuance the notion of joyous and sad affect with the notions of active and passive power.

Consider the paradigm case of fascist joy. The Nazis at the Nuremberg rallies were filled with joyous affect, but this was a passive joy of being swept up into a mass movement. The Nazis' joy was triggered by the presence of a transcendent figure manipulating symbols (flags and faces) and by the imposition of a rhythm or a forced entrainment (marches and salutes and songs). Upon leaving the rally, they had no autonomous power (*puissance*) to make mutually empowering connections repeatable. In fact, they could feel sad only at being isolated, removed from the thrilling presence of the leader (Berghaus 1996; Thamer 1996). I propose an ethical standard: Does the encounter produce repeatable mutually active joyous affect in enacting positive care and cooperation? Does it increase the *puissance* of the bodies—that is, does it enable them to form new and mutually empowering encounters of care and cooperation outside the original encounter?

A final remark. I've tried to keep this Conclusion neutral with regard to classic questions in political philosophy. But I don't think I can make it all the way to the end, for, to develop capacities for active joyous encounters for self and others without qualification we need positive or substantive liberties that enable claims on material support and appropriate care. Despite the anthropological consensus that social evolutionism, in which states are our telos, is dead, if active joy is possible today only by reforming a liberal state toward democratic socialism, then so be it; if we are stuck with states, we might as well make them the best we can. But what kind of state, and what kind of liberalism, are we talking about? If current liberalism, as one might pessimistically think, is just the realization base for racialized and gendered capitalism, a base that is now being replaced as the current wave sweeping many states toward ethnonationalist fascism gains momentum, then revolution is our duty, whether it be anarchist, socialist, communist, or pluralist and polycentric. It's really not up to me to declare which way we will go, reform or revolution; there's only so many things a book can do, so it will be up to us to decide our fate by ballots or barricades.

Whatever the institutional base, one must be protected, cared for, and nurtured to reach one's prosocial potentials. I think there is a possible connection with the Sen / Nussbaum capabilities approach, but it must be "without qualification," to ward off the implicit economic productivity and political performance orientation of Sen and Nussbaum that Eva Feder Kittay detects. That's why I go with the capacity for joy that Kittay finds expressed in her daughter's life: "But I have since learned—from her, from the disability community and from my own observations—that she is capable of having a very good life, one full of joy, of love, of laughter" (Kittay 2005, 110). It's only then, relieved of the anxiety produced by artificial scarcity and its attendant egoism, that we have institutionalized the means to develop our prosocial potentials, whatever the register—art, science, politics, philosophy, love—for singular differenciations of the multiplicity of human nature. It's only then that we can continue to explore what we—self and others, without qualification—can become. It's then that we can truly live nonfascistically.

Notes

Introduction

1. For instance, even in the limit case of the berserker rage we examine in chapter 3, where we find an attenuation of subjective control and holes in autobiographical memory and it seems as if berserkers are possessed, as if someone else has taken over, nonetheless we can still identify cultural triggers of the biologically inherited rage mechanism. No one just snaps, even if it might seem that way because their defense mechanism thresholds have been lowered by previous trauma; they snap because their buttons were pushed, because a social situation—in war or at home—so triggers them that they lash out. Rage is a prey reaction; it differs from atrocity, which is predatory, even if frenzied.

2. As I explain in depth in chapter 2, I use the term "enact" deliberately to refer to the political implications of Francisco Varela's notion of enaction.

3. The term I developed in Protevi (2009) for the biocultural human being is "body politic," with both social and somatic connotations ("body politic" is nominal in referring to a society, while "politic" is adjectival in referring to individuals; in that sense, "body politic" means "politically shaped body"). For the closely aligned "neuroanthropology" school, see Lende and Downey (2012), Kirmayer et al. (2020), and Wexler (2006).

4. Note that, while this is not a focus of this book the way it was in my *Political Affect* (2009) and *Life, War, Earth* (2013), I think these scientific approaches are consistent with Deleuze's metaphysics, with a dose of Simondon, in which pre-individual networks or "multiplicities" of interacting processes produce relatively stabilized individuated beings still in touch with their pre-individual pools of potentials; in other words, individuation is always trans-individual. For more, see Scott (2015) and Read (2015). For essays combining enaction and Simondon, see Di Paolo (2020) and Di Paolo and De Jaegher (2021).

5. Andrews (2023) presents an interesting case for "normative regularities" as "a socially maintained pattern of behavioral conformity within a community" (35) not limited to linguistically mediated explicit rules and including reward as well as punishment.

6. In a justly famous phrase, H. Rap Brown said in 1967: "Violence . . . is as American as cherry pie" (quoted in Singer 2021). The full passage reads, "I say

violence is necessary. Violence is a part of America's culture. It is as American as cherry pie. Americans taught the black people to be violent. We will use that violence to rid ourselves of oppression if necessary. We will be free, by any means necessary."

7. See Miguel de Beistegui (2018) on the imposition of the sexuality *dispositif* as prompted by forensic befuddlement at murders that are irrational for the *homo economicus* that was the object of governmentality; they could be explained only as perversions of a supposedly natural sexual instinct.

8. Various aspects of the notion of violence in Deleuze or Deleuze and Guattari are studied in Milisavljević and Sibertin-Blanc (2017), Milisavljević (2012), Schinkel (2013), and Masset (2013). Sibertin-Blanc (2016) is particularly important for this book because he studies three major regimes of violence: arché-violence, the formation of the state; exo-violence, the violence of the war-machine outside of the state; and endo-violence, the violence of capital and axiomatics.

9. Form of content and form of expression are discussed in chapters 3 and 5 of Deleuze and Guattari (1987). For commentary, see Holland (2013), Adkins (2015), Bogue (2018), and Wasser (2018).

10. Deleuze and Guattari (1987) also discuss urban societies and ecumenical social forms. We will discuss Deleuze and Guattari's notion of capitalism in passing in chapter 6 on marronage (the question of capitalist slavery).

11. The State appropriation of the nomad war machine is not quite the transformation of qualitative into quantitative we see with State capture of primitive societies, as the Steppe nomad war machine had its own form of numbering (Deleuze and Guattari 1987, 387–94). For more on the State regime of violence in particular, see Schinkel 2013, Sibertin-Blanc 2016, Smith 2018, and the sources cited previously in note 7.

12. For commentary, see, *inter alia*, Holland (2013), Adkins (2015), and Patton (2018).

13. Any attempt to outline the vast and constantly expanding literature on terrorism is bound to fail. Just to mention a few prominent works in the realm of philosophy and "Theory," I have found Colebrook (2022), Erlenbusch-Anderson (2018), Puar (2017), and Agamben (2005) to be important and useful.

14. Lawlor finds, in his examination of Derrida, that the singularity of a person or an event must appear to a subject as other than the subject, but this very appearing as other forces upon it an iterability and a generalizing that violates the singularity of the other (2016, 5–6).

15. The social violence in the institutionalized torture of solitary confinement is examined in devastating detail in Guenther (2013).

16. I provide a deconstructive reading of Kant's use of *Gewalt*, which encompasses meanings of force, violence, and authority, in Protevi (1994 and 2001).

17. There is a huge literature on structural violence, racism, and "necropolitics" (Mbembe 2003). My notion here connects with Ruth Wilson Gilmore's definition of racism as "the state-sanctioned or extralegal production and exploitation of group-differentiated vulnerability to premature death" (Gilmore 2007, 29).

18. Although I will not be able to treat Kronfeldner (2018) in this book, I do agree with her claim that we should be "post-essentialist" when discussing human nature.

19. On the whole, experts see humans as actually quite pacific when it comes to incidents of direct physical violence in the vast majority of our daily interactions, as illustrated by the memorable image that opens Hrdy (2009), who contrasts the humdrum deplaning of humans after a long plane ride from the mayhem that would have ensued with chimpanzees as passengers. This everyday face-to-face pacificity of course does not invalidate critiques of oppression, domination, exploitation, and other structural factors in many social formations; you can be harmed even if you are not struck.

20. "Multiplicity" is one of the most commented-on concepts in Deleuze's philosophy. It would be impossible to provide a comprehensive bibliography on the term. I will say a bit more about it in chapter 1. I discuss it at length in Protevi (2009) and (2013); in those works, I am influenced by De Landa (2002).

21. To be precise, while I think you can make sense of the notion of cultural selection, I don't think genes are the units of selection, as opposed to developmental systems (what I'm calling here biocultural ways of life, including child-rearing and prestige gradients for adults). There can be variation of ways of life that under inter-group competition can be selected against: Selection under-determines optimality but weeds out nonviability. So, for instance, a society whose way of life produces defensive capacities that can be overwhelmed in zero-sum competition could be driven to extinction, as the history of genocidal warfare attests, but that's not to say that in all cases all the genes in the victimized population are removed as opposed to their way of life's being destroyed (e.g., in cultural assimilation practices many native peoples suffered after contact with Europeans such as residential schools, forced adoptions, and the like). It is true that all genes might be removed in the case of an utter extermination, caused by overt violence coupled with susceptibility to disease, but not all genocides are utter exterminations.

1. Human Nature

1. The occasion for the essay on which this chapter is based was an invitation by Rosi Braidotti and Rick Dolphjin to contribute to their edited collection, *Deleuze and Guattari and Fascism* (Braidotti and Dolphjin 2022). I am grateful to Edinburgh University Press for allowing me to adapt that essay here.

2. In chapter 3 of Protevi 2009 I use Deleuze and Guattari's gnomic utterance that "the organism is the judgment of God" to examine Aristotle's embodied pedagogy; in so doing, I trace Aristotle's thought of the best life as that in which properly situated and trained adult male citizens have the occasional ability to most fully and most often actualize the identity of divine and human activity in flashes of theoretical intuition.

3. For example, despite his commitment to the *tabula rasa*, Locke does seem to uphold something of a fallen human nature stance, whereby left to its own devices, that is, bereft of properly institutionalized discipline, a fundamental lassitude will triumph. Consider his proposal on the treatment of the poor in England, which, when coupled with his paean to the industriousness found among the proto-capitalists in the state of nature, paints a picture whereby a lack of self-imposed discipline on the part of the poor requires its supplementation by forced labor to keep the tendency to vice and idleness at bay: "If the cause of this evil be well looked into, we humbly conceive it will be found to have proceeded neither from scarcity of provisions, nor from want of employment for the poor, since the goodness of God has blessed these times with plenty, no less than the former, and a long peace during those reigns gave us as plentiful a trade as ever. The growth of the poor must therefore have some other cause, and it can be nothing else but the relaxation of discipline and corruption of manners; virtue and industry being as constant companions on the one side as vice and idleness are on the other" (Locke 2003, 447).

4. Probably the most extreme example of this line of thought is Michael Ghiselin's notorious passage: "The evolution of society fits the Darwinian paradigm in its most individualistic form. Nothing in it cries out to be otherwise explained. The economy of nature is competitive from beginning to end. Understand that economy, and how it works, and the underlying reasons for social phenomena are manifest. They are the means by which one organism gains some advantage to the detriment of another. No hint of genuine charity ameliorates our vision of society, once sentimentalism has been laid aside. What passes for cooperation turns out to be a mixture of opportunism and exploitation. The impulses that lead one animal to sacrifice himself for another turn out to have their ultimate rationale in gaining advantage over a third; and acts 'for the good' of one society turn out to be performed to the detriment of the rest. Where it is in his own interest, every organism may reasonably be expected to aid his fellows. Where he has no alternative, he submits to the yoke of communal servitude. Yet given a full chance to act in his own interest, nothing but expediency will restrain him from brutalizing, from maiming, from murdering his brother, his mate, his parent, or his child. Scratch an 'altruist' and watch a 'hypocrite' bleed" (Ghiselin 1974, 247; cited in Ruse 1985, 88).

5. Wynter 2003.

6. That section tackles the notion of "specificity," or what distinguishes *Homo sapiens* from other primates, the third of three senses of "human nature" considered by Kronfeldner (2018), the most important of recent philosophical works on human nature. For space considerations I omit discussion of the other senses, "fixity" in development, which I gloss as "dynamic interactionism" in Protevi 2013; and the "typicality" of prosociality. For useful reviews of Kronfelder 2018, see Honenberger 2019 and Downes 2019.

7. Among the sources I've consulted to compose this paragraph are Barker 2015 and Downes 2018.

8. For instance, one could say it's a good thing our ancestors developed a fear response triggered by the presentation of potential harmful situations; it's another thing altogether for that to drift into the free-floating anxiety of living in a gig economy with an eroding social safety net. For a comprehensive treatment of fear and anxiety, see LeDoux 2015.

9. As a result, two publications that often appear in Evolutionary Psychology treatments of the regimes of violence in the EEA are Wrangham and Peterson (1996) and Wrangham (1999).

10. Although I will stay within a largely adaptationist, though suitably modified, evolutionary paradigm in this chapter, looking at how joy could function as a proximate mechanism for sharing, whose adaptive character I will argue for, in chapter 4 I will take seriously a nonutilitarian take on joy in sports. I give a reading of what could be called the metaphysics of joy in Spinoza, Nietzsche, and Bergson in Protevi (2020).

11. After composing the bulk of this book, I came across two noteworthy books on moral progress from an evolutionary perspective: Buchanan and Powell (2018) and Kumar and Campbell (2021). Unfortunately, then, I won't be able to note too many points of agreement and disagreement. Among the former, perhaps the most important is a naturalist argument for "adaptively plastic morality" such that institutional frames producing security can allow for "inclusive morality." There are some disagreements, however, especially their portrayal of the EEA as marked by inter-group conflict fueled by competition over scarce resources. While it is true that Buchanan and Powell (2018) take note of positions critical of widespread early inter-group conflict—they cite Sterelny (2014) and Kelly (2005)— they nonetheless place more emphasis on conflict than I do. While war is undoubtedly a large part of late human history, I emphasize anthropological literature on early cooperation and relative abundance and indeed challenge the very notion of "groups." If it is the case that cooperative sharing was risk-buffering, then it's possible we could find conditions conducive to "inclusivist" morality in the EEA because, while Buchanan and Powell are correct that inclusivity is not a "scaled-up" version of group-bond cooperation, if "groups" are not the final word on the social

ontology of the EEA foragers, then networked generalized reciprocity might actually qualify as inclusivity.

12. I provide an extended treatment of my version of human nature as "dynamic interactionism" in a Deleuzean reading of Wexler (2006) in Protevi (2013).

13. I provide lengthy discussions of virtuality and actuality in Protevi (2009 and 2013); I am influenced in those works by De Landa (2002).

14. Mauss (1990). Derrida (1992) sees the pure gift, extracted from any economic relation, as aporetic or "impossible"; for a critique of Derrida's reading of Mauss, see Hénaff (2020), who thinks Derrida throws the baby out with the bathwater by identifying "gift" *simpliciter* with "pure gift," as there are incommensurate kinds of gifts. I delve into Derrida's thought on the gift of life in Protevi (1997); there, it is the asymmetry of the gift of life from parent to child that at least approaches a "pure gift," in that children can extend the life of their parents (give them more life) but can never give them life.

15. I cover the debate among proponents of the "Theory Theory," simulation, and phenomenological conceptions of TOM in Protevi (2013); for the idea that we pick up TOM through narrative practices, see Hutto (2012) and for TOM as a culturally produced "cognitive gadget" see Heyes (2018).

16. On the neuroscience of joy, see Panksepp (1998), chapter 13 (280–99), who ties it to rough-and-tumble play and to touch. The only extended treatment of joy from an evolutionary psychology perspective I've found is Meadows (2013), who focuses on pair-bonding in mating couples and its relation to child-rearing, with a brief mention of friendship with cooperating partners as transcending utilitarian calculation: "When both parties cooperate, the repeated exchanges of help tend to develop a sense of trust and a favorable feeling toward each other. These interactions go beyond pragmatic utility because friendship and fellow feeling transcend this utility. Assistance is given to the other party without the expectation of a pragmatic exchange of rewards" (96). We will pick up on the theme of autotelic joy in discussing sport in chapter 4. For recent work on joy in nonhuman animals with the potential for illuminating the evolution of human joy, see Nelson et al. (2023).

17. I distinguish my approach from that of contemporary positive psychology by my interest in evolutionary anthropology. For a survey of contemporary work on joy in positive psychology, see M. Johnson (2020). The political critique of positive psychology claims it is content with recommending resilience as coping with bad social conditions and is complicit with the pathologizing of those discontents with domination, exploitation, and injustice. For a review of these criticisms, including the claims that positive psychology amounts to "neo-liberal ideology" and is simply a "capitalist venture" selling an impossible ideal, see Van Zyl et al. (2023). For a social constructivist critique, see Burr and Dick (2022).

18. This notion of joy is compatible with a suitably trans-individual reading of Spinoza (Read 2015), as I will explore in more detail in the discussion of relational

autonomy in chapter 4. Trans-individuality points to the relational dimension of selfhood: We are who we are through our relations to others. For Spinoza (1992), joy is the increase in power to affect and be affected, so joy can occur in sharing because we are trans-individual: You increase your power when you increase the power of others to act in ways that recognize their trans-individuality. That is, when we know human beings, we know that, as *Ethics* Part 4, P35, C1 says: "There is no individual thing in the universe more advantageous to man than a man who lives by the guidance of reason." Hence, following P36: Living together in a rationally organized society—one that also supports and encourages rationality—we find that the highest good of virtuous people is common to everyone. There is no zero-sum game here: Seeking your own advantage is seeking to live in a rationally organized society with other rational people.

19. We are on dangerous ground here in particular once we recall the Nazi uptake of a "struggle for existence" as a central motif in their version of Darwinism (Weikart 2013) and Social Darwinism (Hawkins 1997). Nonetheless, the absence of any teleology of the state or hierarchy of races in the Kropotkin position should insulate us from that.

20. For a primer on Kropotkin's Darwinism, see Gould (1988). For an in-depth look at the marginalization of what the author calls Kropotkin's "Socialist Darwinism" in favor of Social Darwinism that is due to fearful reaction against the Paris Commune and other social reform and revolutionary events, see Johnson (2019).

21. Gonzalez-Cabrera (2019) commenting on Tomasello: "[O]ne idea for further exploration would be to think of our capacity for normative guidance as having been selected for to avoid disappointing a relationship partner's expectations in a more tolerant social environment when hominins became more interdependent foragers. . . . Norms would be conceived as shared expectations about how individuals ought to behave in a given situation, i.e., they would be represented as joint intentional states. These expectations were necessary to carry out tasks that required complex coordination such as collaborative foraging and more so to build the kind of collective cultural institutions that are the distinctive feature of behaviorally modern humans" (541).

22. "Everyone" here also includes Rousseau (1997), who is crystal clear about the violence of "nascent society" at the beginning of Part 2 of the *Discourse on Inequality.*

23. Among the modern forms of political experimentation Graeber and Wengrow (2021, 544n48) find interesting is the use of warfare in the "society against the state" thesis put forth by Clastres (1989 and 1994), to which we will return in chapters 5 and 6. Viveiros de Castro (2019, 89) upholds the irreducibly political nature of such warfare by reminding us that Clastres never held that all South American nonstate peoples used warfare as an anti-state mechanism. Hence those who did were not compelled by ecological or social circumstances.

24. I draw the term "legible" here from Scott (1998, 2009, 2017) to denote the accountancy condition for State capture, which is composed of comparison and appropriation. To compare crop yields of a plot of land, state officials need to be able to see and count the produce, hence the dependence of early State societies on grains as opposed to tubers.

25. From a functionalist-adaptationist perspective, ritual wars, with their limited time, space, and mortality, might have evolved as a means, albeit at risk of escalation and hence failing at its goal, of preventing all-out war. Such ritualization may have been thrown off-kilter by European colonialism, resulting in novel forms of genocidal war (Blick 1988).

26. Richard Wrangham (2017) attempts to finesse the psychological implausibility argument by his interesting distinction of hot-headed reactive versus cold-blooded planning aggression, with the former selected against by Boehm-style internal selection and the latter the means by which that selection is accomplished, but also available for inter-group raids. I think this distinction founders, however, as hot-headed anger is needed for many instances of hand-to-hand combat; you can plan all you want, but when the blows start landing your rage is very easily triggered, and once rage is activated in battle, the threshold for its expression back home is lowered to the point where it would be easily triggered in in-group settings, thus attracting in-group selection against it. See chapter 3 for more on the berserker rage, the limit case of hot-headed anger.

27. Note that, according to Tomasello et al. (2012), Sterelny (2014), and others in the interdependency school, cooperation evolves by mutualism and reciprocity, not by group-level selection.

28. This is called "adaptive plasticity" by Buchanan and Powell (2018) and Kumar and Campbell (2022). See note 11.

2. Affective Ideology

1. Portions of this chapter appeared as "Stanley on Ideology" in *Theoria: An International Journal for Theory, History and Foundations of Science* 31 (3): 357–69. I am grateful to *Theoria* for allowing me to adapt that essay here.

2. See Protevi (2009, 2010, and 2013) for a more fully worked-out story.

3. For an overview that distinguishes enactivism from cognitivism and resonates with the notion of a political philosophy of mind, using the congenial term "cultural permeation," see Hutto et al. (2020).

4. The original "extended mind" article is Clark and Chalmers (1998), who propose a "parity principle": If a cognitive process loops into the world in a way that, were the process to occur completely within the brain, it would count as a cognitive act, then the world-involving act should be seen as cognitive as well.

5. For commentaries by Slaby, Gallaher, and others, see Pickford (2022).

6. For a noteworthy discussion of naturalist normativity, which takes seriously politically maladaptive positions, see Rouse (2023).

7. This is not to deny the existence of puzzling experiences, which don't fit the pre-existing concepts, or moral dilemmas, in which an action is susceptible of multiple and conflicting interpretations. Without my wanting to produce a full phenomenological description of those cases but simply to insist on the essential co-presence of affect and cognition in experience, note that there is a characteristic affective tone of puzzlement, or of being stuck, of being pulled in two (or indeed more) directions, or of hewing to-and-fro between commitments. And that we often experience a felt sense of relief in having made a decision, or foreboding at the outcome of our decision, or a sense of resignation to our fate, or a sense of commitment to the type of person we are making of ourselves by this decision, and so on and so forth.

8. For introductory comments on shared intentionality and the cooperative motives that enable it, see Tomasello (2009). For early cultural learning's fulfilling the psychological sense of ideology—transmitting the basic concepts of a society, including those of technical procedures, see Sterelny (2012).

9. Gilbert (2014) provides a genealogy of presuppositions about mass sociality from Hobbes through Le Bon and Freud that must be critically examined, and the practices based on such presuppositions defeated, to rehabilitate a notion of democratic self-organization that would not be liable to neoliberal authoritarianism, which, as we see today, is shading toward outright fascism.

10. The question of desensitization is difficult; one might think that experience in violence, by desensitization, would ease the barriers to the engagement in violence, but burnout is also possible, such that it is sometimes newcomers who are more likely to engage in violent activity, though sometimes, because of their freshness, the results of witnessing the carnage can be emotionally devastating.

11. One of the best works on the social psychology of violence I know, and the study of which is the source from which I draw most of these remarks, is Collins (2009).

3. Berserkers

1. The occasion for writing the text on which this chapter is based was an invitation to present work at a conference on the "inhuman gaze," held at the Centre Culturel Irlandais in Paris in June 2018. It subsequently appeared as "Phenomenology of the Blackout Rage: The Inhibition of Episodic Memory in Extreme Berserker Episodes," in Anya Daly, Fred Cummins, James Jardine, and Dermot Moran, eds., *Perception and the Inhuman Gaze* (New York: Routledge, 2022), 218–35. I am grateful to Routledge for permission to adapt that essay here.

2. I will speculate on the appearance of berserkers in exogenous mechanisms (i.e., those led by maroons in nonstate regimes of violence) of state-formation in chapter 5.

3. That the berserker rage violates the American imperial regime of violence does not exempt actions that conform to it from moral judgment. In this case, even if Bales had followed his rules of engagement, the entire Afghanistan mission that put him there would have to be analyzed. In philosophical terms, granted that Bales violated the terms of just war action (*jus in bello*), was the United States justified in terms of starting a war by invading Afghanistan (*jus ad bellum*)—that is, treating 9/11 as an act of war rather than as a crime to be resolved by nonmilitary means?

4. Regarding its automaticity, our culture substitutes mechanical metaphors for the divine possession metaphors of other cultures. Note then the reference to "autopilot" and "felt something switch" in Vaughan 2015, an interview with Robert Bales, a contemporary American berserker.

5. See Flanagan 2016 for a criticism of this basically Aristotelian position on the appropriateness of some forms and intensities of anger; although he does not advocate a universal condemnation of all forms of anger, he does propose a smaller range of appropriate forms than is the contemporary American norm.

6. The Robert Bales case was multifactorial, but we can note that one of the soldiers he was charged with protecting had lost a leg hours before Bales committed the massacre. The Bales massacre occurred in Afghanistan in March 2012. Bales, who was a staff sergeant charged with providing base security for combat troops, killed sixteen civilians in two villages near base in two trips at 3:00 A.M. while dressed in Afghan clothes over his military uniform. Three other factors besides the injury to one of his soldiers are mentioned: (a) alcohol and steroid use; (b) mefloquine, a malaria drug with possible psychological effects (Miller 2013); (c) domestic and financial trouble, as three days previously his house was put up for sale in an "underwater mortgage" in which the property was listed for less than what he had paid for it in 2005, and less than what he owed the bank (Sherwell 2012).

4. Esprit de Corps

1. The occasion for the text on which this chapter is based was the 2022 Spindel Conference at the University of Memphis, on the theme of "Relational Autonomy and Collective Intentionality." I am grateful to Shaun Gallagher for the invitation, and to conference participants for helpful comments. The essay appeared as "*Esprit de corps* and thinking on (and with) your feet: Standard, enactive, and poststructuralist aspects of relational autonomy and collective intentionality in team sports," *Southern Journal of Philosophy*, special issue, Spindel Conference 2022

(September 2023). I am grateful to Wiley-Blackwell, the publishers of the *Southern Journal of Philosophy*, for permission to adapt that essay here.

2. My thanks to Adriel M. Trott for prompting me to think about shared joy in competitive running.

3. A video clip of the goal can be found at https://www.youtube.com/watch?v=0B4q6di-3fg.

4. In the philosophy tradition, we could refer to Bataille's notion of *dépense* or joyous wasting of energy (Bataille 1984), and to Deleuze and Guattari's (1977) notion of anti-production from *Anti-Oedipus*.

5. On the neuroscience of play, see Panksepp (1998), chapter 13 (280–99).

6. Speaking of exuberant life, allow me to indulge a brief metaphysical excursus. The discontent with the grindingly pragmatic adaptationist orientation of much evolutionary work is displayed by Nietzsche, who complained that what he saw as the Darwinist emphasis on survival and reproduction missed the active power dimension of life (and indeed of being itself; see Ansell Pearson 1997; Richardson 2008). For Nietzsche in *Genealogy of Morality* (1997), what life seeks is self-overcoming and expansion of power, which is only crudely expressed as power over others in the form of command, as opposed to the noble power expressed in self-overcoming. We could follow Deleuze's reading of Nietzsche (Deleuze 1983) and connect that to Spinoza and see beings as expressions of the divinely natural power to be, to affect and be affected (Protevi 2012 and 2020). Spinozist being is constantly modulating itself, growing or shrinking. Joy is the growth in our power to be; as we saw at the end of chapter 1, it is active joy when we are the adequate cause of that growth, which comes down to understanding the contribution of our singular essence to the consequences of our encounters.

7. See also Grosz (2008) for a Deleuzean account of diversifying beauty from sexual selection.

8. For a fascinating poststructuralist treatment of soccer, see Brian Massumi's analysis, where, with typical verve, he makes the ball the subject of the play around which the players gravitate and coalesce (Massumi 2002, 71–82).

9. As Nelson et al. (2023) put it: "Play behaviour is another potentially useful marker of joy. Play in humans is interwoven with joy, pleasure, and happiness. Indeed, by generating positive states, play is self-rewarding" (1559).

10. There's something of a curious reticence in talking about love, once an essential concern of the greats (what would Plato, Aristotle, Augustine be with talk of love?) in contemporary philosophy, though there are signs of a resurgence of interest. A recent essay on love is De Jaegher (2021): "Our most sophisticated human knowing, I think, lies in how we engage with each other, in our relating. . . . [We need a] new, engaged—or even engaging—epistemology of human knowing. The enactive theory of participatory sense-making takes steps towards this, but it needs

deepening. I propose to look at human knowing through the lens of loving. We then see that both knowing and loving are existential, dialectic ways in which concrete and particular beings engage with each other" (847).

5. Statification

1. The occasion for the essay on which this chapter is based was an invitation by Henry Somers-Hall and Jeff Bell to contribute to their edited collection *The Deleuzian Mind* (New York: Routledge, 2024). I am grateful to Routledge for allowing me to adapt that essay here.

2. I use the majuscule "State" for the concept or abstract machine of overcoding or capture (terms I will explain in the text), and the minuscule "state" for empirically real concrete assemblages that effectuate, to one degree or another, that abstract machine. This use of "state" conforms to Deleuze and Guattari's notion of "State apparatus" (Deleuze and Guattari 1987, 223).

3. These are linked but, I believe, analytically separable processes. Overcoding allows comparison while capture denotes appropriation of a portion of a flow. Deleuze and Guattari call the abstract statification process "overcoding" and the concrete assemblage of comparison and appropriation in any statifying society an "apparatus of capture."

4. In addition, "ecumenical" social formations of an economic, religious, or artistic nature are said to link these heterogenous forms (Deleuze and Guattari 1987, 435).

5. Deleuze and Guattari see mutation as made possible by resistance to and escape from order (or conversely, order is the coagulation of mutability). Order, as the result of overcoding and capture, is the goal of the statification process; the limit case of complete order is "the State." Conversely, the most intense empirical form of an anti-order social process supporting mutation is the Steppe nomads and their "war machine." The abstract social formation process of anti-order mutation is then named "nomadism," and the process of mutation is called "installing a war machine."

6. As we will discuss in chapter 6, the term "maroon" comes from the context of Atlantic slavery but is now applied as a general term for those fleeing states.

7. This is the current interpretation of Çatalhöyük (Graeber and Wengrow 2021, 212–25), which Deleuze and Guattari classify as an empire (Deleuze and Guattari 1987, 428).

8. Hence, we need to distinguish my use of "limit" in the mathematical sense of an asymptote from Deleuze and Guattari's quasi-marginalist sense of limit as last exchange that preserves the qualitative behavior of an assemblage.

9. In Protevi (2019) I used James C. Scott for an analysis of the infrastructure of the trans-egalitarian society as "domus" (Scott 2017, 116)—that is, sedentarized

gathering of domesticated animals, plants, and humans. We could say the domus is an economic form and trans-egalitarian chiefdom is a political form.

10. Carneiro (1970) is the archetypal conflict theory, with an emphasis on geographical constraints.

11. I could have ordered these two chapters differently, discussing maroons first, then states. Either way, however, cross-references would be necessary at multiple points, and I ultimately chose to discuss statification first as my discussion of maroons in the Atlantic enslavement system presupposes multiple European states and their New World colonies.

12. I thank Jeanne Etelain for suggesting autonomy as the goal for maroons.

13. In chapter 6 we will investigate the claims that the social structure of the Brazilian seventeenth-century maroon community of Palmares contained State elements.

14. In chapter 3 of Protevi (2013) I speculated on the affective side of the regime of violence of the hill people who served as skirmishers in the imperial armies of Mesopotamia.

6. Marronage

1. I would like to thank the organizers, Rodrigo Nunes and Ulysses Pinheiro, of the conference at which these ideas were first presented ("Tomar os desejos por realidade: 50 anos de O anti-Édipo," Universidade Federal do Rio de Janeiro, Brazil, October 3–5, 2022, https://congressoantiedipo.wixsite.com/my-site-1), as well as everyone working with them. The essay on which this chapter is based appeared as "The Multiplicity of Marronage," *La Deleuziana*, Dossier 50 years of Anti-Oedipus / 2023, volume 1: Taking Desires for Reality, 111–28, http://www.ladeleuziana.org/wp-content/uploads/2023/06/7_Protevi_The-multiplicity-of-marronage.pdf. I am grateful to the editors of *La Deleuziana* for permission to adapt my essay here.

2. I would like to dedicate this chapter to the memory of Gwendolyn Midlo Hall, a great historian of the transatlantic slave trade and author of the masterpiece *Africans in Colonial Louisiana* (1992), who passed away in 2022. Her writings on the resistance and creativity of the enslaved people of Louisiana have inspired me for many years.

3. For the distinction of smooth and striated space, see Deleuze and Guattari 1987 (474–500).

4. I draw the portrait of the multiplicity of marronage from accounts of various instances of maroon communities in Surinam (Price 1976), Jamaica (Patterson 1979; Kopytoff 1978; A. M. Johnson 2020), Brazil (Kent 1965; Freitas 1990; Schwartz 1992; Anderson 1996; Thornton 2008), Haiti (Fick 1990; Casimir 2020; Roberts 2015), and the United States (Aptheker 1979). For treatments of general

178 · NOTES TO CHAPTER 6

themes of marronage, I rely on the introduction to Price 1979, as well as on Scott 2009 and 2016, Roberts 2015, and Bona 2016.

5. Jeanne Etelain helped me greatly by suggesting "autonomous zone" as a name for the geography of maroon societies, as well as reminding me of the possibility that some maroons joined pirate bands.

6. That's not to say that marronage wasn't an important factor in the Saint Domingue revolution (Fick 1990, 7), which did indeed seek to destroy the colonial slave state; the role of former maroons in the turbulence of postrevolutionary Haiti, the struggle between those who wanted to replace the colonial state with another state or with a nonstate "counter-plantation system" (Casimir 2020), is a matter of ongoing historical investigation, whose political economy dimensions are explored in Nesbitt 2022.

7. Deleuze and Guattari write at AO 334F, referring to Jackson's line from July 28, 1970, quoted as the epigraph to this essay, "Il se peut que je fuie, mais tout au long de ma fuite, je cherche une arme!" which is translated by Lane, Hurley, and Seem as "I may take flight, but all the while I am fleeing, I will be looking for a weapon!" at AO 277E. For commentary on the incorporation of Jackson's writings into Deleuze and Guattari's works, see Koerner 2011.

8. Some uses of "enslave" in the English version of *Anti-Oedipus* are translations of *asservissement* (Deleuze and Guattari 1977, 249 and 365). Note also that "machinic enslavement" in the English version of *A Thousand Plateaus* is a translation of "l'asservissement machinique" (Deleuze and Guattari 1987, 451 and 456).

9. The text at Deleuze and Guattari 1987, 569n43, refers to Parain 1969; see also Bert 2013 and above all Badaire 2023.

10. I am grateful to Quentin Badaire for the invitation to attend his seminars with the Collège International de Philosophie in Paris in Spring 2023, which provided me much help with this topic.

11. Deleuze and Guattari here presumably refer to what is known as inter-group "ritual war," an anthropological topic much in debate in the early war discussions we covered earlier in chapter 1. As we also saw in chapter 1, the intra-group regime of violence of nomadic foragers is detailed by Boehm (2012a and 2012b) as a "reverse dominance hierarchy" in which slackers and bullies are ridiculed, exiled, or killed.

12. Compare the notion of necropolitics in Mbembe (2003).

13. John Locke was Secretary for the Lord Proprieters of Carolina when that phrase was penned. The debate over Locke's role in the transatlantic slave system is quite large. Among other pieces, see Bernasconi and Mann 2005, Uzgalis 2017, and Brewer 2017.

14. I examined the "affective ideology" necessary for such torture to occur in chapter 2.

15. Maroon raids terrorized white settlers. Aptheker reminds us of Hobbes when he cites an 1823 *Norfolk Herald* article claiming that whites "have for some time been kept in a state of mind peculiarly harassing and painful, from the too apparent fact that their lives are at the mercy of a band of lurking assassins, against whose fell designs neither the power of the law, or vigilance, or personal strength and intrepidity, can avail" (Aptheker 1979, 151). For Hobbes, the state of war is a length of time of uncertainty; it's the psychological stress of the state of war that motivates the desire to join social contract. Note also that whites have claimed "law" on their side (cf. Deleuze and Guattari's apparatus of capture analysis: The original violence of statification defines resistance as crime that law and police combat in secondary violence or lawful application of force). After the death of a white man, the *Norfolk Herald* article continues, "No individual after this can consider his life safe from the murdering aim of these monsters in human shape" (note here the Lockean animalizing language). The goal of the militia was to kill the maroons and "thus relieve the neighbouring inhabitants from a state of perpetual anxiety and apprehension." Needless to say, that's the intended state in which slaves were to be kept (Patterson 2018).

16. Deleuze and Guattari mention African slaves as a figure of affect in American literature of the beat generation: "[C]aught between two nightmares of Indian genocide and the slavery of the blacks, Americans made of the black a repressed image of the force of affect, of a multiplication of affects" (Deleuze and Guattari 1987, 283).

7. The Capitol Invasion

1. The essay on which this chapter is based was originally formulated in response to an invitation by Gohkan Kodalak. It will appear as "Under the Dome: The Capitol Invasion," in Stavros Kousoulas and Andrej Radman, eds., *The Space of Technicities* (TU Delft Open Press, forthcoming). I am grateful to TU Delft Open Press for permission to adapt the essay here.

2. For an excellent analysis of the peaks and valleys of confrontational energy, including vivid descriptions of the "forward panic" when one side cracks and their opponents break through, see Collins (2009). See also Collins (2021), wherein he describes the "short-term processes" of the January 6 event: "The building guards putting up resistance at first, then losing cohesion, retreating, fading away; some fraternizing with the assaulting crowd, their sympathies wavering. They had weapons but most failed to use them."

3. For a portrait of Chansley's affective ideology, a motley libidinal politics consisting in a mélange of Trump, Q-Anon, and appropriations of Native American and Nordic themes, see Kunkle (2021).

4. I present several case studies and develop their philosophical background at some length in Protevi (2009 and 2013).

5. On the different treatments of events in *Difference and Repetition* and *A Thousand Plateaus*, in which events *qua* intensive "spatio-temporal dynamisms" are no longer schematism-like dramatizations mediating virtual ideas and actual objects but are immanent material haecceities, see Toscano (2006, 175–80).

6. Here I repeat analyses from Protevi (2013).

7. From the website for the Senate chaplain: "Throughout the years, the United States Senate has honored the historic separation of Church and State, but not the separation of God and State. The first Senate, meeting in New York City on April 25, 1789, elected the Right Reverend Samuel Provost, the Episcopal Bishop of New York, as its first chaplain. Since then, all sessions of the Senate have been opened with prayer, strongly affirming the Senate's faith in God as Sovereign Lord of our Nation. The role of the chaplain as spiritual advisor and counselor has expanded over the years from a part-time position to a full-time job as one of the officers of the Senate. The Office of the Chaplain is nonpartisan, nonpolitical, and nonsectarian" (Office of the Chaplain, n.d.).

8. One interesting task would be to compare Chansley's prayer with the one offered by the current Senate chaplain at the conclusion of the joint session ending on January 7, from the lectern in the House chamber: "Lord of our lives and sovereign of our beloved nation, we deplore the desecration of the United States Capitol building, the shedding of innocent blood, the loss of life, and the quagmire of dysfunction that threaten our democracy. These tragedies have reminded us that words matter and that the power of life and death is in the tongue. We have been warned that eternal vigilance continues to be freedom's price. Lord, you have helped us remember that we need to see in each other a common humanity that reflects your image. You have strengthened our resolve to protect and defend the Constitution of the United States against all enemies domestic as well as foreign. Use us to bring healing and unity to our hurting and divided nation and world. Thank you for what you have blessed our lawmakers to accomplish in spite of threats to liberty. Bless and keep us. Drive far from us all wrong desires, incline our hearts to do your will and guide our feet on the path of peace. And God bless America. We pray in your sovereign name, Amen" (*Adventist Review* 2021).

9. On abjection and architecture, see Akahane-Bryen and Smith (2019). For a standard social science look at defecation as sign of disrespect, see Friedman (1968). For a classic in the politics of shit, see Laporte (2002).

8. Covid-19

1. The occasion for the essay on which this chapter is based was an invitation by Julian Kiverstein and Michele Maiese to contribute to their edited forum on

NOTES TO CHAPTER 8 · **181**

"The Shape of Lives to Come." The essay appeared as "Covid 19 in the USA as affective frame," *Frontiers in Psychology* 13 (2022), https://doi.org/10.3389/fpsyg .2022.897215. I am grateful to *Frontiers in Psychology* for permission to adapt that essay here.

2. A full development of this notion, beyond what we can do here, would entail investigating the complex relations of paid emotional labor with traditional feminization practices that thematize caring as essentially or at least characteristically female; Gilligan (1982) would be a key reference here.

3. See Weheliye (2014) for criticism of Foucault's use of the concept of racism.

.

Bibliography

Adkins, Brent. 2015. *Deleuze and Guattari's* A Thousand Plateaus: *A Critical Introduction and Guide.* Edinburgh: Edinburgh University Press.

Adkins, Lisa. 2018. *The Time of Money.* Redwood City, Calif.: Stanford University Press.

Adventist Review. 2021. "Adventist Chaplain Leads Closing Prayer at U.S. Senate's Momentous Session." https://adventistreview.org/news/adventist-chaplain-leads -closing-prayer-at-us-senates-momentous-session/

Agamben, Giorgio. 2005. *State of Exception.* Translated by Kevin Attell. Chicago: University of Chicago Press.

Ahmed, Sara. 2007. "A Phenomenology of Whiteness." *Feminist Studies* 8.2: 149–68.

Akahane-Bryen, Sean, and Chris Smith. 2019. "The Space of the Lacerated Subject: Architecture and Abjection." *Architecture Philosophy* 4.1. https://ojs.library .okstate.edu/osu/index.php/jispa/article/view/7874

Alliez, Éric, and Maurizio Lazzarato. 2018. *Wars and Capital.* Translated by Ames Hodges. New York: Semiotext(e).

Anderson, Robert N. 1996. "The *Quilombo* of Palmares: A New Overview of a Maroon State in Seventeenth Century Brazil." *Journal of Latin American History* 28.3 (October): 545–66.

Andrews, Kristin. 2023. "Humans, the Norm-Breakers." *Biology & Philosophy* 38:35. https://doi.org/10.1007/s10539-023-09918-w

Ansell Pearson, Keith. 1997. *Viroid Life: Perspectives on Nietzsche and the Transhuman Condition.* London: Routledge.

AP News. 2021. Transcript of Trump's speech at rally before U.S. Capitol riot. January 13, 2021. https://apnews.com/article/election-2020-joe-biden-donald-trump -capitol-siege-media-e79eb5164613d6718e9f4502eb471f27

Aptheker, Herbert. 1979. "Maroons within the Present Limits of the United States." In *Maroon Societies: Rebel Slave Communities in the Americas,* edited by Richard Price, 151–67. Baltimore: Johns Hopkins University Press.

Architect of the Capitol. n.d. Senate Chamber. https://www.aoc.gov/explore-capi tol-campus/buildings-grounds/capitol-building/senate-wing/senate-chamber

Ashforth, Blake, and Ronald Humphrey. 1993. "Emotional Labor in Service Roles: The Influence of Identity." *The Academy of Management Review* 18.1: 88–115.

Badaire, Quentin. 2023. *Gilles Deleuze et Félix Guattari face à l'économie politique: usages critiques des sciences sociales dans les années 1960–70.* PhD thesis, École Normale Supérieure. https://www.theses.fr/s175692

Baptist, Edward. 2014. *The Half Has Never Been Told: Slavery and the Making of American Capitalism.* New York: Basic Books.

Barash, David, and Judith Lipton. 2011. *Payback.* Oxford: Oxford University Press.

Barker, Gillian. 2015. *Beyond Biofatalism: Human Nature for an Evolving World.* New York: Columbia University Press.

Barrett, Lisa Feldman. 2017. *How Emotions Are Made.* New York: Houghton Mifflin Harcourt.

Bataille, Georges. 1984. "The Notion of Expenditure." In *Visions of Excess: Selected Writings, 1927–1939,* edited by Alan Stoekl, 116–29. Minneapolis: University of Minnesota Press.

Beauvoir, Simone de. 2012. *The Second Sex.* Translated by Constance Borde and Sheila Malovany-Chevallier. New York: Vintage.

Beck, Ulrich. 1992. *Risk Society.* Translated by Mark Ritter. London: Sage Publications.

Beistegui, Miguel de. 2018. *The Government of Desire: A Genealogy of the Liberal Subject.* Chicago: University of Chicago Press.

Bellah, Robert. 1967. "Civil Religion in America." *Dædalus, Journal of the American Academy of Arts and Sciences* 96.1: 1–21.

Ben-Ghiat, Ruth. 2021. "Trump, the Coronavirus, and What Happens When Strongmen Fall Ill." *The New Yorker* (October 13). https://www.newyorker.com/culture/cultural-comment/trump-the-coronavirus-and-what-happens-when-strong men-fall-ill

Benjamin, Jessica. 1988. *The Bonds of Love: Psychoanalysis, Feminism, and the Problem of Domination.* New York: Pantheon Books.

Berghaus, Günther. 1996. "The Ritual Core of Fascist Theatre." In *Fascism and Theatre: Comparative Studies on the Aesthetics and Politics of Performance in Europe, 1925–1945,* edited by Günther Berghaus, 39–71. Providence, R.I.: Berghahn Books.

Bernasconi, Robert, and Anika Mazza Mann. 2005. "The Contradictions of Racism: Locke, Slavery and the *Two Treatises.*" In *Race and Racism in Modern Philosophy,* edited by Andrew Valls, 89–107. Ithaca: Cornell University Press.

Bert, Jean-François. 2013. "La Méditerranée vue par les anthropologues marxistes," *Yod [En ligne]* 18. http://journals.openedition.org/yod/1749

Bird, Douglas, Rebecca Bird, Brian Codding, and David Zeanah. 2019. "Variability in the Organization and Size of Hunter-Gatherer Groups: Foragers Do Not Live in Small-Scale Societies." *Journal of Human Evolution* 131: 96–108.

Blackburn, Robin. 1997. *The Making of New World Slavery: From the Baroque to the Modern, 1492–1800.* New York: Verso.

Blair, Robert. 2010. "Psychopathy, Frustration, and Reactive Aggression: The Role of Ventromedial Prefrontal Cortex." *The British Journal of Psychology* 101: 383–99.

Blair, Robert. 2012. "Considering Anger from a Cognitive Neuroscience Perspective." *Wiley Interdisciplinary Review of Cognitive Science* 3.1: 65–74.

Bledsoe, Adam. 2017. "Marronage as a Past and Present Geography in the Americas." *Southeastern Geographer* 57.1: 30–50.

Blick, Jeffrey. 1988. "Genocidal Warfare in Tribal Societies as a Result of European-Induced Culture Conflict." *Man* (New Series) 23.4: 654–70.

Boehm, Christopher. 2012a. "Ancestral Hierarchy and Conflict." *Science* 336.6083: 844–47.

Boehm, Christopher. 2012b. *Moral Origins: The Evolution of Virtue, Altruism, and Shame.* New York: Basic Books.

Bogue, Ronald. 2018. "Who the Earth Thinks It Is." In *A Thousand Plateaus and Philosophy,* edited by Henry Somers-Hall, Jeff Bell, and James Williams, 46–63. Edinburgh: Edinburgh University Press.

Bona, Denetem Touam. 2016. *Fugitif, où cours-tu?* Paris: PUF.

Borch-Jacobsen, Mikkel. 1988. *The Freudian Subject.* Translated by Catherine Porter. Stanford, Calif.: Stanford University Press.

Boyd, Robert, and Peter Richerson. 1985. *Culture and the Evolutionary Process.* Chicago: University of Chicago Press.

Brady (Syfers), Judy. 1971. "I Want a Wife." *New York* 4.51 (December 20–27): 56.

Brewer, Holly. 2017. "Slavery, Sovereignty, and 'Inheritable Blood': Reconsidering John Locke and the Origins of American Slavery." *The American Historical Review* 22.4 (October): 1038–78.

Brison, Susan. 2003. *Aftermath: Violence and the Remaking of a Self.* Princeton: Princeton University Press.

Buchanan, Allen, and Russell Powell. 2018. *The Evolution of Moral Progress: A Biocultural Theory.* Oxford: Oxford University Press.

Burr, Vivian, and Penny Dick. 2021. "A Social Constructionist Critique of Positive Psychology." In *Routledge International Handbook of Theoretical and Philosophical Psychology,* edited by Brent Slife, Stephen Yanchar, and Frank Richardson, 151–69. New York: Routledge.

Byrne, Richard. 2015. "The What as Well as the Why of Animal Fun." *Current Biology* 25.1 PR2-R4, 201. https://doi.org/10.1016/j.cub.2014.09.008

Caillois, Roger. 2001. *Man, Play, and Games.* Translated by Meyer Barash. Champaign: University of Illinois Press.

Cairns, Douglas. 2003. "Ethics, Ethology, Terminology: Iliadic Anger and the Cross-cultural Study of Emotion." In *Ancient Anger,* edited by S. M. Braund and G. W. Most, 11–49. Cambridge: Cambridge University Press.

Callaghan, Tara, and John Corbit. 2018. "Early Prosocial Development across Cultures." *Current Opinion in Psychology* 20: 102–6.

Canetti, Elias. 1984. *Crowds and Power*. Translated by Carol Stewart. New York: Farrar, Straus & Giroux.

Cannon, Clare. 2021. "Intersectional and Entangled Risks: An Empirical Analysis of Disasters and Landfills." *Frontiers in Climate* 3. doi:10.3389/fclim.2021.709439

Carneiro, Roberto. 1970. "A Theory of the Origin of the State." *Science* 169 (3947): 733–38.

Casimir, Jean. 2020. *The Haitians: A Decolonial History*. Translated by Laurent Dubois. Chapel Hill: University of North Carolina Press.

Castelli, Luigi, Cristina De Dea, and Drew Nesdale. 2008. "Learning Social Attitudes: Children's Sensitivity to the Nonverbal Behaviors of Adult Models During Interracial Interactions." *Personality and Social Psychology Bulletin* 34.11: 1504–13.

Chemero, Anthony. 2009. *Radical Embodied Cognitive Science*. Cambridge, Mass.: MIT Press.

Chowkwanyun, Merlin, and Adolph Reed. 2020. "Racial Health Disparities and Covid-19—Caution and Context." *New England Journal of Medicine* 383.3: 201–3.

Cisney, Vernon, and Nicolae Morar, eds. 2016. *Biopower: Foucault and Beyond*. Chicago: University of Chicago Press.

Clark, Andy, and David Chalmers. 1998. "The Extended Mind." *Analysis* 58.1: 7–19.

Clastres, Pierre. 1989. *Society Against the State*. Translated by Robert Hurley and Abe Stein. New York: Zone Books.

Clastres, Pierre. 1994. *Archaeology of Violence*. Translated by Jeanine Herman. New York: Semiotext(e).

Cohen, Emma, Robin Ejsmond-Frey, Nicola Knight, and Robin Dunbar. 2010. "Rowers' High: Behavioural Synchrony Is Correlated with Elevated Pain Thresholds." *Biological Letters* 6.1: 106–8.

Colebrook, Claire. 2022. "The War on Terror versus the War Machine." In *Deleuze and Guattari and Terror*, edited by Anindya Sekhar Purakayastha and Saswat Samay Das, 30–43. Edinburgh: Edinburgh University Press.

Collins, Randall. 2009. *Violence: A Microsociological Theory*. Princeton: Princeton University Press.

Collins, Randall. 2021. "Assault on the Capitol: 2021, 1917, 1792." *The Sociological Eye* (January 28). http://sociological-eye.blogspot.com/2021/01/assault-on-cap itol-2021-1917-1792.html

Cooke, Nancy, Jamie Gorman, Christopher Myers, and Jasmine Duran. 2012. "Interactive Team Cognition." *Cognitive Science* 37.2: 255–85.

Cooper, Melinda. 2019. *Family Values*. Princeton: Princeton University Press.

Cooper, Melinda, and Ben Mable. 2018. "Family Values." *Viewpoint Magazine*. https://viewpointmag.com/2018/03/19/family-matters/

Curran, Dean. 2013a. "Risk Society and the Distribution of Bads: Theorizing Class in the Risk Society." *The British Journal of Sociology* 64.1: 44–62.

Curran, Dean. 2013b. "What Is a Critical Theory of Risk Society? A Reply to Beck." *The British Journal of Sociology* 64.1: 75–80.

Curran, Dean. 2016. *Risk, Power, and Inequality in the 21st Century.* Basingstoke: Palgrave Macmillan.

Curran, Dean. 2018. "Beck's Creative Challenge to Class Analysis: From the Rejection of Class to the Discovery of Risk-Class." *Journal of Risk Research* 21.1: 29–40.

Cybersecurity & Infrastructure Security Agency (CISA) guidelines. 2020. March 19. https://www.cisa.gov/news/2020/03/19/cisa-releases-guidance-essential-criti cal-infrastructure-workers-during-covid-19

Davidson, Justin. 2021. "Can an Armored Capitol Still Be the People's House?" *Curbed* (January 13). https://www.curbed.com/2021/01/armored-capitol-troops -peoples-house-after-riot.html

Davis, Arran, Jacob Taylor, and Emma Cohen. 2015. "Social Bonds and Exercise: Evidence for a Reciprocal Relationship." *PLoS ONE* 10(8): e0136705.

De Block, Andreas, and Siegfried Dewitte. 2009. "Darwinism and the Cultural Evolution of Sports." *Perspectives in Biology and Medicine* 52.1: 1–16.

De Dreu, Carsten, and Mariska Kret. 2016. "Oxytocin Conditions Intergroup Relations Through Upregulated In-Group Empathy, Cooperation, Conformity, and Defense." *Biological Psychiatry* 79.3: 165–73.

De Jaegher, Hanne. 2021. "Loving and Knowing: Reflections on an Engaged Epistemology." *Phenomenology and the Cognitive Sciences* 20.5: 847–70.

De Jaegher, Hanne, and Ezequiel Di Paolo. 2007. "Participatory Sense-Making." *Phenomenology and the Cognitive Sciences* 6.4: 485–507.

De Landa, Manuel. 2002. *Intensive Science and Virtual Philosophy.* London: Continuum.

Del Savio, Lorenzo, and Matteo Mameli. 2020. "Human Domestication and the Roles of Human Agency in Human Evolution." *History and Philosophy of the Life Sciences* 42: 21.

Dean, Mitchell. 1998. "Risk, Calculable and Incalculable." *Soziale Welt* 49.1: 25–42.

Debien, Gabriel. 1979. "Marronage in the French Caribbean." In *Maroon Societies: Rebel Slave Communities in the Americas,* edited by Richard Price, 107–34. Baltimore: Johns Hopkins University Press.

Deleuze, Gilles. 1983. *Nietzsche and Philosophy.* Translated by Hugh Tomlinson. New York: Columbia University Press.

Deleuze, Gilles. 1990. *The Logic of Sense.* Translated by Mark Lester, with Charles Stivale. New York: Columbia University Press.

Deleuze, Gilles. 1994. *Difference and Repetition.* Translated by Paul Patton. New York: Columbia University Press.

Deleuze, Gilles. 2004. "The Method of Dramatization." Translated by Michael Taormina. In *Desert Islands and Other Texts,* edited by David Lapoujade. New York: Semiotext(e).

Deleuze, Gilles, and Felix Guattari. 1977. *Anti-Oedipus*. Translated by Robert Hurley, Mark Seem, and Helen R. Lane. New York: Viking.

Deleuze, Gilles, and Felix Guattari. 1987. *A Thousand Plateaus*. Translated by Brian Massumi. Minneapolis: University of Minnesota Press.

Deleuze, Gilles, and Félix Guattari. 1991. *What Is Philosophy?* Translated by Hugh Tomlinson and Graham Burchell. New York: Columbia University Press.

DeRobertis, Jacqueline. 2020. "Port Allen Nursing Home Employee on Oxygen Dies from Coronavirus; She Was 'Backbone' of Family." *The Advocate* (May 18). https://www.theadvocate.com/baton_rouge/news/coronavirus/port-allen -nursing-home-employee-on-oxygen-dies-from-coronavirus-she-was-back bone-of-family/article_c2b7dd12-96e0-11ea-9ff8-9ff8faef31c2.html

Derrida, Jacques. 1992. *Given Time: I. Counterfeit Money*. Translated by Peggy Kamuf. Chicago: University of Chicago Press.

Derrida, Jacques. 1995. *The Gift of Death*. Translated by David Wills. Chicago: University of Chicago Press.

Di Paolo, Ezequiel. 2005. "Autopoiesis, Adaptivity, Teleology, Agency." *Phenomenology and the Cognitive Sciences* 4: 429–52.

Di Paolo, Ezequiel. 2008. "Extended Life." *Topoi* 28.1: 9–21.

Di Paolo, Ezequiel. 2021. "Enactive Becoming." *Phenomenology and the Cognitive Sciences* 20: 783–809.

Di Paolo, Ezequiel, and Hanne De Jaegher. 2021. "Enactive Ethics: Difference Becoming Participation." *Topoi* 41: 241–56.

Di Paolo, Ezequiel, Hanne De Jaegher, and Elena Cuffari. 2018. *Linguistic Bodies: The Continuity Between Life and Language*. Cambridge, Mass.: MIT Press.

Di Paolo, Ezequiel, and Evan Thompson. 2014. "The Enactive Approach." In *The Routledge Handbook of Embodied Cognition*, edited by Lawrence Shapiro, 68–78. New York: Routledge.

Di Paolo, Ezequiel, Evan Thompson, and Randy Beer. 2021. "Laying Down a Forking Path: Incompatibilities Between Enaction and the Free Energy Principle." *PsyArXiv* (April 19). doi:10.31234/osf.io/d9v8f

Diamond, David, Adam Campbell, Collin Park, Joshua Halonen, and Phillip Zoladz. 2007. "The Temporal Dynamics Model of Emotional Memory Processing: A Synthesis on the Neurobiological Basis of Stress-Induced Amnesia, Flashbulb and Traumatic Memories, and the Yerkes-Dodson Law." *Neural Plasticity*. Article ID 60803. doi:10.1155/2007/60803

Dodd, James. 2021. "A Short Prolegomena to the Philosophy of War, in Four Problems." *Labyrinth* 23.2: 99–116.

Downes, Stephen. 2019. "What's Left of Human Nature." Review of *What's Left of Human Nature*, by Maria Kronfeldner. *BJPS Review of Books*. https://www.the bsps.org/reviewofbooks/downes-on-kronfeldner/

Downes, Stephen. 2021. "Evolutionary Psychology." In *The Stanford Encyclopedia of Philosophy* (Spring), edited by Edward Zalta. https://plato.stanford.edu/archives/spr2021/entries/evolutionary-psychology

Drews, Robert. 1993. *The End of the Bronze Age: Changes in Warfare and the Catastrophe ca. 1200 B.C.* Princeton: Princeton University Press.

Erlenbusch-Anderson, Verena. 2018. *Genealogies of Terrorism: Revolution, State Violence, Empire.* New York: Columbia University Press.

Fanon, Frantz. 2008. *Black Skin, White Masks.* Translated by Richard Philcox. New York: Grove Press.

Ferguson, Brian. 2008. "Ten Points on War." *Social Analysis* 52.2: 32–49.

Ferguson, Brian. 2013a. "Pinker's List: Exaggerating Prehistoric War Mortality." In *War, Peace, and Human Nature,* edited by Douglas Fry, 112–31. Oxford: Oxford University Press.

Ferguson, Brian. 2013b. "The Prehistory of War and Peace in Europe and the Near East." In *War, Peace, and Human Nature,* edited by Douglas Fry, 191–240. Oxford: Oxford University Press.

Fick, Carolyn. 1990. *The Making of Haiti.* Knoxville: University of Tennessee Press.

Flanagan, Owen. 2016. *The Geography of Morals.* Oxford: Oxford University Press.

Flannery, Kent, and Joyce Marcus. 2012. *The Creation of Inequality: How Our Prehistoric Ancestors Set the Stage for Monarchy, Slavery, and Empire.* Cambridge, Mass.: Harvard University Press.

Foster, John Bellamy, Hannah Holleman, and Brett Clark. 2020. "Marx and Slavery." *Monthly Review* 72.3 (July).

Foucault, Michel. 1978. *History of Sexuality, Volume 1*, Translated by Robert Hurley. New York: Random House.

Foucault, Michel. 1979. *Discipline and Punish.* Translated by Alan Sheridan. New York: Vintage.

Foucault, Michel. 2003. *"Society Must Be Defended."* Translated by David Macey. New York: Picador.

Foucault, Michel. 2007. *Security, Territory, Population.* Translated by Graham Burchell. Basingstoke: Palgrave Macmillan.

Foucault, Michel. 2008. *The Birth of Biopolitics.* Translated by Graham Burchell. Basingstoke: Palgrave Macmillan.

Freitas, Décio. 1990. *Palmares: A Guerra Dos Escravos,* 5th ed. Rio de Janeiro: Edições Graal.

Freud, Sigmund. 1989. *Group Psychology and the Analysis of the Ego.* Translated by James Strachey. New York: Norton.

Friedmaan, Albert. 1968. "The Scatological Rites of Burglars." *Western Folklore* 27.3: 171–79.

Fry, Douglas. 2006. *The Human Potential for Peace.* New York: Oxford University Press.

Fry, Douglas. 2013. "War, Peace, and Human Nature: The Challenge of Achieving Scientific Objectivity." In *War, Peace, and Human Nature,* edited by Douglas Fry, 1–21. Oxford: Oxford University Press.

Fuchs, Thomas. 2018. *Ecology of the Brain.* New York: Oxford University Press.

Fuentes, Agustín. 2009. "A New Synthesis." *Anthropology Today* 25.3: 12–17.

Fuentes, Agustín. 2015. "Integrative Anthropology and the Human Niche: Toward a Contemporary Approach to Human Evolution." *American Anthropologist* 117.2: 302–15.

Fuentes, Agustín. 2017. "Human Niche, Human Behaviour, Human Nature." *Interface Focus* 7: 20160136. http://dx.doi.org/10.1098/rsfs.2016.0136

Fuentes, Agustín. 2018. "How Humans and Apes Are Different, and Why It Matters." *Journal of Anthropological Research* 74.2: 151–67.

Fuentes, Agustín. 2022. "Humans Are Not 'Tribal.'" *BigThink* (September 23). https://bigthink.com/the-well/tribalism-humans-not-tribal/

Gallagher, Shaun. 2005. *How the Body Shapes the Mind.* New York: Oxford University Press.

Gallagher, Shaun. 2013. "The Socially Extended Mind." *Cognitive Systems Research* 25–26: 4–12.

Gallagher, Shaun. 2017. *Enactivist Interventions: Rethinking the Mind.* New York: Oxford University Press.

Gallagher, Shaun. 2020. *Action and Interaction.* New York: Oxford University Press.

Gallagher, Shaun, and Anthony Crisafi. 2009. "Mental Institutions." *Topoi* 28: 45–51.

Gallagher, Shaun, and Dan Zahavi. 2021. *The Phenomenological Mind,* 3rd edition. New York: Routledge.

Gallagher, Shaun, and Dan Zahavi. 2023. "Phenomenological Approaches to Self-Consciousness." In *The Stanford Encyclopedia of Philosophy,* edited by Edward N. Zalta and Uri Nodelman (Winter). https://plato.stanford.edu/archives/win2023/entries/self-consciousness-phenomenological/

Gaus, Gerald. 2015. "The Egalitarian Species." *Social Philosophy and Policy* 31.2: 1–27.

Gendler, Tamar Szabó. 2008a. "Alief in Action (and Reaction)." *Mind & Language* 23.5: 552–85.

Gendler, Tamar Szabó. 2008b. "Alief and Belief." *Journal of Philosophy* 105.10: 634–63.

Geronimus, Arline. 2013. "Deep Integration: Letting the Epigenome Out of the Bottle Without Losing Sight of the Structural Origins of Population Health." *American Journal of Public Health* 103 (Suppl 1): S56–S63.

Geronimus, Arline, Margaret Hicken, Danya Keene, and John Bound. 2006. "'Weathering' and Age Patterns of Allostatic Load Scores Among Blacks and Whites in the United States." *American Journal of Public Health* 96: 826–33.

Geronimus, Arline, Margaret Hicken, Jay Pearson, Sarah Seashols, Kelly Brown, and Tracey Dawson Cruz. 2010. "Do US Black Women Experience Stress-Related Accelerated Biological Aging? A Novel Theory and First Population-Based Test of Black–White Differences in Telomere Length." *Human Nature* 21.1: 19–38.

Gibson, James J. 1986. *The Ecological Approach to Visual Perception.* Hillsdale, N.J.: Erlbaum.

Gilbert, Jeremy. 2014. *Common Ground: Democracy and Collectivity in an Age of Individualism.* London: Pluto Press.

Gilbert, Margaret. 2003. "The Structure of the Social Atom: Joint Commitment as the Foundation of Human Social Behavior." In *Socializing Metaphysics: The Nature of Social Reality,* edited by Frederick Schmitt, 39–64. New York: Rowman & Littlefield.

Gilligan, Carol. 1982. *In a Different Voice.* Cambridge, Mass.: Harvard University Press.

Gilmore, Ruth Wilson. 2007. *Golden Gulag: Prisons, Surplus, Crisis, and Opposition in Globalizing California.* Berkeley: University of California Press.

Glissant, Edouard. 1997. *Poetics of Relation.* Translated by Betsy Wing. Ann Arbor: University of Michigan Press.

Glissant, Edouard. 2001. *The Fourth Century.* Translated by Betsy Wing. Lincoln: University of Nebraska Press.

Glowacki, Luke. 2024. "The Evolution of Peace." *Behavioral and Brain Sciences* 47. https://doi.org/10.1017/S0140525X22002862

Gonzalez-Cabrera, Ivan. 2019. "On Social Tolerance and the Evolution of Human Normative Guidance." *The British Journal for the Philosophy of Science* 70.2 (June): 523–49.

Gould, Stephen Jay. 1988. "Kropotkin Was No Crackpot." *Natural History* 97.7: 12–21.

Graeber, David. 2012. *Debt: The First 5,000 Years.* New York: Melville House.

Graeber, David, and David Wengrow. 2021. *The Dawn of Everything: A New History of Humanity.* New York: Farrar, Straus, & Giroux.

Gray, Peter. 2017. "What Exactly Is Play, and Why Is It Such a Powerful Vehicle for Learning?" *Topics in Language Disorders* 37.3: 217–28.

Griffiths, Paul. 1997. *What Emotions Really Are: The Problem of Psychological Categories.* Chicago: University of Chicago Press.

Griffiths, Paul. 2011. "Our Plastic Nature." In *Transformations of Lamarckism: From Subtle Fluids to Molecular Biology,* edited by Snait B. Gissis and Eva Jablonka, 319–30. Cambridge, Mass.: MIT Press.

Griffiths, Paul, and Russell Gray. 1997. "Replicator II – Judgement Day." *Biology and Philosophy* 12: 471–92.

Griffiths, Paul, and Russell Gray. 2001. "Darwinism and Developmental Systems." In *Cycles of Contingency: Developmental Systems and Evolution,* edited by Susan Oyama, Paul Griffiths, and Russell Gray, 195–218. Cambridge, Mass.: MIT Press.

Griffiths, Paul, and Russell Gray. 2004. "The Developmental Systems Perspective: Organism-Environment Systems as Units of Development and Evolution." In *Phenotypic Integration: Studying the Ecology and Evolution of Complex Phenotypes,* edited by Massimo Pigliucci and Katherine Preston, 409–31. Oxford: Oxford University Press.

Griffiths, Paul, and Russell Gray. 2005. "Discussion: Three Ways to Misunderstand Developmental Systems Theory." *Biology and Philosophy* 20: 417–25.

Griffiths, Paul, and Karola Stotz. 2018. "Developmental Systems Theory as a Process Theory." In *Everything Flows: Towards a Processual Philosophy of Biology,* edited by Daniel J. Nicholson and John Dupré, 225–45. Oxford: Oxford University Press.

Grossman, David. 1996. *On Killing.* Boston: Little, Brown.

Grossman, David. 2004. *On Combat.* Millstadt, Ill.: Warrior Science Publications.

Guardian. 2020. "Lost on the Front Line." https://khn.org/news/lost-on-the-front line-health-care-worker-death-toll-covid19-coronavirus/

Guenther, Lisa. 2013. *Solitary Confinement: Social Death and Its Afterlives.* Minneapolis: University of Minnesota Press.

Guenther, Lisa. 2019. "Seeing Like a Cop: A Critical Phenomenology of Whiteness as Property." In *Race as Phenomena: Between Phenomenology and Philosophy of Race,* edited by Emily Lee, 189–206. New York: Rowman & Littlefield.

Guidi, Jenny, Marecella Lucente, Nicolleta Sonino, and Giovanni Fava. 2021. "Allostatic Load and Its Impact on Health: A Systematic Review." *Psychotherapy and Psychosomatics* 90.1:11–27.

Gurven, Michael, and Adrian V. Jaeggi. 2015. "Food Sharing." In *Emerging Trends in the Social and Behavioral Sciences,* edited by Robert Scott and Stephan Kosslyn, 1–12. Hoboken, N.J.: John Wiley & Sons.

Hacker, Jacob. 2006. *The Great Risk Shift.* New York: Oxford University Press.

Hall, Gwendolyn Midlo. 1992. *Africans in Colonial Louisiana.* Baton Rouge: LSU Press.

Hames, Raymond. 2019. "Pacifying Hunter-Gatherers." *Human Nature* 30: 155–75.

Hanson, Kara. 2020. "How the Coronavirus 'Wants' to Change Our Lives." *The Apeiron Blog.* May 5. https://theapeiron.co.uk/how-the-coronavirus-wants-to -change-our-lives-2cd1c10f805f

Hare, Brian. 2017. "Survival of the Friendliest: *Homo sapiens* Evolved via Selection for Prosociality." *Annual Review of Psychology* 68 (January 3): 155–86.

Harney, Stefano, and Fred Moten. 2013. *The Undercommons: Fugitive Planning & Black Study.* New York: Minor Compositions.

Harrison, Simon. 2020. "Through the Magical Pink Walkway: A Behavior Setting's Invitation to Embodied Sense-Makers." *Frontiers in Psychology* 11: 1576.

Harvey, David. 2007. *A Brief History of Neoliberalism.* New York: Oxford University Press.

Hawkins, Mike. 1997. *Social Darwinism in European and American Thought, 1860–1945: Nature as Model and Nature as Threat.* New York: Cambridge University Press.

Headrick, Jonathon, Keith Davids, Ian Renshaw, Duarte Araújo, Pedro Passos, and Orlando Fernandes. 2012. "Proximity-to-Goal as a Constraint on Patterns of Behaviour in Attacker-Defender Dyads in Team Games." *Journal of Sports Science* 30.3: 247–53.

Hénaff, Marcel. 2020. *The Philosopher's Gift: Reexamining Reciprocity.* Translated by Jean-Louis Morhange. New York: Fordham University Press.

Henricks, Thomas. 2020. "Play Studies: A Brief History." *American Journal of Play* 12.2 (Winter): 117–55.

Heyes, Cecilia. 2018. *Cognitive Gadgets: The Cultural Evolution of Thinking.* Cambridge, Mass.: Harvard University Press.

Hirstein, William, and Katrina Sifferd. 2014. "Ethics and the Brains of Psychopaths." In *Brain Theory*, edited by Charles T. Wolfe. New York: Palgrave Macmillan: 149–70.

Hochschild, Arlie Russell. 1983. *The Managed Heart.* Berkeley: University of California Press.

Holland, Eugene. 2013. *Deleuze and Guattari's* A Thousand Plateaus. London: Bloomsbury.

Honenberger, Philip. 2019. "What's Left of Human Nature." Review of *What's Left of Human Nature*, by Maria Kronfeldner. *Notre Dame Philosophical Reviews.* https://ndpr.nd.edu/reviews/whats-left-of-human-nature-a-post-essentialist -pluralist-and-interactive-account-of-a-contested-concept/

Horne, Gerald. 2014. *The Counter-Revolution of 1776: Slave Resistance and the Origins of the United States of America.* New York: New York University Press.

Horne, Gerald. 2018. *The Apocalypse of Settler Colonialism: The Roots of Slavery, White Supremacy, and Capitalism in 17th Century North America and the Caribbean.* New York: Monthly Review Press.

Hrdy, Sarah. 2009. *Mothers and Others.* Cambridge, Mass.: Harvard University Press.

Hristovski, Robert, Keith Davids, Pedro Passos, and Duarte Araújo. 2012. "Sport Performance as a Domain of Creative Problem Solving for Self-Organizing Performer-Environment Systems." *The Open Sports Sciences Journal* 5 (Suppl 1-M4): 26–35.

Hughson, D., and J. Inglis. 2000. "Merleau-Ponty in the Field: Towards a Sociological Phenomenology of Soccer Spaces." *Space and Culture* 3.6: 115–32.

Huizinga, Johan. 1980. *Homo Ludens: A Study of the Play Element in Culture.* Translated by Richard Hull. London: Routledge.

Hurley, Susan. 1998. *Consciousness in Action.* Cambridge, Mass.: Harvard University Press.

Hutto, Daniel. 2012. *Folk Psychological Narratives: The Sociocultural Basis of Understanding Reasons.* Cambridge, Mass.: MIT Press.

Hutto, Daniel, Shaun Gallagher, Jesús Ilundáin-Agurruza, and Inês Hipólito. 2020. "Culture in Mind—An Enactivist Account: Not Cognitive Penetration but Cultural Permeation." In *Culture, Mind, and Brain: Emerging Concepts, Models, and Applications,* edited by Laurence Kirmayer, Carol Worthman, Shinobu Kitayama, Robert Lemelson, and Constance Cummings, 163–87. Cambridge: Cambridge University Press.

Jablonka, Eva, and Marion J. Lamb. 2005. *Evolution in Four Dimensions: Genetic, Epigenetic, Behavioral, and Symbolic Variation in the History of Life.* Cambridge, Mass.: MIT Press.

Jackson, George. 1994. *Soledad Brother: The Prison Letters of George Jackson.* New York: Lawrence Hill Books.

Jaeggi, Adrian, and Michael Gurven. 2013. "Reciprocity Explains Food Sharing in Humans and Other Primates Independent of Kin Selection and Tolerated Scrounging: A Phylogenetic Meta-analysis." *Proceedings of the Royal Society B* 280.1768. https://doi.org/10.1098/rspb.2013.1615

Jenkins, Jack. 2021a. "Transcript of QAnon Shaman's Prayer." Twitter. https://twitter.com/jackmjenkins/status/1350827561593532418?lang=en

Jenkins, Jack. 2021b. "The Insurrectionists' Senate Floor Prayer Highlights a Curious Trumpian Ecumenism." *Religion News Service* (February 25). https://religionnews.com/2021/02/25/the-insurrectionists-senate-floor-prayer-highlights-a-curious-trumpian-ecumenism/

Johnson, A. M. 2020. "Jamaica's Windward Maroon 'Slaveholders.'" *New West Indian Guide / Nieuwe West-Indische Gids* 94.3–4: 273–92.

Johnson, Eleanor. 2015. "The Business of Care: The Moral Labour of Care Workers." *Sociology of Health & Illness* 37.1: 112–26.

Johnson, Eric M. 2019. "The Struggle for Coexistence: Peter Kropotkin and the Social Ecology of Science in Russia, Europe, and England, 1859–1922." Electronic Theses and Dissertations (ETDs) 2008+. T. University of British Columbia. doi:10.14288/1.0378937

Johnson, Matthew Kuan. 2020 "Joy: A Review of the Literature and Suggestions for Future Directions," *The Journal of Positive Psychology,* 15:1: 5–24.

Jost, John, Mahzarin Banaji, and Brian Nozek. 2004. "A Decade of System Justification Theory: Accumulated Evidence of Conscious and Unconscious Bolstering of the Status Quo." *Political Psychology* 25.6: 881–919.

Kaplan, Hillard, and Michael Gurven. 2005. "The Natural History of Human Food Sharing and Cooperation." In *Moral Sentiments and Material Interests: The Foundations of Cooperation in Economic Life,* edited by Herbert Gintis, Samuel Bowles, Robert Boyd, and Ernst Fehr, 75–113. Cambridge, Mass.: MIT Press.

Keegan, John. 1976. *The Face of Battle.* London: Jonathan Cape.

Kelly, Raymond. 2000. *Warless Societies and the Origin of War.* Ann Arbor: University of Michigan Press.

Kelly, Raymond. 2005. "The Evolution of Lethal Intergroup Violence." *Proceedings of the National Academy of Science* 102.43: 15294–98.

Kelly, Robert L. 2013. *The Lifeways of Hunter-Gatherers: The Foraging Spectrum.* Cambridge: Cambridge University Press.

Kent, R. K. 1965. "Palmares: An African State in Brazil." *The Journal of African History* 6.2: 161–75.

Kim, Eun Joo, Blake Pellman, and Jeansok Kim. 2015. "Stress Effects on the Hippocampus: A Critical Review." *Learning & Memory* 22: 411–16.

Kirchhoff, Michael, and Julian Kiverstein. 2019. *Extended Consciousness and Predictive Processing.* New York: Routledge.

Kirmayer, Laurence, Carol Worthman, Shinobu Kitayama, Robert Lemelson, and Constance Cummings, eds. 2020. *Culture, Mind, and Brain: Emerging Concepts, Models, and Applications.* Cambridge: Cambridge University Press.

Kisner, Matthew. 2019. "Spinoza on Natures: Aristotelian and Mechanistic Routes to Relational Autonomy." In *Spinoza and Relational Autonomy: Being with Others,* edited by Aurelia Armstrong, Keith Green, and Andrea Sangiacomo, 74–97. Edinburgh: Edinburgh University Press.

Kissel, Marc, and Nam Kim. 2018. "The Emergence of Human Warfare: Current Perspectives." *American Journal of Physical Anthropology* 168.S67: 141–63.

Kitcher, Philip. 1987. "Précis of Vaulting Ambition: Sociobiology and the Quest for Human Nature." *Behavioral and Brain Sciences* 10.1: 61–71.

Kitcher, Philip. 2011. *The Ethical Project.* Cambridge, Mass.: Harvard University Press.

Kittay, Eva Feder. 2015. "Equality, Dignity, and Disability." In *Perspectives on Equality: The Second Seamus Heaney Lectures,* edited by Mary Ann Lyons and Fionnuala Waldron, 93–119. Dublin: The Liffey Press.

Kniffin, Kevin, and Michelle Sugiyama. 2019. "Toward a Natural History of Team Sports." *Human Nature* 29: 211–18.

Koerner, Michelle. 2011. "Lines of Escape: Gilles Deleuze's Encounter with George Jackson." *Genre* 44.2: 157–80.

Kopytoff, Barbara. 1978. "The Early Political Development of Jamaican Maroon Societies." *The William and Mary Quarterly* 35.2: 287–307.

Kraus, Michael, Cassey Huang, and Dacher Keltner. 2010. "Tactile Communication, Cooperation, and Performance: An Ethological Study of the NBA." *Emotion* 10.5: 745–49.

Kumar, Victor, and Richmond Campbell. 2022. *A Better Ape: The Evolution of the Moral Mind and How It Made Us Human.* New York: Oxford University Press.

Kunkle, Frederick. 2021. "Trump Supporter in Horns and Fur is Charged in Capitol Riot." *The Washington Post* (January 9).

Kyle, Chris, Scott McEwen, and Jim DeFelice. 2012. *American Sniper.* New York: W. Morrow.

Lacy, Sarah, and Cara Ocobock. 2023. "Woman the Hunter: The Archaeological Evidence." *American Anthropologist.* https://doi.org/10.1111/aman.13914

Laporte, Dominique. 2002. *History of Shit.* Translated by Rodolphe el-Khoury and Nadia Benabid. Cambridge, Mass.: MIT Press.

Lawlor, Leonard. 2016. *From Violence to Speaking Out.* Edinburgh: Edinburgh University Press.

Leach, Edmund. 1970. *Political Systems of Highland Burma.* London: Athlone Press.

Le Bon, Gustave. 2002. *The Crowd: A Study of the Popular Mind.* Mineola, N.Y.: Dover.

LeDoux, Joseph. 1996. *The Emotional Brain.* New York: Simon & Schuster.

LeDoux, Joseph. 2015. *Anxious: Using the Brain to Understand and Treat Anxiety and Depression.* New York: Penguin.

Lee, Richard. 2018. "Hunter-Gatherers and Human Evolution: New Light on Old Debates." *Annual Review of Anthropology* 47: 513–31.

Lemke, Thomas. 2019. *Foucault's Analysis of Modern Governmentality.* New York: Verso.

Lemm, Vanessa, and Miguel Vatter. 2014. *The Government of Life.* New York: Fordham University Press.

Lende, Daniel, and Greg Downey, eds. 2012. *The Encultured Brain: An Introduction to Neuroanthropology.* Cambridge, Mass.: MIT Press.

Léon, Felipe, and Dan Zahavi. 2018. "How We Feel: Collective Emotions without Joint Commitments." *ProtoSociology* 35: 117–36.

Lindesfarne, Nancy, and Jonathan Neale. 2021. "All Things Being Equal." *The Ecologist.* https://theecologist.org/2021/dec/17/all-things-being-equal

Locke, John. 2003. *Political Writings.* Translated and edited by David Wootton. Indianapolis: Hackett Press.

Lombardo, Michael. 2012. "On the Evolution of Sport." *Evolutionary Psychology* 10.1: 1–28.

Lorenzini, Daniele. 2020. "Biopolitics in the Time of Coronavirus." *Critical Inquiry.* https://critinq.wordpress.com/2020/04/02/biopolitics-in-the-time-of-corona virus/

Loumagne Ulishney, Megan. 2022. "The Evolution of *Homo ludens:* Sexual Selection and a Theology of Play." *Zygon* 57: 564–75.

Luft, Rachel. 2016. "Racialized Disaster Patriarchy: An Intersectional Model for Understanding Disaster Ten Years After Hurricane Katrina." *Feminist Formations* 28.2: 1–26.

MacDonald, Katherine, Fulco Scherjon, Eva van Veen, and Wil Roebroeks. 2021. "Middle Pleistocene Fire Use: The First Signal of Widespread Cultural Diffusion in Human Evolution." *PNAS* 118.31 (Aug. 3): e2101108118. https://doi.org/10.1073/pnas.2101108118

Machery, Edouard. 2008. "A Plea for Human Nature." *Philosophical Psychology* 21.3: 321–29.

Machin, A. J., and Robin Dunbar. 2011. "The Brain Opioid Theory of Social Attachment: A Review of the Evidence." *Behaviour* 148.9/10: 985–1025.

Mackenzie, Catriona. 2000. "Imagining Oneself Otherwise." In *Relational Autonomy: Feminist Perspectives on Autonomy, Agency, and the Social Self,* edited by Catriona Mackenzie and Natalie Stoljer, 124–50. New York: Oxford University Press.

Mackenzie, Catriona. 2019. "Relational Autonomy: State of the Art Debate." In *Spinoza and Relational Autonomy: Being with Others,* edited by Aurelia Armstrong, Keith Green, and Andrea Sangiacomo, 10–32. Edinburgh: Edinburgh University Press.

Maiese, Michelle, and Robert Hanna. 2019. *The Mind–Body Politic.* London: Palgrave Macmillan.

Mameli, Matteo. 2013. "Meat Made Us Moral: A Hypothesis on the Nature and Evolution of Moral Judgment." *Biology & Philosophy* 28: 903–31.

Martin, Randy. 2002. *Financialization of Everyday Life.* Philadelphia: Temple University Press.

Martínez, Quintero, and Hanne De Jaegher. 2020. "Pregnant Agencies: Movement and Participation in Maternal–Fetal Interactions." *Frontiers in Psychology* 11: 1977.

Masset, Thibault. 2013. *La violence chez Deleuze-Guattari et Balibar: Mode de production, subjectivation et politique.* Kindle Edition, Paris: PUF.

Massumi, Brian. 2002. *Parables for the Virtual.* Durham, N.C.: Duke University Press.

Maturana, Humberto, and Francisco J. Varela. 1980. *Autopoiesis and Cognition: The Realization of the Living.* Boston: Riedel.

Mauss, Marcel. 1990. *The Gift.* Translated by W. D. Halls. New York: Norton.

Mbembe, Achille. 2003. "Necropolitics." *Public Culture* 15.1: 11–40.

McCullough, Michael, Marcia Kimeldorf, and Adam Cohen. 2008. "An Adaptation for Altruism? The Social Causes, Social Effects, and Social Evolution of Gratitude." *Current Directions in Psychological Science* 17: 281–85.

McGann, Marek, Ezequiel Di Paolo, Manuel Heras-Escribano, and Anthony Chemero. 2020. "Editorial: Enaction and Ecological Psychology: Convergences and Complementarities." *Frontiers in Psychology* 11: 3176.

McNeill, William. 1995. *Keeping Together in Time: Dance and Drill in Human History.* Cambridge, Mass.: Harvard University Press.

Meadows, Chris. 2013. *A Psychological Perspective on Joy and Emotional Fulfillment.* New York: Routledge.

Merleau-Ponty, Maurice. 1965. *The Structure of Behavior.* Translated by Alden L. Fisher. Pittsburgh: Duquesne University Press.

Milisavljević, Vladimir. 2012. "Une violence qui se présuppose: la question de la violence de Benjamin à Deleuze et Guattari." *Actuel Marx* 52: 78–91.

Milisavljević, Vladimir, and Guillaume Sibertin-Blanc. 2017. *Deleuze et la violence*. OpenEdition Books. http://books.openedition.org/europhilosophie/109

Miller, Geoffrey. 2011. *The Mating Mind: How Sexual Choice Shaped the Evolution of Human Nature*. New York: Anchor Books.

Miller, Greg. 2013. "A Gruesome War Crime Renews Concerns About a Malaria Drug's Psychiatric Side Effects." *Wired* (August). https://www.wired.com/2013/08/mefloquine-robert-bales/all/

Mills, Charles W. 1997. *The Racial Contract*. Ithaca: Cornell University Press.

Minosh, Peter. 2020. "American Architecture in the Black Atlantic: William Thornton's Design for the United States Capitol." In *Race and Modern Architecture*, edited by Irene Cheng, Charles L. Davis II, and Mabel O. Wilson, 43–58. Pittsburgh: University of Pittsburgh Press.

Miranda, Carolina. 2021. "Yes, the Capitol Is a 'Symbol of Democracy.' One with a Really Troubled History." *Los Angeles Times* (January 7).

Miranda, Luis de. 2020. *Ensemblance: The Transnational Genealogy of* Esprit de Corps. Edinburgh: Edinburgh University Press, 2020.

Mirowski, Philip. 2018. "Neoliberalism: The Movement That Dare Not Speak Its Name." *American Affairs*. https://americanaffairsjournal.org/2018/02/neoliberalism-movement-dare-not-speak-name/

Mogelson, Luke, and Sara Ann Wolansky. 2021. "A Reporter's Footage from Inside the Capitol Siege." *The New Yorker* (January 17). https://www.newyorker.com/news/video-dept/a-reporters-footage-from-inside-the-capitol-siege

Moten, Fred. 2008. "The Case of Blackness." *Criticism* 50.2: 177–218.

Murphy, Ann. 2012. *Violence and the Philosophical Imaginary*. Albany: SUNY Press.

Nelson, Randy, and Brian Trainor. 2007. "Neural Mechanisms of Aggression." *Nature Reviews: Neuroscience* 8: 536–46.

Nelson, Ximena, Alex Taylor, Erica Cartmill, Heidi Lyn, Lauren Robinson, Vincent Janik, and Colin Allen. 2023. "Joyful by Nature: Approaches to Investigate the Evolution and Function of Joy in Non-human Animals." *Biological Reviews* 98: 1548–63. https://doi.org/10.1111/brv.12965

Nesbitt, Nick. 2022. *The Price of Slavery: Capitalism and Revolution in the Caribbean*. Charlottesville: University of Virginia Press.

Nietzsche, Friedrich. 1997. *On the Genealogy of Morality*. Translated by Carol Diethe. Cambridge: Cambridge University Press.

Nietzsche, Friedrich. 1999. *The Birth of Tragedy and Other Writings*. Translated by Ronald Speirs. Cambridge: Cambridge University Press.

Norenzayan, Ara. 2013. *Big Gods: How Religion Transformed Cooperation and Conflict*. Princeton: Princeton University Press.

Office of the Chaplain, U.S. Senate. n.d. https://www.senate.gov/reference/office/chaplain.htm

Office of the Governor of Louisiana. 2020. Stay at home order of March 22. https://
gov.louisiana.gov/home/#:~:text=Covid%2D19%20is%20rapidly,military%20
in%20your%20community

Oksala, Johanna. 2012. *Foucault, Politics, and Violence.* Evanston, Ill.: Northwestern
University Press.

Olofsson, Anna, Susanna Öhman, and Katarina Giritli Nygren. 2016: "An Intersectional Risk Approach for Environmental Sociology." *Environmental Sociology*
2.4: 346–54.

Olumhense, Ese. 2020. "For Some Near the Cross Bronx Expressway, Covid-19 Is
an Environmental Justice Issue, Too." *The City* (September 28). https://www.the
city.nyc/2020/9/28/21492252/cross-bronx-expressway-covid-19-environmen
tal-justice-nyc

Ostrom, Elinor. 2005. "Policies That Crowd Out Reciprocity and Collective Action."
In *Moral Sentiments and Material Interests: The Foundations of Cooperation in
Economic Life,* edited by Herbert Gintis, Samuel Bowles, Robert Boyd, and Ernst
Fehr, 253–75. Cambridge, Mass.: MIT Press.

Oyama, Susan. 2000. *The Ontogeny of Information.* Durham, N.C.: Duke University Press.

Oyama, Susan, Paul Griffiths, and Russell Gray, eds. 2001. *Cycles of Contingency:
Developmental Systems and Evolution.* Cambridge, Mass.: MIT Press.

Pallota, Julien. 2019. "Viveiros de Castro au-delà de Clastres: Vers un Brésil mineur
ou un alter-Brésil." In *Politique des Multiplicités: Pierre Clastres face à l'État,*
edited by Eduardo Viveiros de Castro. Bellevaux: Éditions Dehors.

Panksepp, Jaak. 1998. *Affective Neuroscience.* New York: Oxford University Press.

Patterson, Orlando. 1979. "Slavery and Slave Revolts: A Sociohistorical Analysis of
the First Maroon War, 1665–1740." In *Maroon Societies: Rebel Slave Communities in the Americas,* edited by Richard Price, 246–92. Baltimore: Johns Hopkins
University Press.

Patterson, Orlando. 2018. *Slavery and Social Death: A Comparative Study.* Cambridge, Mass.: Harvard University Press.

Patton, Paul. 2018. "1227: Treatise on Nomadology—The War Machine." In *A Thousand Plateaus and Philosophy,* edited by Henry Somers-Hall, Jeffrey Bell, and
James Williams, 206–22. Edinburgh: Edinburgh University Press.

Pepping, Gert-Jan, and Erik Timmermans. 2012. "Oxytocin and the Biopsychology
of Performance in Team Sports." *Scientific World Journal* 2012. doi: 10.1100/20
12/567363

Pessoa, Luiz. 2017. "A Network Model of the Emotional Brain." *Trends in Cognitive
Science* 21.5: 357–71.

Peters, Achim, Bruce McEwen, and Karl Friston. 2017. "Uncertainty and Stress:
Why It Causes Diseases and How It Is Mastered by the Brain." *Progress in Neurobiology* 156: 164–88.

Pickford, Henry, ed. 2022. "The Mind–Body Politic Symposium." *Syndicate*. https://syndicate.network/symposia/philosophy/the-mind-body-politic/

Pigliucci, Massimo, and Gerd Müller, eds. 2010. *Evolution: The Extended Synthesis*. Cambridge, Mass.: MIT Press.

Pilozzi, Alexander, Caitlin Carro, and Xudong Huang. 2020. "Roles of β-Endorphin in Stress, Behavior, Neuroinflammation, and Brain Energy Metabolism." *International Journal of Molecular Science* 22.1 (December 30): 338.

Pisor, Anne, and Michael Gurven. 2016. "Risk Buffering and Resource Access Shape Valuation of Out-Group Strangers." *Scientific Reports* 6: 30435. https://doi.org/10.1038/srep30435

Pisor, Anne, and Martin Surbeck. 2019. "The Evolution of Intergroup Tolerance in Nonhuman Primates and Humans." *Evolutionary Anthropology* 28: 210–23.

Plumer, Brad. 2016. "Full Transcript of Donald Trump's Acceptance Speech at the RNC." July 22. https://www.vox.com/2016/7/21/12253426/donald-trump-acceptance-speech-transcript-republican-nomination-transcript

Popoli, Maurizio, Zhen Yan, Bruce McEwen, and Gerald Sanacora. 2012. "The Stressed Synapse: The Impact of Stress and Glucocorticoids on Glutamate Transmission." *Nature Reviews Neuroscience* 13: 22–37.

Potter-Efron, Ronald. 2007. *Rage*. Oakland, Calif.: New Harbinger Books.

Price, Richard. 1976. *The Guiana Maroons: A Historical and Bibliographical Introduction*. Baltimore: Johns Hopkins University Press.

Price, Richard, ed. 1979. *Maroon Societies: Rebel Slave Communities in the Americas*. Baltimore: Johns Hopkins University Press.

Protevi, John. 1994. "Violence and Authority in Kant." *Epoché: A Journal for the History of Philosophy* 2: 65–89.

Protevi, John. 1997. "Given Time and the Gift of Life." *Man and World* 30.1: 65–82.

Protevi, John. 2000. "'A Problem of Pure Matter': Deleuze and Guattari's Treatment of Fascist Nihilism in A Thousand Plateaus." In *Nihilism Now! "Monsters of Energy,"* edited by Keith Ansell-Pearson and Diane Morgan, 167–88. London: Macmillan.

Protevi, John. 2001. *Political Physics*. London: Athlone Press.

Protevi, John. 2008. "Affect, Agency, and Responsibility: The Act of Killing in the Age of Cyborgs." *Phenomenology and the Cognitive Sciences* 7.2: 405–13.

Protevi, John. 2009. *Political Affect: Connecting the Social and the Somatic*. Minneapolis: University of Minnesota Press.

Protevi, John. 2010. "Rhythm and Cadence, Frenzy and March: Music and the Geo-bio-techno-affective Assemblages of Ancient Warfare." *Theory & Event* 13.3 (September).

Protevi, John. 2011. "Semantic, Pragmatic, and Affective Enactment at OWS." *Theory & Event* 14.4 (Supplement).

Protevi, John. 2012. "Deleuze and Life." In *The Cambridge Companion to Deleuze*, edited by Henry Somers-Hall and Daniel W. Smith, 239–64. Cambridge: Cambridge University Press.

Protevi, John. 2013. *Life, War, Earth: Deleuze and the Sciences.* Minneapolis: University of Minnesota Press.

Protevi, John. 2019. *Edges of the State.* Minneapolis: University of Minnesota Press.

Protevi, John. 2020. "Affect and Life in Spinoza, Nietzsche, and Bergson." In *Affect and Literature,* edited by Alex Houen, 66–82. Cambridge: Cambridge University Press.

Prum, Richard O. 2017. *The Evolution of Beauty.* New York: Anchor Books.

Puar, Jasbir. 2017. *Terrorist Assemblages: Homonationalism in Queer Times.* Durham, N.C.: Duke University Press.

Radman, Andrej. 2012. *Gibsonism: Ecologies of Architecture.* Delft: TU Delft Repository.

Ramstead, Maxwell, Samuel Veissière, and Laurence Kirmayer. 2016. "Cultural Affordances: Scaffolding Local Worlds Through Shared Intentionality and Regimes of Attention." *Frontiers in Psychology* 7: 1090.

Rapinoe, Megan. 2014. "The Cross." https://www.theplayerstribune.com/articles/the-cross

Read, Jason. 2015. *The Politics of Transindividuality.* Chicago: Haymarket Books.

Reich, Wilhelm. 1946. *The Mass Psychology of Fascism.* Translated by Theodore P. Wolfe. New York: Orgone Institute Press.

Richardson, John. 2008. *Nietzsche's New Darwinism.* New York: Oxford University Press.

Richerson, Peter, and Robert Boyd. 2005. *Not by Genes Alone: How Culture Transformed Human Evolution.* Chicago: University of Chicago Press.

Rietveld, Erik, Damian Denys, and Maarten Van Westen. 2018. "Ecological-Enactive Cognition as Engaging with a Field of Relevant Affordances." In *The Oxford Handbook of 4E Cognition,* edited by Albert Newen, Leon De Bruin, and Shaun Gallagher, 41–70. New York: Oxford University Press.

Rietveld, Erik, and Julian Kiverstein. 2014. "A Rich Landscape of Affordances." *Ecological Psychology* 26.4: 325–52.

Roberts, Neil. 2015. *Freedom as Marronage.* Chicago: University of Chicago Press.

Roscoe, Paul. 2007. "Intelligence, Coalitional Killing, and the Antecedents of War." *American Anthropologist* 109.3: 485–95.

Rosen, Michael. 1996. *On Voluntary Servitude: False Consciousness and the Theory of Ideology.* Cambridge, Mass.: Harvard University Press.

Rouse, Joseph. 2023. *Social Practices as Biological Niche Construction.* Chicago: University of Chicago Press.

Rousseau, Jean-Jacques. 1997. *Discourse on Inequality.* In *The Discourses and Other Early Political Writings.* Translated and edited by Victor Gourevitch. Cambridge: Cambridge University Press.

Ruse, Michael. 1985. *Sociobiology: Sense or Nonsense?* Dordrecht: Riedel Publishing.

Ryan, Kevin, and Shaun Gallagher. 2020. "Between Ecological Psychology and Enactivism: Is There Resonance?" *Frontiers in Psychology* 11: 1147.

Sahlins, Marshall. 1972. *Stone Age Economics*. New York: Aldine de Gruyter.

Sahlins, Marshall. 2008. *The Western Illusion of Human Nature*. Chicago: Prickly Paradigm Press.

Sánchez-Villagra, Marcelo, and Carel van Schaik. 2019. "Evaluating the Self-Domestication Hypothesis of Human Evolution." *Evolutionary Anthropology* 28: 133–43.

Sansone, David. 1992. *Greek Athletics and the Genesis of Sport*. Berkeley: University of California Press.

Satz, Debra, and John Ferejohn. 1994. "Rational Choice and Social Theory." *The Journal of Philosophy* 91.2: 71–87.

Scarry, Elaine. 1987. *The Body in Pain: The Making and Unmaking of the World*. New York: Oxford University Press.

Scheidel, Walter. 2013. "Studying the State." In *The Oxford Handbook of the State in the Ancient Near East and Mediterranean*, edited by Peter Fibiger Bang and Walter Scheidel, 5–58. New York: Oxford University Press.

Schinkel, Willem. 2013. "Regimes of Violence and the *Trias Violentiae*." *European Journal of Social Theory* 16.3: 310–25.

Schino, Gabriele, and Filippo Aureli. 2009. "Reciprocal Altruism in Primates: Partner Choice, Cognition, and Emotions." *Advances in the Study of Behavior* 39: 45–69. Cambridge, Mass.: Academic Press.

Schwartz, Stuart B. 1992. *Slaves, Peasants, and Rebels: Reconsidering Brazilian Slavery*. Champaign: University of Illinois Press.

Scott, James C. 1998. *Seeing Like a State*. New Haven: Yale University Press.

Scott, James C. 2009. *The Art of Not Being Governed: An Anarchist History of Upland Southeast Asia*. New Haven: Yale University Press.

Scott, James C. 2017. *Against the Grain: A Deep History of the Earliest States*. New Haven: Yale University Press.

Segovia-Cuéllar, Andrés, and Lorenzo Del Savio. 2021. "On the Use of Evolutionary Mismatch Theories in Debating Human Prosociality." *Medicine, Health Care and Philosophy* 24: 305–14.

Segundo-Ortin, Manuel. 2024. "Socio-cultural Norms in Ecological Psychology: The Education of Intention." *Phenomenology and the Cognitive Sciences* 23: 1–19.

Seth, Anil, and Karl Friston. 2016. "Active Interoceptive Inference and the Emotional Brain." *Philosophical Transactions of the Royal Society, B Biological Sciences*. 371: 20160007. doi: 10.1098/rstb.2016.0007

Shay, Jonathan. 1994. *Achilles in Vietnam*. New York: Macmillan.

Shay, Jonathan. 2003. *Odysseus in America*. New York: Scribner.

Shay, Jonathan. 2014. "Moral Injury." *Psychoanalytic Psychology* 31.2: 182–91.

Sherman, Nancy. 2005. *Stoic Warriors: The Ancient Philosophy Behind the Military Mind*. Oxford: Oxford University Press.

Sherwell, Philip. 2012. "Sgt Robert Bales: The Story of the Soldier Accused of Murdering 16 Afghan Villagers." *The Telegraph* (March 17).

Shilton, Dor, Mati Breski, Daniel Dor, and Eva Jablonka. 2020. "Human Social Evolution: Self-Domestication or Self-Control?" *Frontiers in Psychology* 11. doi:10.3389/fpsyg.2020.00134

Sibertin-Blanc, Guillaume. 2016. *State and Politics: Deleuze and Guattari on Marx.* Translated by Ames Hodges. New York: Semiotext(e).

Siegel, Allan, and Jeff Victoroff. 2009. "Understanding Human Aggression." *International Journal of Law and Psychiatry* 32: 209–15.

Simondon, Gilbert. 2020. *Individuation in Light of Notions of Form and Information.* Translated by Taylor Adkins. Minneapolis: University of Minnesota Press.

Singer, Alan. 2021. "Political Violence: Still as American as Cherry Pie." History News Network. https://www.historynewsnetwork.org/article/political-violence-still-as-american-as-cherry-pie

Singh, Manvir, and Luke Glowacki. 2022. "Human Social Organization During the Late Pleistocene: Beyond the Nomadic–Egalitarian Model." *Evolution and Human Behavior* 43.5: 418–31.

Slaby, Jan. 2008. "Affective Intentionality and the Feeling Body." *Phenomenology and the Cognitive Sciences* 7: 429–44.

Slaby, Jan. 2010. "Steps Towards a Critical Neuroscience." *Phenomenology and the Cognitive Sciences* 9.3: 397–416.

Slaby, Jan. 2016. "Mind Invasion: Situated Affectivity and the Corporate Life Hack." *Frontiers in Psychology* 7. doi:10.3389/fpsyg.2016.00266

Slaby, Jan, and Shaun Gallagher. 2015. "Critical Neuroscience and Socially Extended Minds." *Theory, Culture & Society* 32.1: 33–59.

Smith, Daniel W. 2018. "7000BC: Apparatus of Capture." In *A Thousand Plateaus and Philosophy,* edited by Henry Somers-Hall, Jeffrey Bell, and James Williams, 223–41. Edinburgh: Edinburgh University Press.

Somers-Hall, Henry, Jeffrey Bell, and James Williams, eds. 2018. *A Thousand Plateaus and Philosophy.* Edinburgh: Edinburgh University Press.

Sommerfeldt, Chris. 2021. "Pro-Trump Rioters Smeared Poop in U.S. Capitol Hallways During Belligerent Attack." *New York Daily News* (January 7).

Speidel, Michael. 2002. "Berserks: A History of Indo-European 'Mad Warriors.'" *Journal of World History* 13.2: 253–90.

Spinka, Marek, Ruth Newberry, and Marc Bekoff. 2001. "Mammalian Play: Training for the Unexpected." *Quarterly Review of Biology* 76.2: 141–68.

Spinoza, Baruch. 1992. *Ethics.* Translated by Samuel Shirley. Indianapolis: Hackett Books.

Stanley, Jason. 2015. *How Propaganda Works.* Princeton: Princeton University Press.

Stennett, Lavinya. 2020. "An Exploration of Agency Within Maroon Ecological Praxis: Unearthing the Histories of Maroon Ecology in Jamaica and Brazil from 1630 to 1780." *Decolonial Subversions* 99–119.

Sterelny, Kim. 2012. *The Evolved Apprentice: How Evolution Made Humans Unique.* Cambridge, Mass.: MIT Press.

Sterelny, Kim. 2014. "Cooperation, Culture, and Conflict." *British Journal for the Philosophy of Science* 67.1: 1–28.

Sterelny, Kim. 2021. *The Pleistocene Social Contract.* New York: Oxford University Press.

Stewart, Lindsey. 2021. *The Politics of Black Joy.* Evanston, Ill.: Northwestern University Press.

Stoljar, Natalie. 2024. "Feminist Perspectives on Autonomy." In Edward Zalta, ed., *The Stanford Encyclopedia of Philosophy.* https://plato.stanford.edu/archives/sum 2024/entries/feminism-autonomy

Sutton, John. 2007. "Batting, Habit and Memory: The Embodied Mind and the Nature of Skill." *Sport in Society* 10.5: 763–86.

Sutton-Smith, Brian. 1997. *The Ambiguity of Play.* Cambridge, Mass.: Harvard University Press.

Swihart, Gayla, John Yuille, and Stephen Porter. 1999. "The Role of State-Dependent Memory in 'Red-Outs.'" *International Journal of Law and Psychiatry* 22.3–4: 199–212.

Thamer, Hans-Ulrich. 1996. "The Orchestration of the National Community: The Nuremberg Part Rallies of the NSDAP." In *Fascism and Theatre: Comparative Studies on the Aesthetics and Politics of Performance in Europe, 1925–1945,* edited by Günther Berghaus, 172–90. Providence, R.I.: Berghahn Books.

Theweleit, Klaus. 1987–89. *Male Fantasies.* Translated by Stephen Conway, Erica Carter, and Chris Turner. Minneapolis: University of Minnesota Press.

Thoburn, Nick. 2003. *Deleuze, Marx, and Politics.* London: Routledge, 2003.

Thomas, Greg. 2016. "*Marronnons* Let's Maroon: Sylvia Wynter's 'Black Metamorphosis' as a Species of Maroonage." *Small Axe* 20.1 (49): 62–78.

Thompson, Evan. 2007. *Mind in Life: Biology, Phenomenology, and the Sciences of Mind.* Cambridge, Mass.: Harvard University Press.

Thompson, Evan, and Francisco J. Varela. 2001. "Radical Embodiment: Neural Dynamics and Consciousness." *Trends in Cognitive Sciences* 5.10: 418–25.

Thornton, John K. 2008. "Les États de l'Angola et la formation de Palmares (Brésil)." *Annales. Histoire, Sciences Sociales* 63: 769–97.

Tollefsen, Deborah. 2015. *Groups as Agents.* Cambridge: Polity Press.

Tomaello, Michael. 2009. *Why We Cooperate.* Cambridge, Mass.: MIT Press.

Tomasello, Michael. 2016. *A Natural History of Human Morality.* Cambridge, Mass.: Harvard University Press.

Tomasello, Michael. 2019. *Becoming Human: A Theory of Ontogeny.* Cambridge, Mass.: Harvard University Press.

Tomasello, Michael, and Ivan Gonzalez-Cabrera. 2017. "The Role of Ontogeny in the Evolution of Human Cooperation." *Human Nature* 28: 274–88.

Toscano, Alberto. 2006. *The Theatre of Production: Philosophy and Individuation between Kant and Deleuze.* London: Palgrave Macmillan.

Totterdell, P. 2000. "Catching Moods and Hitting Runs: Mood Linkage and Subjective Performance in Professional Sport Teams." *Journal of Applied Psychology* 85.6: 848–59.

Trevarthen, Colwyn. 1999. "Musicality and the Intrinsic Motive Pulse: Evidence from Human Psychobiology and Infant Communication." *Musicae Scientiae,* special issue: 155–215.

Turecki, Gustavo, and Michael Meaney. 2014. "Effects of the Social Environment and Stress on Glucocorticoid Receptor Gene Methylation: A Systematic Review." *Biological Psychiatry* 79.2: 87–96. https://doi.org/10.1016/j.biopsych.2014.11.022

Tyner, James. 2006. "'Defend the Ghetto': Space and the Urban Politics of the Black Panther Party." *Annals of the Association of American Geographers* 96.1: 105–18.

Uzgalis, William. 2017. "John Locke, Racism, and Indian Lands." In *The Oxford Handbook of Philosophy and Race,* edited by Naomi Zack, 21–30. New York: Oxford University Press.

Vaesen, Krist. 2014. "Chimpocentrism and Reconstructions of Human Evolution (a Timely Reminder)." *Studies in History and Philosophy of Biological and Biomedical Sciences* 45: 12–21.

Van den Linden, Harry. 1988. *Kantian Ethics and Socialism.* Indianapolis: Hackett.

van der Kolk, Bessel, and Mark Greenberg. 1987. "The Psychobiology of the Trauma Response." In *Psychological Trauma,* edited by Bessel van der Kolk, 63–87. Washington, D.C.: American Psychiatric Press.

van Zyl, Llewellyn, Jaclyn Gaffaney, Leoni van der Vaart, Bryan Dik, and Stewart Donaldson. 2023. "The Critiques and Criticisms of Positive Psychology: A Systematic Review." *The Journal of Positive Psychology.* doi: 10.1080/17439760.2023.2178956

Varela, Francisco J. 1981. "Describing the Logic of the Living: The Adequacy and Limitations of the Idea of Autopoiesis." In *Autopoiesis: A Theory of Living Organization,* edited by Milan Zeleny, 36–48. New York: North Holland.

Varela, Francisco J. 1991. "Organism: A Meshwork of Selfless Selves." In *Organism and the Origins of Self,* edited by Alfred Tauber, 79–107. Dordrecht: Springer.

Varela, Francisco J. 1995. "Resonant Cell Assemblies: A New Approach to Cognitive Functions and Neuronal Synchrony." *Biological Research* 28: 81–95.

Varela, Francisco J. 1996. "Neurophenomenology: A Methodological Remedy for the Hard Problem." *Journal of Consciousness Studies* 3.4: 330–49.

Varela, Francisco J. 1999. "The Specious Present: A Neurophenomenology of Time Consciousness." In *Naturalizing Phenomenology: Issues in Contemporary Phenomenology and Cognitive Science,* edited by Jean Petitot, Francisco J. Varela, Bernard

Pachoud, and Jean-Michel Roy, 266–314. Stanford, Calif.: Stanford University Press.

Varela, Francisco J., Humberto Maturana, and Ricardo Uribe. 1974. "Autopoiesis: The Organization of the Living, Its Characterization and a Model." *BioSystems* 5.4: 187–96.

Varela, Francisco J., Evan Thompson, and Eleanor Rosch. 1991. *The Embodied Mind.* Cambridge, Mass.: MIT Press.

Vaughan, Brendan. 2015. "Robert Bales Speaks: Confessions of America's Most Notorious War Criminal." *GQ* (October 21). http://www.gq.com/story/robert-bales-interview-afghanistan-massacre

Viveiros de Castro, Eduardo. 2014. *Cannibal Metaphysics.* Translated by Peter Skafish. Minneapolis: Univocal Publishing.

Viveiros de Castro, Eduardo. 2019. *Politiques des multiplicités: Pierre Clastres face à l'État.* Bellevaux: Éditions Dehors.

Walker, Harry, and Iva Kavedžija. 2015. "Values of Happiness." *Hau: Journal of Ethnographic Theory* 5.3: 1–23.

Wallace, Robert, Alex Liebman, Luis Fernando Chaves, and Rodrick Wallace. "Covid-19 and Circuits of Capital." *Monthly Review* (May). https://monthlyreview.org/2020/05/01/covid-19-and-circuits-of-capital/

Wasser, Audrey. 2017. "How Do We Recognise Problems?" *Deleuze Studies* 11.1: 48–67.

Wasser, Audrey. 2018. "587 BC–AD 70: On Several Regimes of Signs." In *A Thousand Plateaus and Philosophy,* edited by Henry Somers-Hall, Jeffrey Bell, and James Williams, 83–98. Edinburgh: Edinburgh University Press.

Watson, Matthew C. 2017. "Imitation and Society: How Boasian Anthropology Reassembled the Social." *Anthropological Theory* 17.2: 135–58.

Webster, George. 2023. "The Metaphysics Science Needs: Deleuze's Naturalism." *European Journal of Philosophy.* doi: 10.1111/ejop.12909

Weeks, Samuel. 2019. "A Politics of Peripheries: Deleuze and Guattari as Dependency Theorists." *Deleuze and Guattari Studies* 13.1: 79–103.

Weheliye, Alexandre. 2014. *Habeas Viscus: Racializing Assemblages, Biopolitics, and Black Feminist Theories of the Human.* Durham, N.C.: Duke University Press.

Weikart, Richard. 2013. "The Role of Darwinism in Nazi Racial Thought." *German Studies Review* 36.3: 537–56.

Weiss, Gail, Gayle Salamon, and Ann Murphy, eds. 2019. *50 Concepts for a Critical Phenomenology.* Evanston, Ill.: Northwestern University Press.

West-Eberhard, Mary Jane. 2003. *Developmental Plasticity and Evolution.* New York: Oxford University Press.

Wexler, Bruce. 2006. *Brain and Culture: Neurobiology, Ideology, and Social Change.* Cambridge, Mass.: MIT Press.

Widerquist, Karl, and Grant McCall. 2017. *Prehistoric Myths in Modern Political Philosophy.* Edinburgh: Edinburgh University Press.

Williams, Eric. 1944. *Capitalism and Slavery.* Chapel Hill: University of North Carolina Press.

Williams, James. 2005. *The Transversal Thought of Gilles Deleuze: Encounters and Influences.* Manchester: Clinamen Press.

Williamson, Kellie, and Rochelle Cox. 2014. "Distributed Cognition in Sports Teams: Explaining Successful and Expert Performance." *Educational Philosophy and Theory* 46:6: 640–54.

Wilson, Edward O. 1975. *Sociobiology: The New Synthesis.* Cambridge, Mass.: Harvard University Press.

Woods, Carl T., Ian McKeown, Mark O'Sullivan, Sam Robertson, and Keith Davids. 2020. "Theory to Practice: Performance Preparation Models in Contemporary High-Level Sport Guided by an Ecological Dynamics Framework." *Sports Medicine—Open* 6: 36.

Wrangham, Richard. 1999. "Evolution of Coalitionary Killing." *Journal of Physical Anthropology* 42: 1–30.

Wrangham, Richard. 2019. *The Goodness Paradox.* New York: Pantheon.

Wrangham, Richard, and Dale Peterson. 1996. *Demonic Males: Apes and the Origins of Human Violence.* New York: Houghton Mifflin.

Wright, Willie Jamaal. 2020. "The Morphology of Marronage." *Annals of the American Association of Geographers* 110.4: 1134–49.

Wu, X., R. C. Nethery, M. B. Sabath, D. Braun, and F. Dominici. 2020. "Air Pollution and Covid-19 Mortality in the United States: Strengths and Limitations of an Ecological Regression Analysis." *Science Advances* 6.45. doi: 10.1126/sciadv.abd4049

Wynter, Sylvia. 2001. "Towards the Sociogenic Principle: Fanon, Identity, the Puzzle of Conscious Experience, and What It Is Like to Be 'Black.'" In *National Identities and Sociopolitical Changes in Latin America,* edited by Mercedes F. Durán-Cogan and Antonio Gómez-Moriana, 30–66. New York: Routledge.

Wynter, Sylvia. 2003. "Unsettling the Coloniality of Being/Power/Truth/Freedom: Towards the Human, After Man, Its Overrepresentation—An Argument." *CR: The New Centennial Review* 3.3: 257–337.

Young, Iris Marion. 1980. "Throwing Like a Girl: A Phenomenology of Feminine Body Comportment Motility and Spatiality." *Human Studies* 3.2: 137–56.

Zahavi, Dan. 2005. *Subjectivity and Selfhood: Investigating the First-Person Perspective.* Cambridge, Mass.: MIT Press.

Zahavi, Dan. 2021. "We in Me or Me in We? Collective Intentionality and Selfhood." *Journal of Social Ontology* 7.1: 1–20.

Zinn, Jens. 2018. "Risk, Power, and Inequality in the 21st Century." *British Journal of Sociology* 69.4: 1344–46.

Žižek, Slavoj. 2008. *Violence: Six Sideways Reflections.* New York: Picador.

Publication History

Grateful acknowledgment is made to the following publishers for permission to adapt parts of the following chapters from their original publications.

Portions of chapter 2 are adapted from "Stanley on Ideology," *Theoria: An International Journal for Theory, History, and Foundations of Science* 31, no. 2 (2016): 357–69.

Portions of chapters 2–5 and the Conclusion are adapted from *Edges of the State* (Minneapolis: University of Minnesota Press, 2019).

Portions of chapter 3 are adapted from "Phenomenology of the Blackout Rage: The Inhibition of Episodic Memory in Extreme Berserker Episodes," in Anya Daly, Fred Cummins, James Jardine, and Dermot Moran, eds., *Perception and the Inhuman Gaze* (New York: Routledge, 2022), 218–35. Copyright 2022. Reprinted by permission of Taylor and Francis Group through PLSclear.

Portions of chapter 3 are adapted from "The Berserker Rage," in Myisha V. Cherry and Owen Flanagan, eds., *The Moral Psychology of Anger* (London: Rowman and Littlefield International, 2018), 139–56. Reprinted with permission of The Licensor through PLSclear.

Portions of chapter 4 are adapted from "*Esprit de corps* and Thinking on (and with) Your Feet: Standard, Enactive, and Post-Structuralist Aspects of Relational Autonomy and Collective Intentionality in Team Sports," *Southern Journal of Philosophy* 61, no. 1 (2023): 24–38.

Portions of chapter 5 are adapted from "Statification," in Henry Somers-Hall and Jeffrey Bell, eds., *The Deleuzian Mind* (New York: Routledge, 2024).

Portions of chapter 6 are adapted from "The Multiplicity of Marronage," *La Deleuziana, Dossier 50 years of Anti-Oedipus (2023). Volume I. Taking Desires for Reality,* 111–28, http://www.ladeleuziana.org/wp-content/uploads/2023/06/7_Pro tevi_The-multiplicity-of-marronage.pdf.

Portions of chapter 7 are adapted from "Under the Dome: The Capitol Invasion," in Stavros Kousoulas and Andrej Radman, eds., *The Space of Technicity* (TU Delft Open Press, 2024). https://doi.org/10.59490/mg.95

Portions of chapter 8 are adapted from "Covid 19 in the USA as Affective Frame," *Frontiers in Psychology* 13 (2022), https://doi.org/10.3389/fpsyg.2022.897215.

Portions of the Conclusion are adapted from "Human Nature and Anti-Fascist Living," in Rosi Braidotti and Rick Dolphjin, eds., *Deleuze and Guattari and Fascism* (Edinburgh: Edinburgh University Press, 2022), 23–38. Reprinted with permission of The Licensor through PLSclear.

Index

accumulation, primitive, xix, 101, 111, 114

adaptation, 56, 67, 68, 69, 74; adaptationist discourse, 11, 70; autopoiesis and, 32–33; evolutionary, 169n10, 175n6; play as, 82–83. *See also* Environment of Evolutionary Adaptedness (EEA)

Adkins, Lisa: on debt, risk, and financialization, 148–49; on essential workers, 159

affect, 35, 44, 79, 142, 144, 163; affect program concept, 55–56, 58; components of, 67–68; definitions of, 75, 130; in team sports, 80–84. *See also* emotions

affective cognition, xiii, 7–8, 38–39, 40, 133–35, 173n7. *See also* bodies politic; cognition; politics

affective frames, 35–36, 132, 141; Covid-19 pandemic and, 144–46, 151, 160; impacting essential workers, 142–43, 148, 156, 157

affective ideology, xxv, 29–48; component of regime of violence, 30, 141; formation of, xxv, 8, 133, 141; political, 30–37, 127, 138; use of term, 10, 144. *See also* ideology

affordances, 39, 137; political, 128, 130–33, 135; social, 34, 133, 134, 144

aggression: proactive, 53–54; reactive, xxv–xxvi; types of, 52–55; violent, 26.

See also anger; berserker rage; rage

allostatic load, 153–54, 156, 160

altruism: in human evolution, 15; inter- and intra-species and group, 19, 162; prosociality's relationship to, 8–9; psychological, 9, 24. *See also* sharing

amnesia, 64. *See also* blackout rages; Transient Global Amnesia (TGA)

Anderson, Robert N.: social structures of maroon communities, 118

Andrews, Kristin: on normative regularities, 165n5

anger, 53–55, 174n5; in battle, 4, 17, 172n26. *See also* aggression; berserker rage; rage

anthropology, xiii, xxv, xxvi–xxvii, 9, 14; evolutionary, 3, 18, 74, 170n17

anti-fascism, xxviii, 43, 161–62, 164. *See also* fascism

Anti-Oedipus (Deleuze and Guattari), xxvi; Foucault's preface to, 161, 162

apparatus of capture, 91–95, 97, 101, 104–6, 114–15, 118. *See also* capture

Aptheker, Herbert: on maroon raids, 179n15

Aristotle, 168n2, 174n5

Asiatic Mode of Production concept, xix, 92, 108

assemblages, 43, 57, 103, 148, 162, 176n8; of affective cognition, 7–8;

Boehm, Christopher: reverse dominance hierarchy theory, 98; on
violence in forager societies, 22,
23
bonobos, 13, 24–25
Boyd, Robert: dual inheritance theory,
70
Brady, Judy: "I Want a Wife!" essay, 73
brain: Bayesian Brain concept, 153–54;
body in dialogue with, 32, 35, 55–56,
77, 78, 84; central command mode,
33, 155; involvement in rage episodes, 57–59, 65; mind's connection
with, 31, 155; Selfish Brain concept,
153–54. See also amnesia; memories;
predictive processing; Transient
Global Amnesia (TGA)
Brown, H. Rap: on American violence,
165–66n6
Buchanan, Allen, 172n28; on evolution
of morality, 169–70n11
bullies, xxi, 22, 24, 26, 40, 178n11
Burghardt, Gordon: surplus resources
theory of play, 71

Caillois, Roger: on dimensions of play,
68
Campbell, Richmond: on evolution of
morality, 169–70n11
capitalism, xviii, 42–43, 97, 149;
Deleuze and Guattari on, 110–14;
gendered, 163–64; global, 111–12,
121; racialized, 163–64; slavery's
relationship to, 108, 112–13. See also
economy
Capitol building, 136. See also Chansley,
Jacob (Q-Anon Shaman); January 6,
2021, invasion of the U.S. Capitol
capture, 70, 116, 176n2; overcoding
and, xxvi, 96, 176n3, 176n5; states
described in terms of, xviii, 89, 95,

119, 172n24. See also apparatus of
capture
care/caring, 3, 11–12, 14, 24, 26, 65, 73.
See also essential workers
case studies: of Covid-19 pandemic,
xxvii–xxviii, 141, 142–43, 144, 148,
160; of esprit de corps, xxv, xxvi,
67, 71, 75, 77; ethics of, 142–43; of
January 6, 2021, invasion of the
U.S. Capitol, xxvii, 127, 128–29, 130,
136; methodology and ontology of,
129–30
Chalmers, David: extended mind
article, 172n4
Chansley, Jacob (Q-Anon Shaman),
xxvii; prayer in Senate chamber,
128, 133, 135–39, 180n8. See also
January 6, 2021, invasion of the U.S.
Capitol
Chemero, Anthony: on affordances,
131–32
chiefdoms, 96, 98
Chimpanzee Referential Doctrine
(CRD), 13–14, 25
chimpanzees, 17, 25, 167n19
Chowkwanyun, Merlin: Covid analysis
by, 151–52, 159
Clark, Andy: extended mind article,
172n4
class: as Covid illness factor, 159;
Deleuze and Guattari on, 97, 99;
management of, 122–23; race intersecting with, 152; risk intersecting
with, 148, 152
Clastres, Pierre: on meaning of subsistence, 14–15; on state formation,
xxvi, 115, 171n23; study of Amazonian societies, xix, 92; on violence,
115
coercive reproduction, 29–30, 39–41,
45; punishment constituting,

40–41, 44, 45–46, 47, 48. *See also* reproduction
cognition, 33, 76, 77, 84, 130, 173n7; enactivist definition of, 31–32, 36–37, 155–56; 4EA, 31, 138. *See also* affective cognition
cognitive science, xxvii, 34, 131, 134, 144, 153–54
collective intentionality, xxvi, 67–68, 75–78, 79; interfacing with relational autonomy, 77–85. *See also* intentionality
competition, 71, 79, 149; in the EEA, 14–15; inter- and intra-species and group, 16, 167n21; for resources, 12, 169–70n11
conflict, xx, 19, 21; competitive, 12, 20; inter-group, xxiv, xxvi, 4–5, 7, 23–24, 161, 169–70n11. *See also* regimes of violence; violence; war/warfare
constructivism, 131; moderate, 6, 55, 57–59, 72; radical, 55, 56–57; social, xii, 6, 8
Cooper, Melinda, 157; alternative to the welfare state, 148; on neoliberalism, 149
cooperation, xxiv, 12, 14, 70, 73, 149, 170n16, 172n27; communicative, 23–24; inter- and intra-species and group, 16, 19, 22; joy of, 10–11, 26. *See also* sharing
Covid-19 pandemic, 141–60; affective frames related to, 144–46, 151, 160; biopower in, 146–47; bodies politic related to, 144–46; case study of, xxvii–xxviii, 141, 142–43, 144, 148, 160; chronic stress caused by, 153–56; deaths of essential workers during, 156–60; predictive processing and, 153–55; racial weathering's

effects during, xxviii, 150–53, 156, 160; risks encountered during, 141, 142, 143, 148–50, 156–57
CRD. *See* Chimpanzee Referential Doctrine (CRD)
Critical Race Architecture, 135. *See also* race
cultural scaffolding, 134–35
culture, xiii, 9, 51, 155. *See also* bioculturality; bioenculturation; enculturation
Curran, Dean: on risk, 148

Darwin, Charles: emphasis on survival and reproduction, 175n6; evolutionary paradigm, 168n4; mutual aid thesis, 12, 19; war as selection pressure for prosociality, 15, 16. *See also* evolution
Darwinism: inclusive, 16; Social Darwinism, 171n19, 171n20
Dean, Mitchell: on risk, 148
Debien, Gabriel: on marronage, 108, 109–10
De Block, Andreas: dual inheritance theory, 70
decoding, 92, 93, 113. *See also* overcoding
De Jaegher, Hanne: essay on love, 175–76n10; on second-person cognition as participatory sense-making, 33
Deleuze, Gilles, xi; abstract machine concept, 57; on capitalism, 110–14; on class, 97, 99; Clastres's influence on, 14; criticism of Lévi-Strauss, 99; definition of affection, 130; on desire, 95; on flight, 121; on form of content, xvii; on geophilosophy, 103–4; on geosocial tendencies, 120; on human nature, xxiii; on ideology,

thought on Marx and Freud, 161–62; governmentality concept of, 147; on neoliberalism, 149; preface to *Anti-Oedipus,* 161, 162; on sexuality, 146–47

Freitas, Décio: social structures of maroon communities, 118

Freud, Sigmund, 161–62

Fry, Douglas, 7, 20–21, 92

Fuchs, Thomas: brain as a relational organ, 77

Fuentes, Agustín: on integrative anthropology, xiii

Gallagher, Shaun: on ecological psychology and enactivism, 130; operative intentionality, 78; ownership without agency concept, 60

gender/gendering: of capitalism, 163–64; as Covid illness factor, 148, 150–51, 159; division of labor according to, 19; practices of, 135, 145, 146

genes, xiii, xv, 6, 11, 167n21

geography: Black, 121–22; of marronage, 103, 119–21; State, 115, 122

Geronimus, Arline: on weathering, 152–53

Ghiselin, Michael: on competition in nature, 168n4

Gibson, James J.: on notion of mass sociality, 173n9; on ecological psychology, 130

gifts/giving, 9, 11, 12, 13, 170n14

Gilbert, Jeremy: on notion of mass sociality, 173n9

Gilbert, Margaret: on collective intentionality, 82; on group subject, 79

Gilmore, Ruth Wilson: definition of racism, 167n17

Glissant, Edouard: on maroons, 121

Gonzalez-Cabrera, Ivan: on the CRD, 13; on norms, 171n21

governmentality, 147, 150, 151, 166n7

Graeber, David: on nonstate peoples, 17–18; on notion of warfare in Clastres, 171n23

Gray, Russell, xiv

Griffiths, Paul, xiv; affect program concept, 55–56, 58

Guattari, Félix, xi, 162; on capitalism, 110–14; on class, 97, 99; Clastres's influence on, 14; criticism of Lévi-Strauss, 99; definition of affection, 130; on desire, 95; on flight, 121; on form of content, xvii; on geophilosophy, 103–4; on geosocial tendencies, 120; on human nature, xxiii; on ideology, 29, 41–44; on interest-discordant behavior, 40; line of flight, 121; on marronage, 109, 110–14; on multiplicities, xxiii; on Nietzsche, 13, 105; on nomads, xix–xx, 108; on organisms, 168n2; on primitive societies, 96–97; on regimes of violence, xviii–xx, 103–4, 115–18; on resonance, 97–98; on slavery, 110–14, 116, 179n16; on social formations, 118–19; social topology of, 102–4; on Spinoza, 10, 162; on state formation, xix, xxvi, 89, 103–4, 176n2; on statification, 90, 91–96, 100–102, 114, 123, 176n3; treatment of ideology, 29, 41–44; on violence, xviii–xx, 114, 166n8; on war machines, xx, 93, 108, 120

Gurven, Michael: on generalized reciprocity, 11

Hacker, Jacob: on risk, 148

haecceity, xxvii, 128, 129–30

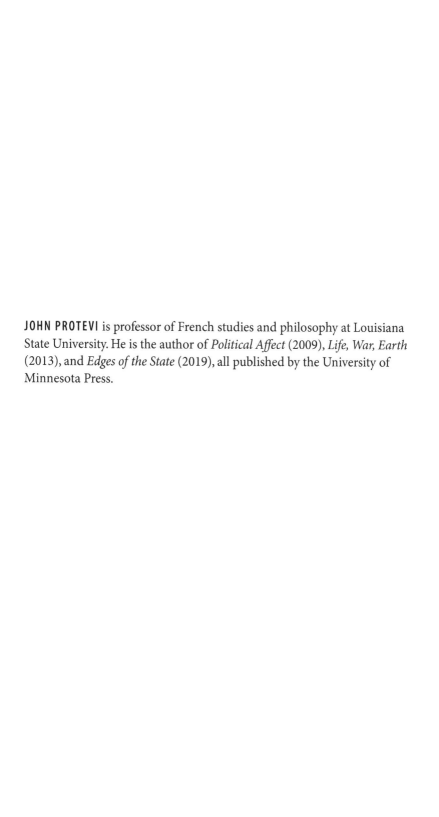

JOHN PROTEVI is professor of French studies and philosophy at Louisiana State University. He is the author of *Political Affect* (2009), *Life, War, Earth* (2013), and *Edges of the State* (2019), all published by the University of Minnesota Press.

www.ingramcontent.com/pod-product-compliance
Ingram Content Group UK Ltd.
Pitfield, Milton Keynes, MK11 3LW, UK
UKHW022355110325

456038UK00004B/76